RUBBLE FILMS

GERMAN CINEMA

IN THE SHADOW

OF THE THIRD REICH

Robert R. Shandley

 Temple University Press

PHILADELPHIA

Temple University Press, Philadelphia 19122
Copyright © 2001 by Temple University
All rights reserved
Published 2001
Printed in the United States of America

Library of Congress Cataloging-in-Publication Data
Shandley, Robert R.
   Rubble films : German cinema in the shadow of the Third Reich /
   Robert R. Shandley.
      p. cm.
   Includes bibliographical references and index.
   ISBN 1-56639-877-0 (alk. paper) — ISBN 1-56639-878-9 (pbk. : alk. paper)
      1. Motion pictures—Germany—History. I. Title.

PN1993.5.G3 S53 2001
791.43'0943'09045—dc21   00–051935

To Linda,
    for all that she is

Contents

Acknowledgments

Writing a book on relatively obscure fifty-year-old German films can be an expensive undertaking, especially from across the ocean. I began gathering the material for the manuscript as a graduate student, with the generous assistance of the Deutscher Akademischer Austauschdienst. Texas A&M University has supported me through its Creative and Scholarly Enhancement grant as well as grants from the Center for Humanities Research and the Film Studies Program. The College of Liberal Arts and the Department of Modern and Classical Languages at Texas A&M have provided me an academic home and generous resources. The Zentrum für Antisemitismusforschung at the Technische Universität Berlin provided both a forum for my ideas and valuable research support. Linda Wiehring von Wendrin and Kirsten Lehmann at the Akademie für Film und Fernsehen in Potsdam went out of their way to provide research materials, as did Peter Latta of the photo archives of the Stiftung Deutsche Kinemathek in Berlin. Among other sources, the Internet Movie Database was helpful in compiling the filmography. An earlier version of Chapter 1 appeared in the *South Central Review*. An earlier version of Chapter 2 appeared in *German Quarterly*.

My work on the manuscript benefited from the intellectual guidance, assistance, and companionship of Jack Zipes, Richard McCormick, Rey Chow, Brent Peterson, Assenka Oksiloff, Gerhard Weiss, Jochen Schulte-Sasse, Ulrike Weckel, Eric Rentschler, Anton Kaes, all of the participants of the German Film Institute at Dartmouth College, Barton

Byg, Lutz Koepnick, Terence Hoagwood, David Pickus, David Myers, Ole Gram, Karyn Ball, Silvia Lopez, Richard Critchfield, Johannes Heil, Arnold Krammer, Betty Joseph, Prudence Rose, Jaimey Fisher, Anke Finger, Eric Williams, Arnold Vedlitz, Rajiv Rimal, and Judith Stallmann. Anja Dehne, Thomas Feldmann, Katharina Lämmel, Antje Korus, and Annekatrin Haß provided support in Berlin whenever I needed it. I would like to thank Constance Hauf for dedicated help in my research. Jennifer Moore was helpful in shaping the manuscript. I am grateful to my editor, Micah Kleit, for his energy and enthusiasm about this project. Naturally, any mistakes that remain are not the fault of those acknowledged. They, of course, are the fault of Richard J. Golsan.

If there is any clarity in my argumentation, it is because of Linda Radzik. She makes my life and my work enjoyable.

RUBBLE FILMS

Introduction

They were deaf, blind and dumb, imprisoned in their ruins as in a fortress of willful ignorance, still strong and capable of hatred, still prisoners of their old tangle of pride and guilt.
—Primo Levi, "The Truce"

The end of the World War II not only brought with it the destruction of a genocidal German nation state, it also signified the end of an entire people's understanding of itself. So bitter was the defeat, so devastating the losses, so violent the reprisals, so one-sided the responsibility, so complete the stripping of the community's ideals that there was very little upon which its members could call in order to organize the complex set of emotions, pathologies, and desires that accompanied the loss. "For the overwhelming majority of the population the entire system of coordinates that determined everyday life under National Socialist rule was derailed."[1] Moreover, the physical environment, especially the cities, from which many had fled and to which they now returned, had been altered completely. The bombings and battles transformed Berlin from a modern metropolis to a peculiar wilderness of rubble. And yet, as Primo Levi indicates, many German attitudes remained untouched.

Germans had, at least temporarily, lost their sovereignty. The cultural institutions that had sustained both the violent regime and the private support of it were dismantled by the Allied powers. All public utterances, whether mediated through the press, radio, literature, universities, theater, or

1

music, were silenced. The Allies then began a thorough and deliberate process of filtering the voices that were allowed to speak. They sifted through journalists to find those least tainted in the regime. They investigated university professors in order to find those who were less implicated in Nazism. Because of the special place film held as a propagandistic tool in the Nazi state and because of the economic potential Germany held as a market for Allied cultural products, the film industry was the last among the media to be allowed to reenter the public sphere. Germany had a highly developed film industry and film-going public. The Allies both wanted a piece of this market and wanted to prevent those who had run the Nazi film culture from reestablishing hegemony.

Rubble films (*Trümmerfilme*) are products of German cinema stemming from the early postwar period, roughly 1946–1949, during which Germany lay in physical, political, and moral chaos. As Thomas Brandlmeier has noted, "the films regarding the past that appear in Germany in shock waves after 1945 are considered generally by German film historians as a kind of miscarriage, both in terms of film and intellectual history."[2] They are topical films from a time often regarded as devoid of topics. For my purposes, they are films that take the *mise en scène* of destroyed Germany as a background and metaphor of the destruction of German's own sense of themselves.

A subset of rubble films are the *Heimkehrerfilme*, films about the return of soldiers from the war. Given the defeat, occupation, and dismantling of Germany, the fate of those who fought to defend it would become fodder for many tales. The *Heimkehrerfilme* offered vivid portrayal of the postwar crisis in male subjectivity, which also had a noticeable impact on the ways in which women and children were portrayed.

Most histories of modern Germany are categorized according to the regimes under which they were made (the Weimar Republic, the German Democratic Republic, the Berlin Republic). In breaking the past into these neat units, history tends to forget times of transition such as the rubble period, between the defeat of the Third Reich and the establishment of the two Cold War German states. This amnesia is unfortunate. Between the end of the war and the beginning of the Berlin airlift this pariah community metamorphosed from the very definition of evil to "the last bastion of freedom" in the face of communist (or, for that matter, capitalist) onslaught. The films of the period tell us much about how that transformation occurred.

For more than fifty years, scholarship on German film has centered on its role as national narrative. Much of this focus can be traced to the stated intentions of National Socialism to instill a sense of a traditional and powerful community in the German cinematic imagination. The Nazis attempted to create a unity of nation and people with the help of the cinematic image. Later generations of filmmakers sought to counter that tradition with a national cinema of their own. Work on German film has covered extensively the aesthetic influence of the Weimar era. Recent works by Eric Rentschler and Linda Schulte-Sasse explore the uses and abuses of the cinematic image in Nazi Germany.[3] In German, Peter Pleyer's important dissertation from the early 1960s continues to prove a valuable source of information on filmmaking in the rubble period, as does Bettina Greffath's 1995 doctoral thesis.[4] Heide Fehrenbach has shown the effects of the church's fight for cultural hegemony on the West German film industry of the 1950s.[5] Scholars have also explored extensively the New German Cinema of the 1960s and 1970s.[6] In 1999, a valuable volume on East German cinema appeared in English.[7] To date, however, there has been no comprehensive study in English of early postwar German filmmaking and its treatment of Germany's Nazi past.

The goals of this book are twofold. First, I seek to provide a critical reading of a set of films made in Germany between 1946 and 1949, thereby filling in a significant gap in German film history. Among the more than fifty feature films that were made in that period, I have chosen those that share the fundamental *mise en scène* of a destroyed and defeated Germany. These films, which range from romances and family melodramas to gangster films and detective stories, constitute a cycle of films insofar as they are all problem films whose problem is the long shadow cast by the legacy of the Third Reich. The films under consideration are:

> *The Murderers Are among Us* (*Die Mörder sind unter uns*, dir. Wolfgang Staudte, 1946)
>
> *Somewhere in Berlin* (*Irgendwo in Berlin*, dir. Peter Pewas, 1946)
>
> *Razzia* (dir. Werner Klingler, 1947)
>
> *In Those Days* (*In jenen Tagen*, dir. Helmut Käutner, 1947; released in English-speaking countries as *Seven Journeys*)
>
> *Marriage in the Shadows* (*Ehe im Schatten*, dir. Kurt Maetzig, 1947)
>
> *And the Heavens Above* (*. . . Und über uns der Himmel*, dir. Josef von Báky, 1947; released in English-speaking countries as *City of Torment*)

Between Yesterday and Tomorrow (*Zwischen Gestern und Morgen*, dir. Harald Braun, 1947)

Film without a Title (*Film ohne Titel*, dir. Rudolf Jugert, 1947)

Street Acquaintance (*Straßenbekanntschaft*, dir. Peter Pewas, 1948)

Long Is the Road (*Lang ist der Weg*, dir. Herbert Fredersdorf and Marek Goldstein, 1948)

Morituri (dir. Eugen York, 1948)

'48 All over Again (. . . *Und wieder '48*, dir. Gustav von Wangenheim, 1948)

The Blum Affair (*Die Affaire Blum*, dir. Erich Engel, 1948)

The Apple Is Off! (*Der Apfel ist ab!*, dir. Helmut Käutner, 1948)

The Ballad of Berlin (*Berliner Ballade*, dir. R. A. Stemmle, 1948)

Love '47 (*Liebe '47*, dir. Wolfgang Liebeneiner, 1949)

The Last Illusion (*Der Ruf*, dir. Josef von Báky, 1949)

My second purpose is to evaluate how Germans of the period treated their immediate past using a medium that had been so exploited by National Socialism. While all of the films presented here make the Nazi past a part of their plot line, either directly or indirectly, not all do so with equal honesty or reflection. The ways in which they are both revelatory and concealing are of critical importance. By intervening in the discourse on the memory of World War II and the Holocaust, these films played an important role in the formation of a collective attitude toward the past, one that shaped many public debates in Germany in the decades thereafter.

The rubble films' treatment of the past is far from morally satisfying to today's viewers. These films only rarely confront the institutions, traditions, and assumptions that led to the catastrophe that was postwar Europe. At best, they mention them; at worst, they lie about them. Helmut Käutner's episodic *In Those Days* tells seven stories of innocent Germans, while neglecting to portray the culpability of others. Most of the films treat the question of guilt as just one problem among many in the postwar period. Worse yet, the rubble films often conflate the wrongs committed during the Third Reich with the Germans' own postwar suffering. The black market is represented as being as distressing as, or even worse than, the presence of war criminals. The German refugees from Silesia and the former German soldiers returning from war often occupy the same symbolic position as the survivors of the death camps.

Early postwar German filmmakers were, I argue, usually so emotionally involved in the hardships of life in postwar Germany that they were largely blind to other concerns such as personal or collective responsibility for the crimes of the war. Thus these films can be seen as training films for the attitude of dismissal regarding the Holocaust that has often prevailed in public discourse in Germany in the ensuing fifty years: "We have so many current problems, why dig up that past again?"

Insofar as I take on the task of discussing Germans and their relationship to their Nazi past, I tread on both fertile and dangerous ground. In so many ways the Nazi question is the easy one. Germans, both individually and collectively, committed the acts that led to the creation of the legal category of "crimes against humanity." I do not try to explicate the history of those crimes. But that history, coupled with the upheaval and material despair of the postwar years, defines the moral situation of postwar Germany.

The narratives of these films seldom depict directly the perpetration of war crimes. Rather, they tend to pursue a litany of issues regarding collective responsibility and passive moral failure. Most Germans supported the regime at one point or another; some were guilty more of sins of omission, willful ignorance, and neglect; others shared the xenophobic attitudes of their neighbors but did not act upon their prejudices; and still others—and this is the category that implicates the film industry the most—profited from a cooperative relationship with the Nazi regime. The fact that most filmmakers of the rubble period shared in the responsibility and moral debt to one degree or another interferes with each film's ability to confront German wartime experiences and actions.[8] But we must also keep in mind that just because Germans were perpetrators, this does not mean that they did not themselves suffer. Certainly, they brought most of that suffering upon themselves. But to ignore the Germans' own postwar anguish is also a failure to pursue the truth. These issues lie at the heart of the rubble films.

In order to understand the place of these films in German historiography, we must ask how they intervene in the narration of history. To paraphrase Hayden White's definition of the task of narrative history, filmmakers had to find a way to fashion the experiences of the recent past into structures of meaning that would then make sense to them.[9] And, indeed, that which "makes sense" was in flux in postwar Germany. The significatory structures upon which German filmmaking had been built were in disarray and filmmakers were at a loss to imagine new ones. Thus, filmmakers had to determine not only the content of historical narratives, but also the form they took.

However, one of the conclusions we can draw from studying rubble films is that, while many of the conditions of production changed overnight, the end of the war did not fundamentally change film culture, at least not at first. The choices of filmic style the directors made were often informed just as much by habit as by concern for new realities. Almost all of these men (this is one of the few eras in German filmmaking where there were no active women feature-film directors) were successful members of the industry before 1945. Just as the agitators who founded the "New German Cinema" in the 1960s charged, there was no discernable difference between the personnel of the industry during and after the war. Almost everyone, from producers and directors to actors and technical staff, found roles for themselves in the downsized and decentralized postwar industry. To the extent that there was blacklisting, it was generally temporary. For example, the one-time artistic director of the dominant film company of the Nazi era, Wolfgang Liebeneiner, shows up again after the war as a director. Thus, it is easy to imagine that the stories these filmmakers tell are influenced by their own ambiguous ideological backgrounds and that they were guided by filmmaking practices established under Nazi management. And, given their drive to legitimate themselves in the new political climate of occupied Germany, we certainly have reason to believe that the pursuit of truth was not always the highest priority among the filmmakers.

Any approach used to study rubble films must be able to evaluate the complex historiographic issues at stake in these films as well as provide a critical appreciation of their aesthetic accomplishments and failures. Likewise, it must reveal something about the potential meanings the original viewers would have attributed to the films. The existing scholarship on these films tends to treat them as transparent historical documents reflecting directly the attitudes of the filmmakers and the audience. This line of inquiry has a long and storied tradition in Germany. Its origins lie in the work of Siegfried Kracauer, whose psychological interpretive model continues to inform German film scholarship. Much of what has been written on the topic of the relationship between German history and film takes up explicitly psychological arguments about both the history of film and filmic depictions of the past. Anton Kaes makes a Freudian connection when he refers to the history films of the late 1970s and early 1980s as the return of a repressed historical discourse.[10] Eric Santner, similarly, sees those films as an acting out of a trauma not yet worked through.[11] Both make more than passing reference to psychologists

Alexander Mitscherlich and Margaret Mitscherlich's 1969 book, *The Inability to Mourn: Principles of Collective Behavior*.[12] The Mitscherlich's thesis is that Germans failed to mourn the losses incurred through their defeat in the war and thus entered into a mass melancholy.

One of the problems with both of these Freudian models is their need to view films as direct psychological reflections of the audience. Kracauer's model has been used to discuss film as a mass-consumed product that is therefore representative of the mentality of those who consume it.[13] Such scholarship often neglects the nuances of the relationships among the filmmaker, the film, and the spectator. For instance, most communication in film is predicated on conventional expectations and the extent to which those expectations are met or thwarted. Thus, films at best reflect a kind of dialogue that occurs between filmmakers and their audiences. Also, films are polysemic texts. Even the worst film (and some of the rubble films are in contention for that title) combines many different media at once to provide a richness of text that cannot be reduced merely to a memorandum on societal attitudes of the moment. But, however reductive the model seems, it does highlight the need to understand the nexus of the social and the psychological significatory structures of these films.

Some might worry whether we can read the rubble films as products of actual postwar German culture at all, due to the omnipresence of the Allied censors in the filmmaking process. Are we seeing the products of German filmmakers' cinematic imaginations, or just what they were directed to create (or believed they would be directed to create) by outside forces? This question ultimately collapses into one of intentionality, a question that is fraught with difficulty under the best of conditions. Although the question of Allied control is addressed in detail in Chapter 1, the fact remains that whether or not these films reflected the values of even those Germans who made them, when they hit the screen they immediately gained access to the audience's imagination. Regardless of intention, the form in which the audience received them was the one that impacted cultural history.

Another useful model for observing and organizing historical narrative is that of "collective memory." First developed by Maurice Halbwachs, who died in Buchenwald, the notion of collective memory also suggests that what gets remembered and how it gets remembered are public issues that are potentially subject to intense contestation.[14] The collective memory model suggests that present concerns (whether those of 1946 or 2001) determine the shape and content of what is to be remembered in the future. Rather than positing these films as a general representation of societal attitudes, Halbwachs's model suggests that these films help construct those attitudes. That is to say, the rubble films cast certain versions of history into the public memory of that period, versions that then serve as models for how that past is remembered. Throughout the book I examine how these films affect the general body of recollection about the Nazi past. While the rubble films themselves ultimately fell into obscurity, they represent a broadly received set of messages about the past that continue to be a part of how Nazism and the Holocaust are remembered in Germany.

Audiences tired quickly of the generally preachy rubble films. By 1947 reviewers used the term "rubble film," which had initially been descriptive, as a pejorative. Shortly thereafter, the rubble film cycle lost its sense of urgency. The growing polarizations of the Cold War changed conditions, and these films were no longer compelling to audiences. While stragglers continued to employ the berubbled *mise en scène*, they failed both commercially and critically. Rubble films were problem films about problems that the German public either no longer wished to solve or claimed to have already solved.

The German film industry was deeply implicated in the crimes of the Nazi era. It is surely unrealistic to expect that the path from Nazism to a full reckoning with the past would be a short one. The question we are left with in the end is not only one of successful treatment of history. The word *Vergangenheitsbewältigung*, which the Germans use to describe the necessary approach toward their past, must be a process rather than a singular act. Rubble films certainly did not deal with the past in a fully satisfactory way. They provided their audiences with ways of thinking about the past that are sometimes deceptive and apologistic. But, at the same time, they represented small yet vital steps along the path to the liberalization of German culture and honest reckoning with the crimes of the Nazi era. German cinema in the shadow of the Third Reich reveals an important first step in the process of working the National Socialist past into the collective cultural imagination of postwar Germany.

1

Dismantling the Dream Factory

The Film Industry in Berubbled Germany

ntil the unconditional surrender of the Third Reich effective at midnight on May 8, 1945, Germany had one of the strongest, most productive film industries in the world. A cartel of studios, producers, and distributors freed the theaters from competition and provided them with an audience positively disposed to domestic films. The film industry was implicated in the National Socialist capture and maintenance of power, and it benefited immediately from the war effort, which gave German films unprecedented access to the cinema market all over Europe. The films filling the schedules of movie theaters throughout the continent were not only the propaganda pieces we have come to associate with the regime but also a heavy fare of popular entertainment films, similar in look and feel to the Hollywood products of the era. In fact, the German film industry of the late 1930s and early 1940s enjoyed a success paralleled only by its American counterparts, and its monopolistic business practices were not radically different from those of the Hollywood studios during the same era.

The Nazis were engaged actively in supporting and controlling all artistic production, but the cinema held a special place in their imaginations and in their plans. As Eric Rentschler has put it, "Adolf Hitler and his minister of propaganda, Joseph Goebbels, were keenly aware of film's ability to mobilize emotions and immobilize minds, to create overpowering illusions and captive audiences."[1] The Nazis achieved control over the industry and employed it to deceive, distract, and mold the German public. The four main German studios, which eventually became a part of the portfolio of Goebbels's propaganda ministry, produced more than a thousand feature films during the Nazi era, and cinemas and spectatorship grew steadily. In 1933 there were 5,071 cinemas and 245 million filmgoers in Germany. At the industry's peak in 1943, there were 6,484 cinemas with over 1.1 billion spectators.[2] Germany's heavily supported and protected film industry played a central role, both socially and politically, in Nazi Germany.

As the Allies began to make inroads into German territory in the final months of 1944, they passed laws halting or radically limiting German cultural and religious activity. On November 24, 1944, the four triumphant powers—the United States, France, Great Britain, and the Soviet Union—passed Law 191 of the Military Government, Germany, which states:

> The printing, production, publication, distribution, sale and commercial lending of all newspapers, magazines, periodicals, books, pamphlets, posters, printed music and other printed or otherwise mechanically reproduced publications, of sound recordings and motion picture films; and the activities or operation of all news and photographic services and agencies, of radio broadcasting and television stations and systems, of wired radio systems; and the activities or operation of all theaters, cinemas, opera houses, film studios, film laboratories, film exchanges, fairs, circuses, carnival houses and other places of theatrical or musical entertainment and the production or presentation of motion pictures, plays, concerts, operas, and performances using actors or musicians are prohibited.[3]

With actions such as these, the Allies transformed the German film industry from an industrial superpower to a cottage industry in a matter of weeks. As a part of Law 191 the Allies dissolved Goebbels's infamous ministry, the Reichsministerium für Volksaufklärung und Propaganda, and its portfolio. Thus, almost six months before the war's end, the Allies completely blacked out one of the primary forces the Nazis had used to create the strong sense of community in Germany.

Not only were all theaters and cinemas taken over, they were also closed, thereby cutting off Germans' ability to see films, as well as the flow of capital back into the industry. Cinema owners were prevented from using their theaters for any purpose whatsoever. The studios were turned into storage spaces and barracks for invading soldiers. The stock of films owned by the German distribution companies was confiscated. Film stars were restricted from appearing in public. All raw film stock and film equipment was confiscated and, in some cases, taken as war bounty. By the time of surrender on May 8, 1945, the once powerful German film industry had ceased to exist.

Having obtained Germany's unconditional surrender, the Allies amended Law 191 on May 12, 1945. The amendment set up a licensing system for print media as well as for all broadcasting, film presentation, and performance activities. Four regional occupational zones replaced the Allied Supreme Command of the Invasion and were established under the sovereignty of the United Kingdom, France, the United States, and the Soviet Union. Each zone then set up its own military government and policies of governance. Control of cultural activities came under the command of each separate military government. Initially, there was little commerce or even movement among the four zones due to the overall disrepair of the systems of transport and communication as well as a consensus among the Allies that decentralization of power in Germany was necessary. Even before the Allied victory, tensions between the Western Allies and the Soviets were manifesting themselves, leading to even less cooperation between the Soviet zone and its Western counterparts.

The ruling body of the American sector, the Office of Military Government of the United States (OMGUS), pursued a bifurcated policy of both economic colonization and reeducation. The latter was not to be a process of self-discovery but of acceptance of history as told by the victors. This policy was especially evident in the mission of the Information Control Division, the branch of OMGUS charged with overseeing the Germans' reentry into public discourse. The overriding directive of the Information Control Division was to

> provide the Germans with information, which will influence [changed on April 16, 1947, to "enable"] them to understand and accept the United States program of occupation, and to establish for themselves a stable, peaceful, and acceptable government. Such information will impress upon the Germans the totality of their military defeat, the impossibility of rearmament, the responsibility of the individual German for war and atrocities, the disastrous effects of the structure and system of National Socialism on Germany and the world, and the possibility that through work and cooperation Germany may again be accepted into the family of nations.[4]

While this was the policy only in the American sector, it not only influenced the other Allies' decisions, it also affected any media product that hoped to be allowed into the American sector. This policy both set out guidelines for how Germans were to behave in the present and mandated what their relationship to their history would be. By 1946, when German filmmakers were allowed into the public sphere to tell their history, they had to compete with the rest of the world for the attention of the German audience. However, there is no real indication that, had they been given more freedom initially, they would have constructed more honest or critical version of the past.

Shortly after the capitulation of the German forces, ships and planes were sent to Europe by the thousands to retrieve the victorious soldiers. Those vehicles not only carried provisions for the occupying forces, they also contained thousands of publications readied by the Americans for use in reeducating Germans. Along with political writings of the American founding fathers, the occupational forces also distributed canonical works of American literature deemed representative of the ideals they wished to instill in the Germans, such as the writings of Benjamin Franklin and James Fenimore Cooper. This literature was also meant to fill a void left by much of the German literature that was to be removed from bookstores or restricted in libraries.

The onslaught of American cultural products was not confined to the literary arts. The American film industry, which had been so cooperative with the military during the war, was looking for a repayment for its efforts. Under the guise of a similar mission of reeducation, Hollywood also sent dozens of American films to fill the vacuum left by the removal of German films from circulation. Only unlike the publishing industry, whose products were often given away, Hollywood intended to make money in a market that had, for many years, been closed to American films. In a reversal of the war years, the European film market was now closed to German films.

The American occupational authorities imagined Hollywood film as a democratizing force, though just how this was to function is unclear. They did not set out to find the most didactic or socially relevant films available from Hollywood. Instead, they hoped that the most common of films would suggest supposedly ingrained American values of equality, justice, and hope that were lacking in the German tradition. Robert Joseph, an American film officer in Berlin, voiced this conception of the Germans most succinctly. "The film people who valorized Siegfried for twelve years cannot understand that Joe Smith (for Germans, Johann Schmidt) is a guy who looks like John Garfield, thinks like Spencer Tracy, and acts like James Cagney, and that he is just as valuable as anyone else and not a bit more."[5] It is hard to imagine someone who behaves like James Cagney being a model for the ideal democratic subject.

OMGUS had prepared the way for Hollywood and was counting on a steady supply of re-released American films. The problem was that, in the months and years following the war, there was no money to be made. There was no Reich backing the value of the Reichsmark, and almost all activity was conducted on a barter market. While Germans still possessed currency, it was not convertible in any way that would be of value to the Americans. Through film, the occupational authorities had hoped to provide both distraction and education to the vanquished nation. But having discovered there were no profits to be made, Hollywood stemmed the regular flow of films late in the summer of 1945. Tensions between Hollywood and OMGUS were mounting on other fronts as well.

Hollywood, Expatriate Germans, and the Struggle for Control in the Western Sectors

If German filmmakers seemed generally happy no longer being under the watchful eye of the propaganda ministry, they were resentful about the supposed spoils the victors' studios were enjoying. Billy Wilder's first experience with postwar Germany provides a good example of the reasons that tension and distrust arose between the German and American film industries. A German immigrant and filmmaker who had become successful in Hollywood, Wilder returned in the summer of 1945 as part of a visiting crew of Hollywood officials. The trip was supposedly intended to seek out ways in which the industry could assist the military government. In reality, the team sought ways for the Americans to establish a monopoly in Germany.[6] Wilder represented the conflicts of interest that were inherent in the Hollywood encounters with OMGUS. One of his reasons for being in Germany was that he was under consideration for the job of overseeing the resumption of German film production in the American sector.

Wilder was asked to write a report about the state of the production facilities and personnel available for use in the industry. Before doing so, he wrote a report regarding the use of film in the reeducation process, in which he expressed appreciation for the films being presented to Germans in order to expose them to their own guilt. Wilder himself provided technical assistance to the most famous of these, *The Death Mills*, which Germans were often forced to watch in order to receive their ration cards. Wilder argued that such films would only have a limited effect. In the summer of 1945, Germans were happy about the fact that theaters were open at all. Initial audiences showed appropriate respect and contrition while viewing these films, many of which were made up of footage taken as concentration camps were liberated. And yet, Wilder asked in late July, "will Germans come week after week in the cinema in order to play the guilty little school boy?" He presumed not. Likewise, he doubted that the initial films sent by Hollywood would serve their supposed purpose, namely democratic reeducation.[7]

As we shall see, the Russian impulse was to find ways in which the Germans could begin reeducating themselves about their history. Wilder presented a different model, one that showed his Hollywood colors. He pitched his own idea for a film that would serve as the ideal reeducation film: a romantic comedy between a German woman and an American G.I. (which eventually became his *A Foreign Affair*, released in 1946). Rather than the information films with which the Germans were being deluged, Wilder felt that entertainment films dealing with German–American relations would be the ideal propaganda.[8]

In Wilder's report on the German film industry, he laid out many of the existing barriers for the resumption of filmmaking, most of which were political in nature. Despite Wilder's private comments to the contrary, the report characterizes the Soviets as adamant yet reasonable adversaries interested in the general success of a postwar German film production. It shows both a concern about the activity in the Soviet zone and a willingness to cooperate with the Soviets in reshaping film culture in Germany. Wilder reported that the Soviets were insisting that any German film have access to all zones. Meanwhile the Soviets, who at that point were the Allied power placing the fewest censorship constrictions on the Germans, nevertheless insisted that all films shown in Germany be submitted to each of the film control boards for approval. Wilder and the Soviets agreed that a German film industry would be viable only if it could function in all zones. This would only be possible, according to Wilder, through the institution of a committee of the film officers from each of the four military governments that would govern the logistics of the industry.

Given the conditions in August 1945, shortly after the Potsdam Conference, it would seem that Wilder's remarks must have been either disingenuous or uninformed. To be sure, the Soviets were the most friendly toward reestablishing filmmaking in Germany. And yet, one of the first things that any visitor to Germany in the summer of 1945 would have noticed was the discord between the U.S. and Soviet occupational authorities. And, even if the two larger powers would have been able to agree, the French were also in no hurry to see Germany unified economically or otherwise.

If Wilder's recommendations had a hidden agenda, what was it? In part, Wilder may have been trying to prove his suitability for the job of film officer, a position OMGUS was preparing to create. The post would centralize film policy in the American sector. And yet, it is hard to imagine why Wilder would want such a post, having established for himself a stellar reputation in Hollywood. Given his solid standing within an industry determined to take over the German market, why would he propose a solution for rebuilding the German film industry that was the most reasonable and positive one for the Germans? It was, I believe, a foil. That is, it was an attempt to make Hollywood look like it was cooperating in the reeducation effort by proposing the best solution knowing that it was politically impossible.

Why would Billy Wilder, a member of the Hollywood establishment, put up such a façade? In June 1945 the major Hollywood studios had formed the Motion Picture Export Association (MPEA), a lobby group whose goal was to recapture international markets. As Thomas Guback puts it, "In bringing together the majors and allowing them to act in concert through a single organization, the MPEA presented a 'united front' to the nations of the world, and by legal internal collusion prevented possible ruinous competition among American film companies overseas."[9] The film industry clearly was gearing itself up immediately after the war to expand if not completely take over foreign markets. And while OMGUS and the American government in general may have been grateful to Hollywood and willing to assist it in its mission, this mission also ran contrary to OMGUS's more idealistic attempts to foster democratic discourse on German soil. More directly, the cartel being formed by the major studios was problematic for OMGUS, which was trying to maintain alliances with the British and French while at least appeasing the Russians. The MPEA's formation also threatened to justify Soviet claims of American capitalist imperialism. Hollywood seemed to understand these machinations and coordinated its own policies with those of the government.[10]

Taken together, Wilder's film pitch and his proposal for the rebuilding of the German film industry can be seen as the bait-and-switch policy of Hollywood's major studios. The job of film officer ended up being filled by successive representatives of Hollywood interests. However, the Americans' choice of Eric Pommer turned out to be one much more satisfactory, at least initially, to the Germans than to the Americans.

Meanwhile, Hollywood was conceiving of ways to reap financial benefits from its newly won access to the German market. A complicated arrangement between Hollywood and OMGUS meant that the studios were receiving no royalties on the films they were showing in Germany. The money was frozen in OMGUS accounts and was neither retrievable nor convertible. As Johannes Hauser notes, the MPEA proposed a solution, namely: "the employment of Reichsmarks for the outright acquisition of German motion picture theatres, for the production by them in German studios of newsreels for release both in Germany and other countries, and for the purchase of German raw stock to make positives of pictures to be shown in Germany as well as outside of it."[11] In other words, the Hollywood studios proposed to use the resources gained through the large market share they had immediately following the war to consolidate permanently that oligopoly.

Late in the summer of 1945, the Information Control Division rejected the MPEA's suggested solution, after which Hollywood refused to send enough films to meet the demand in occupied Germany. Given the need for entertainment and the fact that Germans had not yet been allowed to make films, a procedure was established whereby German films made before 1945 could be put through a censor system and then re-released. Thus, by autumn of 1945, German films were again appearing in the theaters, but only if they met the detailed standards published by OMGUS:

> No German films may be shown in the United States Zone of Occupation which glorify the ideology of Fascism, Nazism, or racial distinction; glorify or idealize war or militarism; politically subvert or pervert German history; glorify or idealize the German Army; seem derogatory or uncomplimentary of or ridicule Allied peoples, their governments, their political or national leaders; deal with German revenge; ridicule or criticize religious feelings and religious attitudes; glorify or idealize the thoughts and/or acts of German leaders whose opinions, notions, or political philosophy was imperialistic; are based upon a book or script of a known Nazi Party member or supporter, or

which originate through the creative efforts of known Nazi Party members or proven active supporters.[12]

The other Western Allies seem to have followed the American lead in writing strict censorship rules regarding the flow of information. Either the Americans were by far the least active censors or the German distributors practiced effective self-censorship: The Americans approved every one of the 845 films presented to them for review. Given the thousands that would have been available, selection had to have taken place somewhere. Most engaged in the activity were the British, who pursued a thorough review and censor policy.[13] The British reviewed over half again as many films as the Americans, approving even more, but also refusing more than three hundred. The French followed a pattern similar to the Americans, although they did refuse thirty-nine films. There is no published record of similar Soviet censorship activity.

Soviet Film Policy and the Founding of the First Postwar Film Company

Unlike the other Allies, the Soviets were less interested in establishing their own economic system in Germany than they were in establishing ideological control. Their colonial gestures were directed mostly toward winning over their former foes to a Soviet-style political culture. Those efforts were sometimes contradictory. To be sure they included many of the brutal tactics that Cold War rhetoric has come to associate with the Soviet Union. And yet, many of their policies toward Germany and Germans were, at the close of the war, much more conciliatory and humane than those of their Western counterparts. Thomas Heimann claims that many of the Soviet cultural officers sought to improve upon the models they had seen in their own country.[14] For example, Soviet film policies tended to allow Germans ways to discuss and understand their own history, rather than having their history lessons imposed upon them. By early 1946, a committee of Soviet officers, returning German expatriates, and resident German filmmakers came together to start the first active postwar German film company, DEFA (for Deutsche Film AG). It would become the sole film company of the German Democratic Republic.

Christiane Mückenberger, the *doyen* of DEFA history, notes that there existed an atmosphere of political tolerance in the studio's early days. "Both parties—artists and politicians—were united by one over-riding concern, namely that of overcoming fascism. . . . This was important since it created a special climate in which artists could develop their ideas without fear of censorship and in which they could feel confident that they were both wanted and needed."[15] Most studies of the founding years of DEFA confirm that the atmosphere and work conditions were certainly as open as in any of the Western sectors and perhaps even more liberated than in some of the Allied countries themselves.[16] Although most of the directors of DEFA films in the early years actually lived in the Western sectors of Berlin and were active filmmakers in the Nazi years, DEFA itself made a greater effort to produce films that confronted the Nazi past directly. The heads of DEFA showed from the start openness toward what they coined "antifascist" film projects and therefore attracted many such projects.

By late 1945 the Americans began to realize that they were lagging behind in the struggle for cultural hegemony in Germany. The Russians were more engaged in encouraging and promoting a German cultural life. The British were most active in reorganizing the broadcast industry in their zone and licensed the first film in the Western sectors. Even the French were beginning to license filmmakers. The Americans did not want to be seen as being drawn into a race to restart German filmmaking. The film officer for the Office of Military Government Berlin Sector (OMGBS), Robert Joseph, stipulated that the licensees in the American sector would not just produce films to make the audience laugh. This is most likely a reference to Heinz Rühmann, an actor who became popular in the Nazi era and was among the first to attempt to get a license to produce a film. His initial efforts failed, perhaps because he eschewed the attitude toward filmmaking the Americans demanded. A director was, according to Joseph, meant to awaken contemplation in audience members.[17]

The audiences the Allies were faced with, however, were made up of a defeated, displaced, and unsettled German population. There were few employment opportunities, though plenty of work to be done. A large percentage of the population was homeless either because they had been driven by the Soviets from the eastern provinces or because of the heavy wartime damage to German cities. Germany in 1945 faced the largest migration and displacement problem in European history. Thus, not only did the Allies need to find ways to occupy an idle urban population, they also had to fill the days of the millions living in Displaced Persons (DPs) camps. This was the role film would play much more so than the idealistic democratic reeducation plans of the occupational governments.

By the autumn of 1945, one of the oddities of the film market in all sectors was the increasing presence of the second-run German films the Allies were gradually allowing back into the cinemas. DEFA had a stock of films Goebbels had censored, which it used alongside Russian imports to fill its cinemas in the early days. In fact, the money gained from the release of a filmed version of *Die Fledermaus*, a Nazi-era production shot toward the end of the war and put together in 1946, was used as start-up capital for DEFA. "Thus, Goebbels' film apparatus indirectly financed the first postwar film company, one that inscribed on its flag the working through of Germany's fascist past."[18] DEFA would continue to use these films as a part of its repertoire until at least 1950.

The unreleased films from the Nazi era and those that appeared in the cinemas before 1945 were occupying an increasing market share. The products of Ufa, Tobis, and other German studios, many of which had entertained the German troops at war, were playing next to the Hollywood, Soviet, British, and French films that served a similar function among the Allied troops. The spectator no longer had to choose sides. A visit to any of these films would have provided two hours of warmth and, in most cases, escapism. So, while German filmmaking was suspended for a year, German films only had to sit out a summer before enjoying a comeback. For the spectator this certainly provided the illusion that little had changed. The films of the Nazi "Dream Factory" that had occupied and transformed the German visual imagination for a decade and the films that had been conceived in order to help Germans escape the heavy realities of war were again available. The cycle of depressing postwar diagnostic realist films had yet to appear.

By the winter of 1945–46 other considerations contributed to the growing interest in film, the greatest of which was a severe energy and food shortage. Any two hours that a household spent in a movie theater were two hours during which their apartment would not have to be heated or lighted. And going to the cinema was a cheap alternative to the miseries of everyday life. Peter Pleyer notes that "the need to find this distraction in the cinema is shown by the fact that most movie theaters were filled to the last seat almost every evening." This was made even more feasible by the economic conditions. "A movie ticket neither required a ration card nor did one have to pay black market prices."[19] Thomas Brandlmeier offers a comparison that helps us understand the economics of movie-going: "A visit to the cinema cost approximately 1 Reichsmark. A half-pound stick of butter on the black market cost 250 Reichsmarks."[20] Thus, demand for films to fill the theaters was high.

The *Filmpause:* Rethinking Cinema and the State

Despite the country's high demand for films and Hollywood's reluctance to release enough features to fill that demand, it took more than a year for Germans to start feature film production. The Allies had wiped out one of the Nazis' most effective weapons, and Hollywood had overseen the dismantling of its potentially most forceful competitor. This year-long cessation of production by the once mighty German film industry, which came to be known as the *Filmpause*, gave rise to a public reflection on the role of film that would continue well after German film production resumed.

Robert Joseph's demand for serious filmmaking was not far out of line with the Soviets' requirement that German films should, in the words of the Soviet Commander Tulpanov, "become a sharp weapon in the fight against war and militarism and for peace for the friendship of the peoples of the world."[21] The two Allied representatives demanded both artistic quality and moral guidance from filmic production. Film should be a serious, valuable, and, above all, moral undertaking. These intimidating stakes would serve as the discursive guide for the rubble film cycle.

Already having been refused a filmmaking license by the British and American authorities, Wolfgang Staudte, a minor actor and filmmaker during the Third Reich, wrote a letter to the Soviet cultural authorities on October 9, 1945. It was the second round of letters between Staudte and the Soviet military administration. In the first one he asked to make the film *Der Mann, den ich töten werde* (*The Man I Am Going to Kill*), which would become *The Murderers Are among Us.* The Soviets responded by asking him to propose his film as a part of founding a film studio, another plan of Staudte's. So, in his October 9 letter, Staudte was not trying to justify his film's narrative, but rather to legitimate restarting the German film industry. He gave exactly one reason for wanting permission to start a new film studio—namely, to prevent the dissolution of the energies and talents that comprised the German film industry.[22]

Ignoring the common knowledge among filmmakers that the Allies were intentionally breaking up the monopoly of German film, Staudte suggested creating a centralized studio under which numerous filmmakers unburdened by the Nazi past could provide continuity with the less compromised aspects of pre-1945 German cinema. He did not argue for a break with the past, nor did he even hint that German film might no longer be a major cultural force. Indeed, had Staudte had his way, most of those who were to become the leading directors of the era would have again formed a viable industrial force. "I believe I speak for all filmmakers when I note that a quick decision is necessary in order to address a deplorable social state of affairs and to take a substantial step on the way toward the political renewal of Germany."[23] Whether or not Staudte understood the forces that were working against his plans, he certainly understood the language needed for any proposal made to the occupational authorities.

Not all filmmakers were as active in trying to get restarted—or perhaps as ignorant of the conditions causing the *Filmpause*—as Staudte was. Harald Braun was an active small-budget filmmaker during the Third Reich most noted for his filmic adaptation of Henrik Ibsen's *A Doll's House* and a biographical film about Clara and Robert Schumann. He did not contribute to the large, war-glorifying, antisemitic, or otherwise propagandistic filmmaking of the war era, nor was he a part of the large studio star system of Nazi Germany. But, like many members of that circle after the war, he found himself without work and without a chance to participate in the public arena. The *Filmpause*, as well as the lengthy process of legitimation to which each filmmaker would have to submit her/himself, provided Braun with an occasion to reflect upon film work and the role of film. In a November 1945 article in Munich's newly founded newspaper, *Neue Zeitung*, Braun acceded to the idea that German film had been absolutely delegitimated through its close association with the National Socialists. Like many of his contemporaries, Braun avoided mentioning the Nazis by name: "German filmmaking of the last 13 years has had the questionable advantage of enjoying the attention and 'supervision' of the dictatorship."[24]

Although Braun was among the many who worked hard to get film production underway again after the war, he also expressed some understanding of the obstacles to doing so. For instance, he admitted that the film industry might not have been the most crucial sector to restart in a land where people were hungry and homeless. While it is impossible to know whether to take his comments as simply mouthing Allied policy or as honest expression of need, Braun also asserted that because of filmmaking's close ties to dictatorial power, the break from production could in itself be productive. In fact, Braun's comments were very much in line with the *Zeitgeist* that demanded taking stock of one's moral record. He postulates that "perhaps the *Filmpause* will help us [filmmakers] to come to some insights that will allow postwar necessities to appear as virtues."[25]

The virtue that should rise out of the destruction of Nazism was, according to Braun, artistic and intellectual freedom. After giving examples of how closely the Nazis controlled many artistic decisions, he suggested that eventually German filmmakers lost the will toward autonomy. The end of the war did not immediately bring with it a reestablishment of that autonomy. Braun asserts that desire for independence should be the most important outcome of the reeducation. The break from filmmaking should be used "to formulate and apply new fundamentals to film work."[26] Presumably, the most important of these fundamentals would be the separation of studio and state.

The *Filmpause* implied a practical but not aesthetic break with the recent film past. Braun shared an affinity with the Hollywood understanding of what film should be—namely, entertaining—an attitude that differs little from that of the later Goebbels. There is no call in his writing for filmmaking that would teach the German audience about the dangers of their old ways of thinking and the need for democratic values. Yet, he still saw film as a medium with a moral mission that should "help people to deal more easily with their heavy lives."[27] Paraphrasing his own Schumann film, Braun ends his comments with the claim that to "work on German film, for German film is both a duty and a comfort." Even in his contemplation of reform, Braun remained tied to the language of the older value structure. Culture remains a place of commemoration and reaffirmation, not of challenge or change.

When Braun's article was published there was as yet no nationwide media outlet. His comments were reprinted in trade journals in the other zones prompting comments from other filmmakers seeking to establish a role for themselves in postwar Germany. It is likely that their taking up the pen was an attempt to gain attention for the film projects they were proposing to the Allied authorities, showing that they understood the new rules of the game. This discussion of the German film industry would continue for years in both the trade and the popular presses. Often, those contributing were doing so in order to promote their own political fitness, a presumed prerequisite for filmmakers.

Helmut Käutner was something of an outsider to the wartime film industry. He had made artistically successful films that were, for the most part, censored and shelved by the Nazis. The close of the war found him, not in Berlin or Munich, the major locales of German filmmaking, but in Hamburg and Munich, where he spent most of his efforts trying to get a license to begin filming. Although Staudte had included him in his proposal to the Soviets, by the end of 1945 Käutner, because of the initial cooperation of both the Americans in Munich and the British in Hamburg, had reason to believe that he was well under way to being given the needed permission to make a film. Just days after Staudte and DEFA were set in motion in Berlin, Käutner received his license to make what would become *In Those Days*, a film about an automobile whose "life" spanned the twelve years of the "Thousand Year Reich." A year after production began, the film appeared in cinemas, though its range was painfully limited as there were only four copies in circulation. Far from successful under the Nazis, Käutner found himself after the war with even worse working conditions. And yet, this time he claimed that the governmental authorities were not to blame.

In an article written for a film trade publication in June 1947, Käutner pointed his finger at what he saw as the decisive reason for the failure of German film, namely, the audience.[28] His biggest complaint was that the German audience was not interested in "the intellectual reformation of German film." German filmgoers were used to the entertainment films of the Nazi era's Dream Factory, which was precisely what the Allies had destroyed and supplanted, albeit only partially. Thus, the serious, reflective films German directors were in a position to make were not the kind of films German audience was used to seeing.

Georg Klaren, a colleague of Staudte's in Berlin, also bemoaned the state of the industry. Writing in November 1946, just after the release of the first postwar German film, *The Murderers Are among Us*, Klaren, a director and executive at the DEFA studios, decried the state of screenwriting in the wake of the war.[29] He noted that most of the materials were reactions to everyday realities in Germany. Given the turn-around time and the rapidly changing reality of Germany, topical scripts would, according to Klaren, become dated by the time they arrived in the theaters. "Time runs faster and filmmaking slower than ever. This has to be considered when one demands of a film that it be 'today.' " He claimed to have a ridiculous number of self-pitying coming-home stories and scripts about postwar marital problems. Only a few such films were in the works when the studios began to see the audience and critics grow weary of them. And yet, according to Klaren, screenwriters remained hung-up on these increasingly less relevant problems. He stated that he was looking for a film script that addressed the problems of working women in postwar Germany. (Women made up an overwhelming majority of the German population and, presumably, the filmgoing audience. And yet, filmmaking in those early years fixated on the problems of men returning from the war.)

Not only do Klaren's comments emphasize the disarray of an industry that could not find good scripts to produce, they also suggest an inability of the creative forces in Germany to narrate beyond the scope of their immediate experience. Klaren himself refused to see his inability to find scripts worthy of filming as a sign of imaginative poverty. The fact is that the German film industry found itself in an imaginative vacuum regarding its own role and possibilities in occupied Germany. The parameters in which filmmakers could feasibly fit a story, the realm of action for the characters, the technical dimensions the films could assume, and the plot outcomes were all remarkably limited by both the screenwriter's imaginations and the studios' technical capacities.

The first German films following World War II were moral events. They were serious, pedantic, and anchored in the depressing psychological and material reality of Germany's absolute defeat. They bespoke the Allies' stated wishes that German films should address the gravity of the country's mistakes over the twelve years of Nazism and should reject all forms of militarism and national pride. Whether these were the only films they were allowed to make or whether they had so internalized the censorship guidelines that they attempted nothing else is unclear. The OMGUS rules were restrictive in word, but often quite liberal in enforcement. Thus, filmmakers had little indication as to what would and would not be allowed.

The rubble films were forced to seek out a film language strong enough to confront recent German history while avoiding a confrontation with their German audience. Many of them were well attended and received a significant amount of critical acclaim. However, it is hard to tell if the audiences were generated by the desire to see moralistic films about the recent German past or by the need to find a warm place to sit for a few hours. Whether compelled by force or desire, the rubble films engaged in working through the Nazi past as directly as films from any other era. However, filmgoers who had been offered a seductive international film language often resented being confronted with their own miseries. Rubble films had to find ways to adopt, adapt, or counter the cinematic practices of their competition.

2

Coming Home
through Rubble Canyons

The Murderers Are among Us
and Generic Convention

**A good German is recognizable in how or whether or not he is
affected by this film.**

—Walter Lenning, *Berliner Zeitung*, October 17, 1946

The premiere of Wolfgang Staudte's *The Murderers Are among
Us* (*Die Mörder sind unter uns*) on October 16, 1946, was a
cinematic event unlike any other in German film history.
Not only was it the opening act of postwar German filmmaking and the first feature film of the newly founded
DEFA, it was also a test of the medium. The cinema was
rightfully subjected to the controlling gaze of the occupying
forces in Germany, who were, at best, skeptical of Germans'
relationship to film. What stories Germans would seek to tell
in film, and how they would go about doing so, were topics
of considerable interest and debate among the Allied censorship authorities, filmmakers, and the press. While these
players disagreed on the scope of influence German cinema
should assume in the wake of its misappropriation by the
National Socialists, they did agree on at least one point:
They all seem to have reached consensus that filmic narrative was compelled to provide moral guidance.

The idea that cinema should assume a functionalist char-

25

acter was not novel. Certainly, during the war, cinematic production everywhere mobilized itself in the service of one national narrative or another. But narrative cinema had played such a notorious role in the Nazi regime that Germans, more than others, had to interrogate their relationship to filmmaking. Whether because German filmmakers had abused the power of the image so egregiously during the Third Reich or simply because they lost the war, many of cinema's generic and narrative codes had been thoroughly delegitimated. It was unclear what cinematic language filmmakers would be able to call upon once they were able to resume production.

The Murderers Are among Us seeks a solution to these dilemmas in some surprising places. In its presentation of the landscape, the hero, the heroine, and much of the plot, it echoes the filmic codes of the American Western. A lone, troubled man is lost in a wasteland, where he struggles against his own dark past as well as his lawless surroundings. Likewise, Staudte works with another familiar genre, the domestic melodrama, in which the drive is toward the subject's integration with community values and social harmony. This theme, which acts as a counternarrative to create internal tension in the plot, often occurs in Westerns. Understanding the complex interplay of the Western with the domestic melodrama will go a long way toward explaining the film's relation to the Nazi past.

I do not claim that Wolfgang Staudte intended to make a Western, nor that *The Murderers Are among Us* should be classified as one. What is certain is that the filmmaker chose certain filmic motifs that, upon closer study, parallel generic film patterns, predominantly those of Hollywood Westerns made prior to 1946. And perhaps this is not surprising. The things that get done in Westerns are the things that needed doing in postwar Germany—the establishment of a moral order, confrontation of one's own shady past, and confrontation of evil within a community.

In using Western tropes to exorcise the ghosts of recent history, *The Murderers Are among Us* is putting the genre to a familiar task. The Western genre, according to Andrea Bazin, is the American "historical film par excellence."[1] Quite often the cathedral-like canyon spires and desolate horizons of the American West act as sites of displacement for entirely different histories. The Western often is called upon to perform social commentary, whether about the threats of industrialization, post–Civil War racial politics, rising xenophobia as a reaction to increasing immigration, or what it means to establish a state. Despite the variety of questions the genre positions itself to address, certain formulaic constructions usually remain in place.

Genres have been defined as "coherent and controllable structures of meaning,"[2] which helps explain why resorting to implicit codes would appeal to Staudte. It is precisely coherence and control of meaning that are at stake in *The Murderers Are among Us*. The adoption of accepted cinematic narrative norms provides a seemingly easy fix to the strained legitimacy of filmic discourse. Hollywood genre films were well-established and popular structures that had again become the main stock for the German film spectator.

According to Thomas Schatz, film genres are sets of "interrelated narrative and cinematic components that serve to continually reexamine some basic cultural conflict."[3] Based on their narrative and spatial thematics, Schatz divides genre films into two categories: those of social order and those of social integration. Social order films, which include Westerns, gangster films, and detective films, often take place in contested, determinate spaces. In these films, the struggle is for ideological control, since "fundamental values are in a state of sustained conflict."[4] Social integration films include domestic melodramas, comedies, and musicals. These films are distinguished by conflicts that derive from a "struggle of the principal characters to bring their own views in line either with one another's or more often, in line with that of the larger community."[5] As we will see, Staudte needed elements from both codal sets.

In its search for a narrative foothold, *The Murderers Are among Us* calls upon many generic tactics. German Expressionism is an obvious tradition for Staudte to draw from, but the less obvious gangster genre also gives us a model for understanding the film. The gangster film's hero is often driven by a troubled past and seeks solace in a domesticating woman. But *The Murderers Are among Us* also draws upon the domestic melodrama, in which the domicile itself plays an important narrative and visual role. The film also beckons to the cinematic styles of the Weimar era, which had either been banned or neglected for thirteen years. But the return of that forbidden aesthetic to *The Murderers Are among Us* does not take a direct route. Both narratively and stylistically, the film vaguely echoes Fritz Lang's *M*, a similar story of shell-shock, murder, and revenge in an anxiety-ridden Berlin. The film certainly evokes the Weimar era street films, if only to give an emptied-out counterversion. Among concurrent filmmaking trends, Staudte's work can also be contextualized with Italian neo-realism, though what might at first be taken as raw documentary or location footage in Staudte's film is, in fact, carefully staged and stylized filmmaking. As Thomas Brandlmeier points out, many of the rubble films can also be seen in the context of Hollywood's generic filmmaking of the period.[6] *Film noir* stylistics certainly draw upon Weimar cinematic practices. In fact, given the mass migration from Berlin to Hollywood in the early thirties, they were often practiced by the same people.

Thus, in analyzing Staudte's film, we cannot remain dogmatically tied to a specific genre code. Yet, postwar Germany is as obvious a setting as Tombstone, Arizona, in which to situate a contestation of fundamental societal values. Staudte's film presumes that the most urgent task facing his characters is the restoration of a moral order in a place where almost all legal, religious, and political discourse has lost legitimacy. In fact, given the loss of these legitimizing anchors, the simple task of telling a story has become difficult.

Westerns take as their fundamental conflict questions of how the subject deals with "his" personal history and how communities are brought back into legal discourse. As such, the genre can be said to function as a booster to a narrative economy that needs reinvigorating and guidance. In Staudte's case, it supported the fantasy of an individualistic moral hero in a society that had, up to then, praised mass actions.

The Story

A young woman, Susanne Wallner, returns to Berlin from a concentration camp at the end of the war to find a man living in her apartment. Hans Mertens, a doctor before and during the war, is now lost in shell-shock and self-pity. He remains in Susanne's apartment after her return, usually showing up drunk. She reestablishes herself there and makes a life for her and Hans, who becomes her lover. Possessed by his memories of the war, Hans seeks out his former captain in the army, Ferdinand Brückner. The one-time commander who ordered the execution of an entire village of innocent civilians during the war, Brückner is now owner of a factory that turns battle helmets into cooking pots. Hans seeks to avenge the deaths of the innocent villagers through a vigilante execution of his former captain. Susanne thwarts his plans in the last moment. The film ends with an appeal to the justice system to convict the murderers in their midst.

The film leaves the audience uncertain about how it treats the recent German past. The murderer escapes vigilante execution. Susanne and Hans call for a legal prosecution of Brückner and other war criminals at the very end of the film, and the final shot of Brückner shows him standing behind an iron gate that suggests prison bars. But, since this is the first evidence in the film that any sort of state apparatus even exists, it is hard to place our confidence in an outcome grounded in an institutionalized legal structure.

A second disturbing aspect of the film is the character Susanne. We are told that she has just returned from a concentration camp, where she was sent "because of her father," but no other details are given. Further, Susanne is the most beautiful, healthy-looking, and mentally well adjusted person in the film. Her main activity is helping Hans, the former soldier. Dealing with the Nazi past requires dealing with the Nazis' victims. Why does *The Murderers Are among Us* present us with a victim and then leave her so completely undeveloped?

Establishing Place

We find evidence of competing generic structures from the very start of Staudte's film. The background music that accompanies the opening credits is at once somber and dramatic, in no way a break with pre-1945 cinematic conventions. As the credits finish, the screen goes black with a white text appearing, placing the story both temporally and spatially: "Berlin, 1945 . . . the city has capitulated." Before any image has been projected, we know that the story is set in perhaps the world's most contested space and its most troubled time.

The camera opens on two dark mounds that fill the screen. As the shot cranes upward, the mounds reveal themselves to be graves, marked by flowers, a *Wehrmacht* helmet, and a cross—Berlin as "Tombstone," a place where violence and chaos reign. As the camera continues to lift, we are provided a view of a berubbled landscape, littered in the foreground with a disabled tank and other debris. This establishing crane shot is a cinematic practice often found in the Western. John Ford's film of the same year, *My Darling Clementine*, establishes its site of contestation as one rising out of the unsettled and unsettling atmosphere of the Wild West.

The opening shot is canted slightly, suggesting to viewers that they are going to be presented with a world that is askew. The tinny piano music is in discord with the framed shot of the grave. It is annoyingly cheerful and lively, given the image of death it accompanies. A lonely figure dressed in a long coat and a brimmed hat, framed in the canyons of destroyed buildings, stumbles along a rocky, treacherous path. He moves slowly and tentatively toward the camera while young children move easily and swiftly around him. As the character approaches the camera it cranes upward, providing a shot of this drifting wanderer from above. The character's movement indicates no particular goal. But the music gets louder, suggesting that, while the camera is not subjective, we are hearing what the character does.

The man approaching the camera is held deliberately in the dark. The camera simultaneously zooms in and rises slowly.[7] This move serves to keep his face dissected by a shadow. Slowly he makes a three-quarter turn in search of the source of the music. The music draws the man, who otherwise appears to be walking without direction, into a brothel advertising "Dance, Good Times, and Humor." Although the intertitle announced "Berlin," the ragtime-like music and landscape suggest an uncanny combination of the former "Reichshauptstadt" and a ghost town. It is a deliberate construction of Berlin that is in contrast to the actual city in 1945, with its 3.5 million inhabitants.

Both the music and the image now blend into the second half of the opening sequence, leaving the Western analogy temporarily. The brothel sign dissolves into an extreme canted shot of a train speeding past. The music changes to an orchestrated, dramatic non-diegetic score. While in the first half of the sequence the staging was slow and evocative of death, the rhythm picks up in this second part. Everything about this *mise en scène* indicates an edgy vitality; the city is alive but not well. The shot is framed with a metal beam, cutting it in half diagonally. Passengers are dangling from the sides of the cars. The wagons appear to have no interior. The film cuts to a countershot, supposedly a point-of-view shot from the train itself. The camera does not survey the landscape as the train arrives but remains fixed on the ruins of the platform itself. This is a very urban clutter, different from the clutter in the first shot. As the locomotive enters the station, the film cuts back to a fixed shot from inside. It pans slowly, following the train as it is partially blocked from view by a twisted metal beam.

As the train enters the station, the images gradually change from angular to rounded. The film cuts to a still slightly canted eye-level shot of a crowd walking down the train platform. The figures are dressed darkly and looking away from the camera. As an old man crosses in front of the camera he reveals a young woman in a white coat. The music turns from the driving symphonic score to soft strings. The woman occupies the center of the shot and is fully lighted from the front as she moves in for what becomes a medium close-up. The woman, who will shortly be introduced as Susanne Wallner, is clean, beautiful, and bears no signs of trauma, apart from an apparent shock at the sight and bustle of the city in which she has just arrived.

The train, the movement, the sharp angles provided by the canted camera and the orchestral music draw upon yet another film history, namely the urban fascination of the Weimar cinema. In this case, it looks as if the actors are returning to the set of Walter Ruttman's *Berlin, Symphony of a City* (1929). Susanne is most clearly a part of something; that is, in contrast to Hans, she is not visually alienated from her surroundings.

The film then cuts to a countershot, presumably a subjective one. Her gaze is directed toward a group of broken men lying or sitting next to a wall. One of them crosses in front of the others toward the camera, revealing the prisoner-of-war marking on the back of his coat. As the man crosses, the camera zooms in on what is apparently the object of her attention, namely a travel poster of Nuremberg that hangs crookedly on the wall. The camera zooms in on the poster, which dissolves into a shot of towering ruins, reminiscent of Monument Valley. This shot then dissolves to one of Susanne walking among these ruins. As she passes, it then closes in on an intact statue of a woman and a child framed by the destroyed buildings.

The film's opening sequence introduces the two main characters in a discordant manner; we suspect that the plot is about bringing them together, whereas the film's task ends up being much larger. *The Murderers Are among Us* is experimenting with filmic convention, language, and images, seeking a device that will tell their stories. This leads to other discords in the opening seconds between the spectator's expectation of a Berlin cityscape and the film's presentation of an image that bears a far greater resemblance to the set of a Hollywood Western. The presence of a torn auto carcass, a destroyed tank, and the ruins of a

European metropolis on this set creates a dialogue between the recent European history and film traditions on one hand, and, on the other, a cinematic narrative code that could still produce the moral lesson the film will have to present.

The Murderers Are among Us and the Western

The analogy with the Western derives from three cinematic elements: the film's *mise en scène*, its use of narrative convention, and the development of the characters. In each, Staudte's film shares qualities with the Western. Moreover, the connection is made more vivid through the relationship to the domestic melodrama, a common element to the resolution of many Western storylines. The Western traits, first presented in the opening sequence, continue throughout the film. The landscape of destroyed Berlin, with its scattered bricks and destroyed tanks and cars, mimics the rocky terrain, scrubby brush, and bleached-out bones of familiar desert scenes. The obvious example to which Staudte might have had access is John Ford's *Stagecoach*, which was approved by the Allies for public showing in 1946, and which marked Ford's first use of Monument Valley as a backdrop for moral tales. The blocks of bombed-out buildings in Staudte's film form urban canyons. We are not being shown what Berlin really looked like in 1945; rather, Staudte's Berlin shares with *Stagecoach*'s Monument Valley the conflation of great empty landscapes with the character's inner life. This goal of conflating character and landscape, often stated by Ford, was echoed by Staudte in 1946: "The connection of man to his current environment, that is the basic theme of the film. We want to take the camera to the landscape of the human face, to travel the world of human sensibilities."[8] Other important Western tropes are adapted; at various points in the film, we even see trash and papers blowing by that are reminiscent of tumbleweeds. These function in the film in the same way tumbleweeds are often used in Westerns—as symbols of the past being delivered to a character.

Hans Mertens is, in many ways, a stock genre hero, be it gangster, *film noir*, or Western. He is a man with a mysterious past that he refuses to discuss. The opening shot pins it down more specifically. He arrives in a lawless wasteland where he at first occupies himself with alcohol and brothels. He is both driven and hindered, both strong and depressed. He is reluctant to take up his calling. A typical Western hero meets a typical Western heroine. She is a woman who is pure, civilized, and out of place in the lawless wasteland. But, analogous to the Western, their love affair seems out of place, in fact, inappropriate to the Westerner's character. "If there is a woman he loves, she is usually unable to understand his motives; she is against killing and being killed."[9] And yet, the woman plays an important role in the Western. "Women are often portrayed as possessing some kind of deeper wisdom, while the men, for all their apparent self-assurance, are fundamentally childish."[10] In the case of *The Murderers Are among Us*, Susanne provides a moral compass to Hans's disturbed personality. She keeps his righteousness from becoming criminal.

In the typical Western, the hero's sense of justice becomes refined through his confrontation with evil in the showdown. Robert Warshow notes, "No death can be paid for and no stain truly wiped out; the movie is still a tragedy, for though the hero escapes with his life, he has been forced to confront the ultimate limits of his moral ideas. This mature sense of limitation and unavoidable guilt is what gives the Westerner a 'right' to his melancholy."[11] Until almost the final moments of the film, we see Hans either as a righteous vigilante or a self-righteous ass. But, once informed of his past, we do not dispute the justness of his cause, even when he is preparing to murder. Why not? In part, it is because the film foils the first plot to ambush Brückner. Hans's underlying desire to do good by performing an emergency tracheotomy legitimates him as a moral and social authority figure. Furthermore, we could see the murder plot literally through his eyes as a necessary act taken in the name of bringing justice to chaos. He is *not* the "murderer" among us. In justifying the vigilante legal sense of the Westerner, André Bazin notes, "where individual morality is precarious it is only law that can impose the order of the good and the good of the order. But the law is unjust. . . . If it is to be effective it must be dispensed by men who are just as strong and daring as the criminals."[12] Only the Western has the generic force to allow a man's redemption to come through marshaling social order by direct, vigilante confrontation. Unlike the urban dramas, in the West, morality has more force than legal code. Because the viewer can identify with the hero, who is going to commit a murder in order to bring justice to the community, this film became an ethical benchmark for the reviewer Walter Lenning, who wrote, "A good German is recognizable in how or whether or not he is affected by this film."

But there is an important difference between *The Murderers Are among Us* and the typical Western, one that complicates the moral mes-

sage of the film—there is no final shootout. Hans pulls a gun on Brückner at the end of the film, but he does not kill him. Has Hans, at this
moment, found "the ultimate limits of his moral ideas," as Warshow
claims Western heroes usually do? Or is the moment a triumph in
which Hans abandons vigilantism and embraces a new and better ethic?
Our understanding of the film will depend crucially on our reading of
this scene.

Berlin as Tombstone, or Why Make a Western in 1946 Germany?

Westerns were already a very familiar genre to German filmmakers in
the 1920s. As Lutz Koepnick has shown, the American Western occupied an integral part of the urban fantasy space in Weimar Germany.[13]
After 1940, American films did not find their way into German cinemas,
but Goebbels held screenings of the top Hollywood films to which he
would invite selected members of the filmmaking community. Westerns were a part of the immediate postwar onslaught of approved films
with which the Americans flooded the German cinemas.[14]

The idea of a German Western clearly has precedence, both in popular literature and in film. Adolf Hitler's favorite author, Karl May, is
the obvious literary example. May wrote tales of the Wild West popu-
lated by German emigrants. Luis Trencker's "mountain films" share
the same signature fascination with landscape. Koepnick claims that
"the long-standing German pre-occupation with the iconography of
the Far West" constitutes "a discursive site at which Germans negoti-
ated and contested the meaning of modern culture and society."[15] If
May, and Hitler's attachment to him, compromised the genre, its return
in the form of Hollywood Westerns immediately following the war
would have reclaimed the moral potential of the genre.

The German relationship to the Western is not a simple one. Cultural specificities, such as a different relationship to violence and to language, affect the narrative parameters of German versions of the genre.
That Staudte would call upon the Western codes in their German man-
ifestations, whether consciously or not, seems quite likely. Why could
one not simply have made a Western set in the nineteenth-century
American West? The fact is, and this will become clearer throughout
the book, that a high degree of cinematic discourse in the immediate
postwar era was bound by the demands of realism. The audience and

critics made it clear over and over again that, at least from German film, they wanted Germany's story to be told in recognizable terms.

Given a whole century's worth of German fascination with America, it might seem easy to establish one-way communication between the American Western and German culture. However, the influence actually went in both directions. In a land of immigrants, especially in Hollywood, the nineteenth-century German fascination with the American West was instrumental in creating the Western mythology. Furthermore, John Ford, who was more influential than anyone in creating the generic rules for the Western, drew much stylistic inspiration from 1920s German cinema. F. W. Murnau was a major influence on Ford, and thereby on the Western tradition as a whole. Although many directors and all the major Hollywood studios produced Westerns in the first half of the twentieth century, John Ford's name was already synonymous with the genre by 1940. In his biography of Ford, Tag Gallagher has noted how the filmmaker was "enchanted by the intense stylization of Murnau's painterly invention, in which a character's conscious rapport with his physical world seemed suddenly palpable."[16] As is so often the case in Weimar-era German films, the milieu and the landscape in Ford films becomes a part of the character. Gallagher writes that "contrasts between subjective and objective reality, theater and documentary, character and directorial presence become vital aspects of John Ford's cinema."[17] After his encounter with Murnau, Ford's characters share with Murnau's a simultaneous resistance to and respect for communal codes. Gallagher also notes Ford's use of a Murnau psychological tactic, namely the close-up of the horrified face to portray a startling event taking place in view of the character.[18] Western filmmakers, especially Ford, adopted many such Weimar-era filmic conventions.[19]

Shutting Out the Past with the Domestic Melodrama

It is a common theme in Westerns, especially those of the postwar years, that a cultured woman is introduced into the story in order to establish a bourgeois value structure in the plot. If the Westerner brings law and order to the town, the woman brings shared principles and rootedness. The combination of traits creates community out of the Wild West chaos.

Domestic melodramas, on the other hand, generally include a couple, a civilized space, the conflation of domestication with societal integration, a maternal-familial code, and community cooperation.[20] Susanne's introduction of exactly those elements gives rise to what amounts to the film's generic tension. Their forced co-domestication undermines Hans's declared status as a loner; she tames him against his will. She clears the rubble, the signifier of Hans's alienation, from the house, reclaiming it for civilized functionality. The domestic space becomes increasingly more comfortable and critical to Hans's well-being. Susanne provides the moral code that runs the household, one that Hans's self-pity and drunkenness confront constantly.

The opening sequence announces at least two structural possibilities by introducing Susanne and Hans simultaneously, though entirely differently. Her cinematic structure is highly controlled. The cuts are quick. Shots occasionally dissolve into one another. The general effect is artificial. Shots of Hans are medium to long. The takes are much more extended and editing is almost nonexistent. The film ties her to the desire for communal integration and domesticity. Her reaction to having been cast out—that is, to having been incarcerated in a concentration camp—is to seek to reengage herself in the community. In the famous shot of the couple looking out onto the ruins of Berlin, the window contains Susanne while Hans's frame is still open (Photo 1). Domestic order belongs to the value structure with which she becomes identified. In fact, once she regains her apartment, the only activities we see her engaged in are either domestic, maternal, or both.

One of the film's most memorable images occurs in a canyonesque, low-lighted nighttime sequence (Photo 2). After an argument, Hans follows Susanne out into the landscape that has defined him. The sequence marks the high point of this film's domestic melodrama, as Susanne attempts to extract Hans from the emotional ruins and back into her domestic fantasy. He overtakes her along the winding moonlit path and declares his intention to fall in love with her. It is also a harbinger of the return to the Western. The *mise en scène* is most convincingly a depiction of canyons at that point, with ruined buildings lit from below to exaggerate the imposing character of the environment out of which Susanne retrieves Hans. The argument itself seems contrived in order to remove them to this moonlit rubble set.[21]

This sequence commands further attention because of its obviously deliberate break with cinematic consistency. In this painfully con-

Photo 1. *The Murderers Are among Us:* Susanne and Hans look out over a war-torn city. (Courtesy of Stiftung Deutsche Kinemathek)

Photo 2. *The Murderers Are among Us:* Staudte resorts to a studio to create the perfect rubble. (Courtesy of Stiftung Deutsche Kinemathek)

structed cinematic realist studio set, consistency would have had the two walking away from the camera. Instead, the film's blocking has them move toward the camera. As they do so, the dramatic night shot of ruins diminishes in comparison to the characters. In the course of a minute, the shot goes from an extreme long shot to an extreme close-up.

Shot composition varies widely between the two generic structures in this film. The interior shots are primarily medium-close to close. In fact, the insertion of the facial close-up shots disrupts conventional expectations. As in Westerns, much of *The Murderers Are among Us* is constructed primarily of medium and long shots, often so long that Hans is dwarfed by the landscape. The move from one cinematic form to the other often makes for the most impressive imagery of the film.

Subplot Contextualizations

It takes thirty minutes to introduce the Brückner plot strand into the film. Before that, a number of subplots are introduced, any one of which could have provided interesting cinematic material. The old neighbor and patron of the apartment building, Mondschein, has worked hard to reestablish a life for himself out of the rubble of the war. It is unclear whether or not he may have belonged to the list of those persecuted by the Nazis. Susanne expresses surprise that he is still alive after the war. The hope that his son, who has obviously emigrated to America, will eventually return motivates Mondschein to continue living. His role in the film is to cast a moral gaze upon the unfolding drama of Hans and Susanne. In many ways, he is Susanne's reinforcement in the task of resocializing Hans.

The other characters in the house serve similar functions in the film. The house gossip provides the audience with information about Susanne that establishes her moral authority. By having the neighbors convey the information about her past and about their growing domestic and love relationship, Susanne is protected from being forced to become either self-righteous or defensive.

Herr Timm, the soothsayer, is Brückner's moral *Doppelgänger* in his ability to exploit postwar conditions. Timm exploits individuals' fears and desperation about the future and provides a false comfort. He is exposed as a fraud in the sequence where he predicts Mondschein's imminent reunion with his son. In fact, the film uses the exploitation subplot to introduce the moral poverty of the period, of which Brückner, who appears in the following sequence, is the greater example.

The last of the subplots contrasts Ferdinand Brückner as war criminal and loving father with Hans Mertens, righteous drunk. Just as Hans uses alcohol to conceal his moral indignation, the scenes of domestic tranquility and prosperity in the Brückner household are used to set up an ideal that the film will gradually unveil as false. The film works to replace the domestic fantasy based on lies and exploitations, as embodied in Brückner, with one based on a sense of social justice and altruism, the position gradually established for Hans. Brückner sees the world through new glass windows, while Mertens sees it, literally, through objects of his past (the x-rays saved from Hans's medical school days). These subplots, along with the one in which Hans performs the emergency operation, give the appearance of a community context in a Berlin that is otherwise depicted as empty.

The Final Sequence: A Showdown between the Western and the Melodrama

The move between the two generic structures and the rhythm that it establishes become critical for understanding the film's final sequence and its outcome. For the end of the film amounts to a showdown, not only between Hans and Brückner, but also between the order-oriented Western and the domestic melodrama's drive toward social harmony. The generic structures will demand different resolutions of the problems the narrative sets out to solve. These differences account for the ambiguities regarding the film's treatment of the questions of crime and punishment.

The sequence begins with domestic order having been established. Hans and Susanne have set up a comfortable bourgeois existence together, celebrating Christmas. The outside, which throughout the film has represented the primary threat, has been shut out with the relic of Hans's past, the x-ray film he saved from his days as a medical student. The x-ray photos are polyvalent signs of his personal history. He is able to use this medium to discuss his distant past as a successful young doctor, until memory of the intervening history arises. Hans is reminded of the war and Brückner's order to liquidate the population of a village. His mood turns dark and he takes out his gun.

Right as Hans picks up his gun, the film's generic duality reemerges. Hans immediately turns from an eloquent storyteller to a silent shadow. The shots of him pull back so that, in the next scene, when he stops to listen to "Silent Night" being sung inside a ruined church, his long shadow is projected onto a darkened facade. He is again portrayed as an alienated and haunted figure whom we know to be headed for a showdown.

As Hans strolls through the city witnessing its Christmas Eve activities, his eyes reveal the discord underlying this supposed harmony. The words of peace and reconciliation are but a thin ice covering the sea of moral chaos. What Hans sees, Susanne speaks. In his absence, she finds and reads his written account of Christmas Eve three years earlier, when the village massacre took place. Since Susanne has told us the history, in the final showdown (Photo 3) Hans need only tell Brückner that he is demanding revenge, restating the statistics of the brutal village liquidation. Words do not interfere with his desire, they only justify it.

Hans increasingly closes in the space. If the community is endangered by the "murderer among us," the camerawork and staging slowly entrap the criminal, as in the final sequence of Fritz Lang's *M*. The shadow that Hans has become will be the very location of the showdown. Nothing else occupies the space. The diegetic and non-diegetic music is gone. Hans confronts Brückner in an empty space, a hallway.

Photo 3. *The Murderers Are among Us:* Brückner is called to account by a "ghost of Christmas past." (Courtesy of Stiftung Deutsche Kinemathek)

As Brückner backs away he is consumed by Hans's shadow, gradually shrinking in the space. Hans is prepared to kill the murderer who is, in fact, now visually internal to him. As Photo 3 shows, Brückner is now consumed inside Hans's shadow. Hans has indeed contained the evil and needs only to eliminate it. He is, in that moment, purely external, nothing but surface and gaze. He has installed fear in the eyes of his enemy.

One sound brings the showdown to an end—not the sound of a shot, but that of Susanne calling of Hans's name, calling him back to himself. The series of medium close-ups of him, her, and Brückner breaks up the action. The tension is relieved, space is expanded. Her final statement that "we don't have the right to be judge and hangman," followed by accession to democratic due process, is clearly integrationist. The Western structure has given way to the domestic melodrama. Hans is drawn away from quick and immediate justice into the slow narrative of legal discourse. Brückner ends up visually/symbolically behind bars.

The Missing Shootout

The analogy to the Western lacks a critical element: a final gun battle. The missing shootout in *The Murderers Are among Us* is very important to understanding the film. Typically in a Western, the shootout is the tool by which the hero reestablishes a moral order in a lawless land. It is quick justice. The purpose of such a cathartic bloodletting is to allow the spectator the fantasy of pure justice triumphing over evil, unadulterated by legal stratification.

In a number of John Ford's Westerns the final showdown has a precarious relationship to the law. In *Stagecoach* we sympathize with John Wayne's character's need to avenge the death of his brother and father. The shooting of Liberty Valance is, in legal terms, a murder.[22] In almost all of the portrayals of Wyatt Earp and Doc Holliday, the showdown at the OK Corral is an ambush.[23] The pursuit of justice in these and many other classic Hollywood Westerns suggests that law functions without clear moral boundaries between good and evil.

But in *The Murderers Are among Us*, the showdown is cut short. Why is there no final shootout? The most obvious explanation is that the Soviet censors would not let Staudte make such a film. The Soviet censors' reasoning was that they could not allow an endorsement of vigilante justice to be shown in postwar Germany. They had to maintain public order. Cathartic bloodlettings may work in film, but they are unacceptable in occupied territories. As Staudte explains it, "The Soviet officer was enamored of the material, but had only one objection: I should change the ending. He refused that type of vigilantism and painted for me a picture of the consequences that could come from the effects of the film if everyone were to go and shoot everyone else, regardless of how understandable their wishes might be. Such criminals must be handed over to the proper courts for judgment."[24] The officer's reason for demanding a different ending reveals an attitude about film that would influence DEFA throughout the rest of the decade. The Soviet authorities had an agenda for film as a tool of education and socialization. The projection of a private fantasy that would be in conflict with a public value was not acceptable. And they clearly believed that film made a direct connection between the two.

Staudte's pitch to the Soviet authorities was not completely in line with the standard Western's lawless answer to justice. In it, Hans becomes the test case of criminal law instead of Brückner. The proposal also takes the story through a trial where the former captain is painted as a pillar of society and Hans a cowardly murderer. The story of the wartime "liquidation" becomes Hans's defense testimony. Staudte's proposal had the film end with the court's deliberation, that is, without a verdict.[25] Ultimately, this test of the legal system was not one that the authorities were willing to allow in a film.

Neither the trial sequence in the original proposal nor the conclusion in the actual film gives *The Murderers Are among Us* closure. The film sets us up for a showdown that does not happen. The solution of relying on the legal system is ungrounded in the rest of the film and inexplicit. Legal authority, whether in the form of Allied forces, local justice, or even bureaucratic restriction, is completely absent, as are all institutional forces.[26] That is not to say that Staudte's original proposal, in which a legal system was depicted, would have provided such a narrative. It too would have failed to produce the moral drama necessary to bring the film to a satisfactory conclusion. It is an important artifact of 1946 that the film leaves open the significant legal and moral questions of guilt.

The failure of the final showdown to produce catharsis is largely a function of the generic restlessness of this text. But, at the same time, the lack of a shootout adheres to the conventions of the distinctively German Western.[27] While the Western can, in many ways, be said to be as much a part of German popular imagination as it is American, the traditional German rendition varies somewhat from its New World counterpart. German Westerns seldom have final shootouts, and the heroes are often more communicative, choosing to talk their way out of potentially violent situations. Koepnick claims that German Westerns "rewrite the quest for law and order as a romantic search for spiritual refinement and communal harmony."[28] Koepnick argues elsewhere that "the removal of the gunfight from publicness in the German Western expresses an aspiration to collapse private and public realms . . . by exposing the striking role, not of bullets, but of words."[29] When Hans resorts to the legal system at the end of the film, it could be argued that he is adhering to the generic code of the specifically German Western. It could also be argued that the film picks up on the inherent domesticating tension within most Westerns, choosing a different resolution to the conflict.

If the German Western is, to use Schatz's terms, more integrationist than its American counterpart, that would still leave us with some incongruities. For the shadows that serve throughout the film to define and determine Hans's alienated character would confuse our comparison of *The Murderers Are among Us* with the generic patterns of the Hollywood Western. A typical German Western hero, Sutter in Luis Trencker's *The Emperor of California*, for instance, seeks integration. He desires acceptance by the community.[30] In contrast, the American Western hero often becomes integrated despite himself. He avoids community, but community seeks him out. Hans behaves more like the latter. He is driven to carry out vigilante justice. In Staudte's original proposal, Hans succeeds and then asks for public affirmation of his decision. In the final version, Susanne prevents him from carrying out his own justice. A man of few words, his justification for killing Brückner consists of the raw numbers of those the latter had "liquidated." According to the proposal, Hans would have hoped for the verdict to go his way, that is, to have become at one with community values. An American Westerner would do what he had to do and thereby *establish* community values.

What does the film's relationship to Western narrative practices, both of the American and German variety, tell us about how this film works with the Nazi past? The Western provides an interesting model for a relationship to the past, even if following the model to its end was in this case impossible. Staudte and, perhaps, the audience desire quick justice—they want to purge the murderers from their midst (and perhaps from themselves). Given the very guilt that they would have liked to purge, this possibility is obviously closed. So the characters, the film, and the audience are left to appeal to a democratic legal system, one for which there is not yet a public discourse or understanding. The film does not know how to portray it. And, in 1946, there would have been no reason why an audience would have had any confidence in such a system, nor satisfaction in a film ending that would evoke such an appeal.

Innocence *sans* Victimhood

Susanne remains a puzzle. Why is her character so undeveloped? What is her role in the film? Why are we told that she is a concentration camp survivor and then given no more details? Why is this concentration camp survivor represented as healthy, redeeming, and optimistic? We can answer these questions by thinking about the role of women in Westerns and domestic melodramas.

Susanne is no more out of place than most women in Westerns, nor is her story any less developed. Since Hans is defined through a different set of generic characteristics, her motivations and desires lie in a wholly different drama than Hans's, namely in a domestic melodrama. Hans and Susanne seem like characters in different films that have been forcibly merged. From the very start, these differences cause tension between the two of them and between the viewer and the film. But this is a tension common to the classical Western narrative.

In Westerns, women are symbols of civilization, innocence, and community. They are non-ideological bearers of language. To be sure, Susanne is all of these things in *The Murderers Are among Us*. But why make Susanne a concentration camp survivor? Because of the discourse of guilt that included all Germans in 1946, the film needs to find a position of innocence from which it can civilize Hans. Any ordinary woman who had been living in Germany at the time would have been burdened with a morally questionable past. And since the point of the film is to rehabilitate Hans, it is all the more convenient to exclude Susanne's past through resorting to a genre that, by definition, is a male frontier.[31]

Only in the fantasy of the filmmakers, however, was someone in a concentration camp as naive, unburdened, and optimistic as Susanne is portrayed as being. Obviously the filmmakers elide the realities of concentration camps. Germans in the immediate postwar years were often heedless of all suffering other than their own. They had plenty of information regarding Nazi atrocities, but few intellectual and emotional tools to process it. And they, like Hans, assumed guilt to a blindingly selfish degree. In this questionable view of the world, victims were seen as lucky in comparison.

Conclusion

Reading *The Murderers Are among Us* as analogous to a Western—and seeing the ways in which it stops short of being a Western—helps answer some of the film's more enigmatic elements. It also serves as a good introduction to the many ways in which films of the early postwar period in Germany resort to generic convention in order to give life to filmic narrative in postwar Germany. This film's answers to Germany's past are grounded in Hollywood narrative schematics. Susanne remains a disturbingly underdeveloped character, as do women in most Westerns. The generic codes that best suit her story, namely the domestic melodrama, serve to insert legal discourse into the film. All this leaves us with the big question with which we started. Does *The Murderers Are among Us*—the first German postwar film—redeem the medium of filmmaking in Germany?

Not quite, I would argue. The film's end, even if Staudte had been free to pursue his original version, leaves us with troubling generalizations. To be sure, one would not have wanted to legitimate, even in a feature film, informal executions as a method of dealing with the past. But one would also not necessarily want to portray the crimes of the Nazi past as a distant problem with distant solutions. Likewise, the end of the film sets up German soldiers like Hans and dead Christians (represented by a zoom shot of hundreds of gravemarking crosses) as the victims of the murderers among us, rather than the liquidated villagers (presumably Jews). In a film that either set for itself or was granted by others such high moral aspirations, this sloppiness is critical.

At the very least, the appeal of *The Murderers Are among Us* both to the occupying authorities and to audiences showed filmmakers that historical truth and accuracy were not values that the censors would enforce. The premiere of Staudte's film was followed shortly thereafter by the premiere of Gerhard Lamprecht's *Somewhere in Berlin* (*Irgendwo in Berlin*), a realist drama of the perils of family life in destroyed Berlin, and Milo Harbich's *Free Land* (*Freies Land*), a propagandistic film about the need for Soviet-style land reform in the eastern occupation zones. Both other films failed.[32] While they portrayed actual conditions in Germany, they provided little of the fantasy sought by film audiences. *The Murderers Are among Us* offers redemption to its troubled male subject, the potential for domestic happiness to the long-suffering woman, and a promise of restoring moral order (albeit a weak one) to a confused community.

Renarrating a moral course for its audience is an unrealistic task to assign to a film, especially when the audience also expects some form of entertainment. At best *The Murderers Are among Us* speaks to the ability of film to include moral questions. To be sure, it labors under delusions about what it means to be a concentration camp survivor. It gives no clear message about justice, guilt, or the problems of the German past. Schatz is correct in claiming that "movies are considerably more effective in their capacity to raise questions than to answer them. This characteristic seems particularly true of genre films."[33] In calling upon generic storytelling, Staudte creates a space in film where such questions can at least be posed if not answered. As many of the postwar German historical debates have taught us, opening space in the public sphere for debate on Germany's Nazi past is a significant task. Jürgen Habermas has argued in a much more recent debate that "how we see the distribution of guilt and innocence in the past also reflects the present norms according to which we are willing to accord one another mutual respect."[34]

The Murderers Are among Us sets the tone for an entire set of DEFA films in the late 1940s that thematize the *Schuldfrage* (question of guilt) from varying perspectives.[35] It is an often overlooked cinematic legacy that tells us much about the politics of the past in early postwar German culture. It reveals both the willingness to approach narratives regarding the recent Nazi past and the tendency shy away from a complete critical confrontation with that past. *The Murderers Are among Us* is an introduction to the ambivalence of rubble filmmaking.

3

It's a Wonderful Reich

Private Innocence
and Public Guilt

**In these attempts to shake off guilt, it is remarkable how little
attention is paid to the victims. . . . Now there is only feeling
enough for the cathexis of one's own person, hardly any kind
of sympathy with others. If somehow, somewhere one finds
an object deserving of sympathy, it usually turns out to be
none other than oneself.**

—Alexander and Margaret Mitscherlich, *The Inability to Mourn: Principles of
Collective Behavior*

The blindnesses that the Mitscherlichs describe in their semi-
nal book on the postwar German work of mourning can be
found in much of the early postwar filmic discourse. The
rubble films portray the Nazi past as, at best, one problem
among many. Filmmakers often overlooked the horrific
destruction their community had wrought upon the rest of
the world and concentrated on the alienation of Germans
from their own value structures and worldviews. The filmmakers' refusal to alter their own worldview is visible quite
literally in their failure to find new ways of seeing cinematically. As I discussed in the previous chapter, the legitimacy
of the filmic medium itself was under suspicion in Germany.
Narrative film was the primary suspect; the Allied censors
allowed Germans to begin producing other filmic media
such as newsreels earlier. Germans only succeeded in mak-

ing a case for restarting the feature film industry insofar as they acceded to the demands of the Allies to produce narratives that at least thematized if not confronted the recent German past. Perhaps narratives constructed through cinematic conventions with which the Allies, especially the Western Allies, were most comfortable were seen as the least apt to raise objections. That is to say, the more it looked like Hollywood, the better. In fact, this required little shift from the practices they had adopted under the Nazis.

The directives stated by the Allies at the end of the war required a number of cognitive switches on the part of filmmakers and screenwriters, especially regarding the ideological content of film narratives. By the time filmmaking commenced in the western occupation zone, the censorship apparatus was hardly visible. The filmmakers' interest in pleasing the censors was much more of a factor than actual censorship. In a surprisingly short time, those who were invited back onto the lot included not only those whose wartime films were considered apolitical or even subversive by the Allies, but also others who were favored by and complicit in the old regime. And yet, even those directors considered to have been outsiders in the film industry managed by Goebbels were apprehensive about pleasing the new regime.

Even if filmmakers were successful in finding film genres and styles appropriate to the new political and social reality of the era, they also had to struggle with the actual stories to be told. What could be said about the current life in Germany? And, given the widespread connection between many of the storytellers and the Nazi regime, how did one find a legitimate perspective from which to narrate the troubled past?

Much has been made of the aesthetic success or failure of postwar German filmmakers in relation to their Italian counterparts. Italian neo-realism has become the standard in Europe against which German films of the period are measured. Not only have the films of Roberto Rossellini, Vittorio De Sica, and others established themselves in the cult world of art cinema, intellectuals take them to represent the state of European film discourse at the end of the war. Like their Italian contemporaries, German filmmakers sought a narrative perspective most appropriate to the radically altered political, social, and aesthetic conditions of the postwar era. Unlike the Italians, most German filmmakers did not undertake this questioning on the level of film structure. They employed the cinematic medium to reimagine the past and present, not to reproduce it. They move away from the reality on the street, not toward it.

Neo-realism should not be used as a yardstick for German rubble films. They arise out of entirely different conditions. Neo-realism in Italy originated under fascism as an aesthetic resistance movement, showing from the start a willingness to take not only aesthetic but also political risks.[1] German filmmakers in the late 1940s show no will toward taking political risks and little toward taking aesthetic ones.

Given the onslaught of foreign films filling the German cinema, the only niche German filmmakers could occupy was as mediators of the specificity of Germans' experience. The rubble-era filmmakers tried to speak to the identificatory needs of an audience that was suffering from hunger, homelessness, disillusionment, and subjective confusion. Three of the best-known films of the era, Helmut Käutner's *In Those Days* (1947), Harald Braun's *Between Yesterday and Tomorrow* (1947), and Wolfgang Liebeneiner's *Love '47* (1949), appealed to what Klaus Kreimeier has referred to as the "economy of emotions."[2] Two of these films are among the most successful films of the era; one failed, both critically and financially. All three films provide us with an important insight into the development of a cinematic discourse for use in discussing the Nazi past.

These films do not divulge a German "neo-realism" arising out of the postwar berubbled landscape, in great part because they do not have the resistance impetus of the Italians. Resistance was morally difficult for the German filmmakers. If they expressed resistance, it was against the conditions under which they worked, in which they lacked autonomy, material necessities, and moral authority. Their films are confined to describing the environment and telling small stories of small lives. In some sense, they resist realist tendencies, aspiring instead to an idealism that ignores the basic facts about the past that they are discussing. In this way, the films in this chapter represent a view quite the opposite of their Italian counterparts. Eschewing factual representation, they create a fantasy space that seeks to replace a troubled national past.

Peter Pleyer, in discussing the minimal difference in aesthetic between much of "UFA [the Nazi era studios] dramaturgy, mentality and iconography" and the films of the rubble years, notes critically that

apart from the more or less forced political reorientation at the end of the war most directors' attitudes about the nature of a feature film did not change. The result was that the directorial style of the new films was oriented around older standards of quality. The drive toward originality or new communicative possibilities and thus the expansion of filmic syntax was not predominant. More so was the tendency toward technical perfection of more traditional filmic production methods.[3]

Pleyer goes on to suggest what technical perfection might mean.

> The initial technical difficulties, specifically the lack of studio space, did not provoke German filmmakers, as it did their Italian colleagues, to document real experience regardless of technical difficulties. That would have required a social and political engagement that most postwar German directors were lacking. Instead the directors used technical innovation to reproduce reality as perfectly as possible.[4]

To be sure, postwar German filmmakers did not establish a new trend in filmmaking that could then be exported to other national cinemas. Pleyer is also accurate in noting the degree of control they strove to maintain. But he errs in claiming that this control was put to the task of reproducing reality. Had that been their task, filmmakers would have paid more attention to life in the streets, whether like their Italian contemporaries or in a different manner, to record the incredible and heart-wrenching story of berubbled Berlin. Instead, they employed every cinematic device at their disposal to create an entirely new space, one close to but uncannily different from their German *Heimat*.[5]

Postwar German filmmakers were not interested in opposing or undermining the occupational authorities under which their films were made. They were, however, trying to recapture the filmic idioms for themselves. An important way to accomplish that was to produce a counternarrative to that the one presented by the Allied authorities. The Allies saw in Germany a story of a morally inept people suffering a well-deserved destruction. The three films discussed in this chapter depict the varied response to that Allied narrative. They use the materially trying conditions of postwar Germany as a starting point for reasserting the dignity of the German people. In order to do so, they had to ignore or efface much of the world's case against Germany.

The obedient relationship between political power and cultural production has a long history in Germany. The very notion of a *Kulturnation*, which produced liberal cultural institutions while failing to demand liberal political entities, is part of the traditional historiography of Germany from the Enlightenment to 1945. Quite in tune with this idealist tradition, filmmakers in berubbled Germany set out to try to change the fundamental personal attitudes of the community, while accepting the political conditions as given. The feature films they produced resort to interpersonal discourse as both the problem and the solution. They are all narratives about personal relationships in a horrific past. They share a belief that cinematic narrative can form and change personal moral values, while avoiding seemingly public political values. *In Those Days, Between Yesterday and Tomorrow*, and *Love '47* all look for their model of change in the crisis of the individual.

Pleyer's comments notwithstanding, to the degree that these films experiment at all, they do so at the level of narrative rather than style. Hollywood's Frank Capra provides a more likely analogy than does Rossellini. While Rossellini seemingly would provide a good example for dealing with marginalized cultural figures such as black marketeers and returning soldiers, this marginalization is itself the trauma the rubble films refuse to accept. Characters depicted as powerless at the beginning of film are gradually redeemed and reintegrated into the community. Whether morally, sexually, or physically, the characters regain their centeredness.

In Those Days: Good People in Bad Times

The anecdotes surrounding the making of *In Those Days* encourage fables of their own. There are stories about rampant hunger prevailing on the set.[6] An admirer of one of the film's stars is said to have brought small amounts of sausage to the set to at least ease the hunger pangs of the actors. Toward the end of the filming, Käutner is reported to have broken down in tears on the set, fearing his project would never come to fruition for want of the bare necessities of his cast and crew and the lack of raw film stock.[7] If true, these stories tell us much about the conditions under which the film was produced. Indeed, the actors were likely depicting some of their own experiences in the film. The hardships the crew endured, as well as Käutner's presumed moral legitimacy at the end of the war, brought the project to the attention of the film press well before it was released. Because of his unconventional work during the Third Reich, critics anticipated Käutner's first postwar film to be a standard-bearer for postwar production.[8]

In Those Days opens with the standard rubble film establishing shot over the ruins of a destroyed city, though there is no clear indication of which one. The shot follows an old bearded man and his one-legged companion who are gathering sticks for a fire, passes over a makeshift cemetery and finally settles on two men in a junkyard dismantling an old car. This shot sets up the milieu of berubbled Germany, while the opening dialogue tells us almost everything the film intends to do. The very first sentence uttered reveals the brooding emotional state of Germans as the film hopes to portray it. Willi, one of the two men working on the old car in the junkyard begins the conversation.

Willi: You're thinking again, huh, Karl?

Karl: I can't help it.

Willi anticipates Karl's bemoaning of his rotten existence, listing what must have been a very common litany of postwar complaints.

Willi: What, that broken record again? Nothing to smoke, nothing to drink, nothing to eat, no coal, no real job, no apartment, no money, no news from Susanne, no future, nothing . . . nothing . . . nothing.

Karl: No humanity! There is no more humanity. None, Willi. Just like there was none in all those cursed years. That's why we are all so decrepit.

This is the film's attempt to quantify the vacuum. It first lists the problems that it cannot solve, namely the postwar material hardships. It sets its sights squarely on recovering the subjective losses. Willi asks the more learned Karl what means he when he says that there is no more humanity.

"What is a *Mensch*?" This is the question the film places at the center of its narrative project. *Mensch* is a complicated word in German. In general, a *Mensch* is a human being; more specifically, it refers to a good person. "Humanity" seems to be the object here. Willi laments a loss of human dignity, which he sees as the cause of "those cursed years." How can these two men, implicated in both the horrific history and its miserable aftermath, plausibly counter the claim that humanity has disappeared? The way the film seeks to answer these questions constitutes one of the more bizarre concoctions of the rubble years. As the two men quietly puzzle over Willi's ontological question, a disembodied voice-over interrupts their conversation. The camera zooms in on the car they are dismantling, from which the voice emanates.

Voice: Excuse me if I intrude on your discussion. You, of course, cannot hear me, for fate has dealt you a lack of understanding toward us, those which you call dead objects. But, I have heard you for days, in fact, ever since you have been tearing me apart. Dear Sirs, I have been witness to the endless and depressing considerations with which you have tried to excuse your own incompetence and injustice toward your fellow man. An automobile has no right to an opinion, according to you. And, I don't want to interfere in your discussion. I only want . . . you spoke of humanity and I believe Herr Willi was the one who asked, "What is humanity." And Herr Karl, if I am not mistaken, claimed there is no such thing, not now, and certainly not in those days, those days which were my life. Allow me to tell a few stories my way, which is not the human way. Let me report objectively, heartlessly, without prejudice as only a dead object can. My life is behind me. I have, if you will, closed my eyes forever.

This technological apparatus, the automobile Karl and Willi are busy dismantling, speaks up (with Käutner himself supplying the voice). It is to become the vocal "red thread" of the film. The first thing the car bemoans is the fact that while it has a story to tell, the humans will not be able to hear it. The car encounters a paradox. At first, it bemoans anthropocentrism, that is, that humans are unable to listen to anything but other humans. Yet, the possibility of the car's role as narrator lies in its having experienced humanity in a way the humans did not. As a "dead object" it would like to correct the telling of history to which Karl pretends. It can intervene precisely because it is not human. In 1947 in Germany that means it does not share the intense subjective crises of its human companions, nor could it have any share in the guilt of the war. If it failed to be a *Mensch*, it was not the car's fault. This is a desperate, or perhaps the most inspired, attempt to reconstruct or recoup a sense of narrative perspective. The film claims that it has found a place from which the story of the last twelve years can be told, a place that is "objective, heartless, and without prejudice." The car will tell the stories of seven of its owners. Each episode is triggered by an object removed from the car by Karl and Willi. And each centers on a character who remained a *Mensch* despite the times.

The film is interestingly dialectical. While it sets up an object that can narrate history, this history is told through the dismantling of the object itself. Thus, while the film establishes a perspective for telling stories of the Nazi years, it also takes apart that perspective. Or, even more accurately, the dismantling triggers the storytelling. This dialectic is what is meant, in its most useful sense, by deconstruction. It is not just dismantling, which is the way most critics of poststructuralism use the word. Rather, it is the act of construction through taking apart. It is the act of putting together a new narrative with the parts of an existing one. History-telling, in this sense, becomes contingent upon what you peel off.

The most important gesture of *In Those Days*, then, takes place in the opening sequence. The premise of the story is to retell the history of the Third Reich through the stories of good Germans in bad times. The film tries at different points to set up the car, not only as the narrative perspective on the Third Reich, but also as an allegorical figure of the Third Reich itself. The car says as it begins its saga, "When I was young, I believed my life would span a thousand years, and they would be wonderful." The shot then fades into one of men marching in jackboots. "But a thousand turned to twelve and they were not so wonderful." The car hits the road on January 30, 1933, the day the Nazis come to power. This identification with the Third Reich continues a few seconds later when the car speaks of its own early life. The shot depicts the efficient and clean assembly line, technology at its most utopian and hopeful moment. The car, and thus the image of the Third Reich, emerges out of the sequence as an optimistic return to historical progress.

Just after the film's premiere on June 13, 1947, reviewer Wolfdietrich Schnürre wrote:

> Let us have a glance at the content: It begins with a framed narrative. Two men dismantle a car. In the process they find a few objects, each of which has its own story. A series of numbers on the windshield of the car refer to January 30, 1933, the day on which the first owner of the car, torn between two men, chooses the one who would be persecuted by the regime. A comb reminds the narrator of an ostracized composer whose affair with a married woman forces an emotional conflict with the woman's daughter. A hatpin creates a connection to two people from a "mixed marriage" who commit suicide at the beginning of the Jewish pogroms. A picture frame on the sideboard points to a woman who loses her husband twice: first to her own sister and then later to the bullet of an SS gun. Bullet holes recall a night trip through Russian partisan territory. June 20th [*sic*] checks in.[9] A note leads back to an encounter in the last days of the war between a dispatch rider and a young refugee. The actual collapse, the apocalypse, only flickers on the margins in short but impressive dissolving shots. What remain are simply the car carcass and its voice. What remains is the frame: the two men dismantling the wrecked car. One of them, a former student, posed the

question about humanity. And now the car has answered him: it exists. And, it existed "in those days."[10]

In Those Days initially escaped the "rubble film" pejorative with which all films from *The Murderers Are among Us* onward were labeled. Schnürre's one-liner can serve as a headline for the rest: "As of July 13, 1947 there is again a German film to be taken seriously."[11] His comment is important, for as we shall see in subsequent chapters, the film industry that DEFA represented was not one to which he was willing to give any credence. Schnürre would soon establish himself as East German filmmaking's biggest detractor.

The Western press was enthralled. *In Those Days* enjoyed a different kind of reception from that of *The Murderers Are among Us*. Its aesthetic accomplishment was foregrounded, rather than its moral message. Every reviewer mentioned Käutner's ability to turn the hardships of the filmmaking conditions into creative opportunities. But his treatment of the Nazi past also gains him favor with almost all of the contemporary critics. "Helmut Käutner has proven with this film that he is capable of creating an image of Germany's saddest era that is objective and unprejudiced."[12] In the *Allgemeine Zeitung*, the reviewer compares the film to *The Murderers Are among Us*, noting that Käutner's film does not "seed hatred" as Staudte's film supposedly did. "What establishes itself here as the highest command is the song of humanity that could never, not even in those days, be silenced."[13] Clearly, the tone of these reviews makes it clear that *In Those Days* carried the message the public wanted to hear—that Germans are not so bad after all.

The reception of this film also indicates to what extent Germans kept at least one eye on their conquerors. Each critic makes some note of how this film might be received abroad. It did receive a showing at the 1947 Locarno film festival and was eventually made available for foreign film distribution. Although Allied pressure on filmmakers had lessened by this time, there was still plenty to be lost by failing to account for the opinions of the occupying forces. This film raised no ire. But, unlike *The Murderers Are among Us*, it also failed to find much of an audience outside of Germany.

The question to pose of a film that so directly addresses the Nazi past, both in intention and form, is: What picture of that past emerges from the film? Many early reviews hailed it as being true and just to that past. And yet, the film did not age well with the critics. By the early sixties, when discontentment with the German film industry and its relationship to the Nazi past was rampant, *In Those Days* began to lose its place among significant historical films. In 1961 a journalist writing under the initials R.B. claimed that "dirt and rubble, death and persecution serve as nothing but scenery for [Käutner]. He has taken characters directly from the tiredly recognizable society and problem film genres and put them in front of the truly apocalyptic scenery of those days. . . . *In Those Days* is the exact opposite of a realistic film."[14] Approximately twenty years later, Siegfried Zielinski was even more critical of the film and its early positive reception: "This claim of the existence of humane behavior under the rule of fascism serves as an offer of self-cleansing to those who were then attempting to reestablish themselves among the ruins."[15]

The early reception of the film marveled at both the aesthetic achievement and the historical sympathy of the film, while the later critiques point out some of the film's ideological failures. Much of the early criticism treats the film's political approach too superficially. But perhaps the later criticism makes ahistorical demands upon the film. That is to say, later critics fail to understand the limits and imperatives of filmmaking in the period. *In Those Days* states its intention as addressing the history of the Third Reich as seen by the everyman. Since it was the first postwar German film to focus entirely on that past, we must go beyond previous criticism to ascertain how the film engages with the recent past.

The use of a wrecked car as the vehicle for telling the twelve-year history of the "Thousand Year Reich" admits to the difficulty of the task. The car claims a position that no human could occupy, namely one outside of ideology. This fantasy construction by the filmmaker implicates how shots are constructed throughout the film and how the story is told. Almost without exception, all of the shots in the film are either done from the point of view of the car or at least placed in a position where the car would have "seen" the events. In Photo 4, for example, the car occupies the position of witness of Sybille's romantic dilemma.

Käutner made deliberate efforts to efface the traces of the means of production in the film. That is to say, the film rarely calls attention to itself. Except for during the fade shots into and out of the episode sequences, the film makes next to no use of non-diegetic music. The editing is never jarring and remains rigorously consistent. Apart from the complete dependence on location shooting, the film exhibits all of the qualities of a standardized studio product. The medium does not compete with the narrative for attention; rather, it remains subservient to the narrative.

Photo 4. *In Those Days:* Our omnipresent narrator in his younger days. (Courtesy of Stiftung Deutsche Kinemathek)

In all seven of the episodes, the barrier between public and private morals breaks down. Often this breakdown is constructed in the form of the love triangle. In the first episode, Sybille is torn between two men, the one who gives her the car and the one who wants to take her with him to Mexico. She has clearly attached herself to both of them. Steffan, the latter suitor, does not entrust her with enough information to make the decision he wants her to make. The former, Peter, seems to know something from which Sybille should be protected, indicating that the "public" discourse appears to be between men. Once she is made aware of the significance of the events of January 30, 1933, her decision is radically different from the private one she was otherwise prepared to make. She decides to join Steffan in his Mexican exile. It seems that all three characters in this sequence are endowed with an ahistorical prescience that makes them immediately aware of the consequences of Hitler's rise to power on that day. This awareness is portrayed without direct mention of Hitler or the Nazi party.

Peter returns to the film briefly in the fourth episode, in which

Dorothea discovers that her sister, Ruth, has been having an affair with her husband. The husband, who was arrested for subversive activities, is killed in prison and the authorities are in search of his accomplice, that is, the woman with whom he has been. Dorothea realizes that Ruth is about to be arrested and arranges for herself to be taken instead. Thus, the love triangle into which she had unwillingly entered becomes a device by which she can "resist" the will of the regime. But, because she is not the one who was engaged in the underground and is motivated merely by a love for her sister, her resistance is devoid of political content. Most of this information is revealed through a series of phone calls Dorothea makes from a truck stop phone booth "witnessed" by the car. While she is on the phone, Peter rediscovers the car that he had once given to his beloved. Well into the film, this scene reminds us that the car represents the vessel of the *Zeitgeist*.

Themes of private resistance to the political demands of the Nazi era dominate the film. A *Mensch* turns out to be someone who, however privately, expressed opposition to some aspect of Nazism. But, *Menschlichkeit* (humanity) turns out to be the destination of "inner emigration," that is, those who stayed in Germany but opposed the regime privately. The second episode thematizes the dichotomy between public and private morals. It tells a story, not unlike Käutner's most critically acclaimed film, *Romance in a Minor Key* (1943), of a composer who has an affair with a married woman. This time it is his friend's wife. The couple's daughter becomes aware of the affair and prepares to tell her father when the composer announces that he has been banned. This announcement of public trauma convinces the daughter that the private inconsistency that she was about to reveal is immaterial. Curiously enough, the film makes no judgment regarding the affair. The composer is seen as the ultimate victim of political circumstances. This time the public problem intervenes to prevent the child from revealing the private betrayal of the lovers.

The ability of *In Those Days* to sustain a series of such narratives is based upon how "the enemy" is constructed. Nazis go totally unmentioned and do not appear on screen. The perpetrator is the time, "those days." Every episode emphasizes this construction. The era was evil, not the people in it. Officials on screen appear generally sympathetic and share the recognition that they are mere passive victims of bad times. The film portrays neither perpetration nor perpetrators. More importantly, the film gives no moral judgment as to how the characters (and, by extension, the audience) should have behaved.

The missing Nazi carries over a trait from the Third Reich. As Eric Rentschler has noted, Nazi films "did not show Nazi emblems and Hitler salutes or proclaim party slogans. . . . The decision to eradicate signs of the times and to take flight from present was not made by subversive forces or oppositional artists. It came from the top."[16] Thus, the postwar films break with the Nazi tradition by portraying current times, but they hold true to the rule of keeping Nazis hidden.

The most dramatically convincing episode centers on an older petty bourgeois "mixed marriage" couple facing both the traumas of middle age and the Nuremberg laws restricting the activities of Jews. As they witness the destruction during the *Reichskristallnacht*, Willi, the gentile member of the couple, bashes in the window of his own shop, rather than watch others do it. The shot composition with the Hitler Youths and others supposedly doing the damage consists primarily of long shots with the actor's faces looking down, that is, nondescript masses rather than individuals. No one is depicted as actually doing anything. The political circumstances give the couple the opportunity to show their dedication to each other. They die in their own private gas chamber, committing suicide by leaving on the gas in their home. The film depicts their suicide as a sentimental act of love rather than an act of desperation in the face of persecution.

In Those Days certainly portrays no glorious heroes; no one openly rebels against the system. There is no system to rebel against, since the Nazi regime does not appear in the film. The camera often opens wide, since almost the entire film consists of location shots. In much of the Italian film of the time, location shots are used to open up the private sphere into the public one. In Käutner's film, private concerns screen off public ones. Technically this is done by combinations of medium close-ups of the film's characters and long shots of "those days." The location shots are all designed such that they are within the "sight" and "hearing" of the auto that is to tell the story. As the critical review in 1961 put it, the camera "stylizes where it should show the naked, undecorated truth. On the other hand, it does not have the ability, such as, say, the Italians had, to discover the important and exemplary detail in banal reality."[17]

In general, the critical reviewers can easily justify their dismissal of whatever historical truth the film purports to offer. The film quite simply avoids the difficult questions. In order for Käutner to reestablish himself in the film industry, this film needed to attract an audience. Like all newly founded production companies in West Germany, Käutner's Camera Film Produktion, needed the income from this production to finance further films. A highly political film would have been a box-office failure. As one reviewer noted, the audience's desire to avoid political narratives often damned the first night of the run of the film. "People do not want to hear stories from that time, especially kids. They will be chased away by anything that remotely resembles politics." The review goes on to note that once the potential audience learned that it was not a political piece, the film met with success.[18]

If commercial concerns were not enough, political ones hovered over the production as well. The Western Allies expressed frequent and contradictory skepticism of the political content of filmic treatments of the recent past and/or lack thereof, although actual decisions to censor them were relatively rare. The filmmakers were caught in a quandary. While the Allies demanded that filmmakers confront their recent history, anecdotes suggest that the censors were critical and suspicious of highly politicized treatments of the past.

Nothing suggests that Käutner actually presented a historical narrative with more teeth to the censorship authorities. His previous films were quite similar to *In Those Days* in that they eschewed political confrontation in favor of the portrayal of private fates set against tense, albeit vague, social backgrounds. Käutner's Nazi-era films that were censored by Goebbels, *Romance in a Minor Key*, *Under the Bridges*, and *Freedom Street No. 7*, all were praised as works that subverted the fascist aesthetic.[19] That praise centered on precisely those aspects of Käutner's aesthetic that are dismissed as acritical in his postwar work, namely his utopian humanism. And yet, all of those film narratives were organized around the metaphor of torn loyalties, often represented in a love triangle. It is hard to find commitment portrayed as a desirable characteristic in his films. Thus, after the war, Käutner, who even among filmmakers was seen as a Third Reich outsider, simply chose to continue to make films as he had before. They no more rose to the political tasks of the era than did those he made in Nazi Germany.

The moral problem with Käutner's film is that he takes things too lightly. The conditions demanded that he make a political film. So, he establishes the frame of a film that is supposed to talk about how private lives were affected by the Third Reich. But he does not have the strength to make the moral situation too threatening. The characters all face dilemmas that, at most, amount to sacrificing themselves for their loved ones. A far greater moral test is to take a stand when a stranger is being treated unfairly. Such a story would have actually replicated the greater moral problem of Germans under the Third Reich. Käutner simply avoids it, and sets up a fiction that allows his audience to avoid it as well.

Regardless of the outcome, Käutner's reappearance resonated in the film world. He was looked to as a director who might provide guidance for the industry. Therefore, how he would treat "those days" was important to filmgoers and filmmakers alike. It would help determine the "realism" that other directors might follow and to which the audience would accustom itself. In this case, Käutner's realism excises the most uncomfortable symptoms of the Nazi past and highlights his characters' private histories.

Kirsten Burghardt has argued that the films of the immediate postwar era all took part in a project of "Moral Rearmament."[20] They were, according to Burghardt, not only concerned with the immediate problems of living in the occupied zones. "Beyond that, they reflect the inner condition of a society whose moral-ethical foundation had been severely shaken. . . . In this sense, these films in their anthropocentric discourses offer social, moral, and ethical values and norms that were believed to have been or were actually lost. These values were meant to regain their position after the collapse of the Third Reich."[21]

The lesson provided by *In Those Days*, according to Burghardt, is "protect your belief in humanity."[22] This seems reasonable enough, as does the assertion that many of the rubble films, *In Those Days* included, display moral agendas. As I noted with *The Murderers Are among Us*, they certainly were received as moral events. Yet, the blanket treatment of these films as a part of such a narrow project both ignores each film's specificity and the range of questions to which these films sought answers. It reduces *In Those Days'* treatment of the Nazi past to a question of not losing humanistic faith.

To be sure, that is the program of *In Those Days*. But even the choice of the story's lesson and how it is constructed is more complicated than Burghardt's abstraction can account for. It is a film, not a pamphlet. There is not one morally relevant message in the film, but several, most of them unintentional. Moreover, the film grounds its entire project of rebuilding lost faith in humanity in a strange version of the past. If *In Those Days* teaches its audiences to have faith in humanity, it also encourages them to ignore the public sphere and to overlook the worst of the crimes.

National Socialism is completely effaced in Käutner's film. It is not even mentioned. As Wolfgang Becker and Norbert Schöll have noted, "the characters react to the politics of which they are victims, not with a political opposition against it, but by shifting their reaction to the private sphere. They take the political suppression as a challenge to protect and express themselves privately and personally, to deny their own differences in the face of the—forced—general pressure."[23] In fact, this is how the specific horrors of the Third Reich, the evils great and small that were perpetrated under that regime, are metamorphosed into a general gray notion of "those days." The characters in the film simply back away from the nondescript evil with which they are confronted, whether it is the wife who sacrifices herself to save a sister who has betrayed her or the gentile husband of the Jewish woman who smashed his own shop window. They simply take away the Reich's ability to damage them by making personal sacrifices. I would agree with Becker and Schöll when they say that in so doing, "a solidarity emerges among the good people with which they subject themselves to political domination *together*."[24] The film creates solidarity around primarily gentile German victimhood.

Not only is the Third Reich reduced to just a bad period, the politics of the regime are never once criticized. There is no warning that the spectator should beware never to let it happen again. Rather than dwell on the dark history of Germans in the Third Reich, it picks up a lighter human trait, namely the characters' overcoming of their own selfishness.[25] These individual acts of resistance do not coalesce in a larger movement in any form. They are either stories of death as a form of innocence or glorifications of inner emigration as a form of shutting out external political realities. Becker and Schöll claim that it "is a film in praise of all of those who did not see the political consequences of the Third Reich but only the personal ones."[26]

What is a failure in one dimension may well be a success in another. Resistance even in the narrow personal sense is not an experience of National Socialism with which most Germans could identify. This film does attempt to expand its audience's imagination. *In Those Days* is the most profound example in its era of a narrative designed to reaffirm the spectator's image of him or herself as a private resistor to a public injustice. As depressingly modest as that fantasy might be, it may well have been the only one that had a chance of resonating with the public. While such fantasies circulated in many cinematic narratives, maintaining this skewed worldview must have been a difficult project in 1947, primarily because articulating a fantasy space that remained within a German context was tricky business.

If this fantasy construction succeeds, it does so because *In Those Days* creates a communal spectatorship by referring to so many things that belonged to the collective experience of "those days" and shifting them ever so slightly to create an acceptable collective fantasy. Already the title refers to a specific time that immediately takes on meaning for the audience. In 1947, however, this meaning is far from fixed. The film's intervention is clearly designed to assist in countering the dominant image defeated Germans held of themselves by salvaging their moral character: collective humanity contra collective guilt. Of course, as Benedict Anderson argues, the imagination of a specific time and the certainty of the reader/spectator that thousands of others imagine this time in approximately the same way are the fundamentals of "imagined community."[27] As such, if the film is political, it is in resistance to much of Allied occupational politics. This narrative vehicle will recount stories not of barbaric German monsters, but of fragile humans.

By pretending to reveal the inner lives of those who were opposed to Nazism but did not rise up against it, each episode reaffirms apolitical attitudes to an extreme. "Inner emigration" served as one of the most effective cognitive structures with which many postwar Germans organized their individual innocence in the face of so much collective responsibility. It allowed for an absolutely unfalsifiable story. No matter what you did, in your own heart you were resisting. The characters in this film take small actions, in some cases invisible ones, that show that they were not Nazis. It gives every viewer the opportunity to justify her or his action as remaining true to human solidarity in the face of faceless inhumanity. The moral of the story as given by the now fully dismantled car is, "The times were stronger than they were, but their humanity was stronger than the times." It is hard to imagine a viewer in 1947, save perhaps an extraordinarily critically aware one, who would not want to identify with that statement. The spectator will find in this film a way to justify his own inaction "in those days" as a form of resistance. In the end, Käutner addresses a different question than the surface would suggest. To be sure, this is a story of how to represent the Third Reich. The only question is to whom. This film clearly interprets the question as: How do we represent ourselves to ourselves?

Käutner's film parallels another film that was made almost simultaneously, namely Frank Capra's episodic *It's a Wonderful Life*. Again a nonhuman narrator is forced to intervene when a human is disillusioned with the past. Both films use flashbacks to create passive victims in a predetermined narrative. In both films we know that the episodes will culminate in the catastrophe of the present, which we are shown at the beginning of the film. In the end, both narratives attempt to redeem the destroyed illusions of the past by showing that even in those troubled days, there was much that was worthwhile. Capra's film does this by also investigating the inner turmoil this past has caused in his character. George Bailey is torn by his own contradictory desires and failures. The characters of Käutner's film are, curiously enough, much more self-assured. It is as if the background of the terrorist Nazi state provides them a moral certainty that is missing in the frame narrative's postwar present. It is a curious nostalgia in 1947 Germany.

Between Yesterday and Tomorrow and Narrative Debt

The title of Harald Braun's first postwar film, *Between Yesterday and Tomorrow*, was used for many a publication and discussion in postwar Germany. It depicts precisely the temporal limbo of the German and European predicament. Given the content of the film, however, it seems misplaced. Rather than describing the film, it perhaps describes the lives of those who would come to see it.

Between Yesterday and Tomorrow belongs to a cinematic cycle referred to as the hotel film. The fascination with hotels as a location is perhaps due to their function as gathering places for transients of varying social and economic backgrounds, nationalities, desires, and intentions, all forced to interact relatively intimately with one another. It was a successful genre in Germany in the Nazi era as well as in Hollywood. One contemporary reviewer in the *Westdeutsches Tagesblatt* describes the film's plot as follows:

> It begins and ends in Munich's Regina Hotel, the one-time primary meeting place in the south of Germany for globetrotters, artists, intellectuals, diplomats from all over. . . . The story sways back and forth from yesterday to today. Survivors and shadows move across the screen. . . . the Jewess [Nelly Dreyfuss] who escapes the grip of the executioners by jumping off of the stair rail, the actor [Alexander Corty] who then apathetically follows his wife into death, the stubbornly dogmatic Nazi official who is on both of their

Photo 5. *Between Yesterday and Tomorrow:* Michael Rott returns to the ruins of the world he left behind. (Courtesy of Stiftung Deutsche Kinemathek)

trails, these are characters from the past. The cartoonist [Michael Rott] who flees abroad with his persecutors on his tail and the suddenly lonely co-ed [Annette Rodenwald] who allows herself to be comforted by the Regina Hotel manager [Rolf Ebeling], the art historian who, disillusioned by God, people, and himself, believes books to be the only consolation. . . . they are madly driven through a time between the past and the future. Only one human is there—a girl [Kat], wide-eyed and trusting—who recognizes that life must go on, despite the rubble, despite memory, despite misery and dishonesty.[28]

It is difficult to reconstruct the parallel story lines of the film. This particular review does, however, recognize that the film uses Kat to bring closure to its various plot strands. In so doing, the review also bases the outcome of its realist analysis on her status as the postwar version of Nelly, namely a victim of nameless historical circumstances.

Kat's story begins in 1944, when she works in the hotel as a waitress. Alexander Corty returns to the hotel still mourning the death of his ex-wife, Nelly Dreyfuss, who plunged to her death there in 1938. As Kat approaches him to take his order, Corty opens a small case containing Nelly's jewelry. Corty explains to Kat: "The necklace saved my life. A few years ago I did not know how I could go on living. Then I received this jewelry as a gift. And, in exchange for it I received a lot of money from a bank with which I was able to start anew. And now I have it back and won't give it up again." Shortly thereafter, a bomb alarm is sounded and Corty asks Kat to store his jewelry in her locker for safekeeping. Instead of going to the cellar like the rest of the guests, Corty goes to the lobby and sits in a chair in approximately the same spot where his ex-wife met her death six years earlier. The hotel lobby collapses onto Corty in a bomb blast. The bombing buries the locker and the jewelry, where they stay till after the war, when Kat finally digs them out again.

Kat becomes the key to solving a series of conflicts that are all, in one way or another, tied to Nelly Dreyfuss: debts, duties of gratitude, broken hearts, and mysterious disappearances. Shifting these problems from Nelly Dreyfuss to Kat is an ideological switch from the problems of the past to the problems of the present. While the past reaches closure through Kat's retrieval of the necklace, her problems (as a Silesian refugee, who is deeply dependent upon the black market for her and her brother's survival) go unaddressed.[29] The hardships of the present stand in front of the problems of the past. In keeping with the rubble film pattern, *Between Yesterday and Tomorrow* merely adds the Nazi persecution of the Jews to the list of symptoms, including poverty, depression, and reconstruction, that serve as the obstacles the characters must overcome.

Back in 1938, the hotel staff was visibly shaken by Nelly Dreyfuss's arrival at the front desk. Presumably because of the Nuremberg laws, Ebeling hesitated before checking her in. As Herr Ebeling tells the story, Michael Rott had absconded with the necklace Dreyfuss gave him to give to her ex-husband, Corty. Thus, in Ebeling's eyes, Rott is burdened with a material debt to the deceased Nelly Dreyfuss. Kat's version of the story—that Corty did, in fact, receive the necklace—is intended to release Rott from this material burden. But in doing so Kat passes that debt on to Corty, who had used the necklace as collateral to finance a successful career for himself after his acting career is ruined by the Nazis.

This necklace, which serves as the signifier for Dreyfuss, functions as a currency, always borrowed from her even after she is dead. Her persecution and death serve as a certain collateral for others to begin again. This is not only performed figuratively but literally. She gives the necklace to Rott to give to Corty, so that he can pawn it to start a new life for himself. When plans change, she goes to retrieve the necklace, bumping into the Gestapo while doing so. Thus, the necklace actually becomes her noose. Corty eventually ends up with the necklace anyway, thus remaining in her debt. After the war, Kat is now in search of this same necklace, with which she plans to finance her postwar fantasies. This chain of signification is complete when Rott is able to use the necklace to prove that he owes Dreyfuss no debt and so should be freed from the others' scorn. Dreyfuss is inserted into the plot to create a debt, and paying off this debt is what drives the story. Narrative closure means settling accounts.

Representing Dreyfuss as a Jewish character is a problem the film must solve. As I will discuss in more detail in the next chapter, since film during the Nazi era was responsible for propagating terrible stereotypes of Jews, rubble filmmakers had to be careful not to fall into old patterns of signifying Jewishness. Their efforts meet with mixed success. Braun identifies his heroine as a Jew not through gestures, physical characteristics, or mannerisms, but rather by naming her. With the name Dreyfuss she becomes associated immediately with one of the most famous antisemitic incidents of the nineteenth century. From the mere semiotics of her name we know instantly not only that she is a Jew, but also that something will happen to her. Coupled with the frightened manner with which the characters approach her, this seems designed to create an atmosphere in which we understand her predicament well before the characters are brought to admit it.

Even though Braun's film was referred to as a detective story, it does not keep the spectator in the dark about the truth. The film constructs the events such that we know Rott is innocent and need only have our curiosity sated as to why there is any suspicion of him. More so than intrigue, the audience's need for a redemptive narrative drives the plot. We keep watching until all of the contradictions are resolved such that everyone except the Nazi is exonerated.

The reaction to *Between Yesterday and Tomorrow* in the press was tentative. The title and substance of the film begged comparison with *In Those Days*, and many reviewers did so. Käutner's film was viewed as the more appropriate look at Germany's recent past, because, as one reviewer argued, "holding back is a more effective means than intentional demasking. . . . Käutner's film showed that objective reporting need not fall into flat and sober representations if the director is capable of poetically artistic reportage."[30] In other words, Braun's failure lies in having represented the past too directly. The film confronts and provokes the reviewer. In the end, this critic shows signs that he or she has learned to relativize: the review asserts that the German public does not need this film's lessons about the past because it has learned that "these demons exist everywhere in other clothing."[31] The reviewer resorts to playground moral reasoning: other countries do bad things, so Germans need not beat themselves over the head with their own past.

Not all reviews were negative. One positive critic claims, "It could have been a depiction of a true experience . . . it is thought-provoking and a bit exciting."[32] Revealing one of the more pressing problems of the film industry, the review claims for the film quality equal to any of the Hollywood films that were then filling the cinemas. This was certainly the kind of advertising the struggling German film industry required in 1947, when it had to compete not only with Hollywood, but with the former version of itself. Insofar as *Between Yesterday and Tomorrow* is a crime film, the *Frankfurter Rundschau* review claims, "it is one that shows the criminal era from 1938–1947."[33] Once again, we see a film about the crimes of "those days," not the crimes of any particular people.

Günter Groll, critic for the *Süddeutsche Zeitung*, picks up on the film's lack of formal innovation by noting that "the fact that Nazi films about current problems have been replaced by more agreeable tendencies is fine, but it is of little use if everything else remains stylistically and substantively the same."[34] Munich's other paper at the time, *Die Neue Zeitung*, devotes even less space to discussion of the film. Luiselotte Enderle dismisses *Between Yesterday and Tomorrow*, claiming that in it "the present and the past remain remote, as if we are not experiencing or had not experienced them."[35] Picking up on a theme that almost all reviews share, Enderle notes, "we suffer from this past too much to accept its use as a backdrop for an unsubstantial detective story."[36] Either she would have the film address the problems of the past and present more directly or not at all. Again, we see evidence that, for the culture at large, the past is troubling mostly because it is the cause of so much current misery.

The most negative review is to be found in Berlin's *Der Abend*, where it is referred to as a "pure kitsch, superstar, hotel ruin picture."[37] The reviewer continues: "it is false to the core. The way from yesterday to tomorrow looks much different."[38] Either the reviewer was demanding a political realism that confronted the issues of the past and present more directly, or he or she would have preferred a completely apolitical film. *Between Yesterday and Tomorrow* is neither.

Braun's decision to make a star-studded hotel film certainly does result in a product that looks a lot like the standard entertainment fare of the Ufa system. Apart from Hildegard Knef (Kat), all of the stars are identifiable from that system. And the camera work, costumes, editing, and *mise en scène* evoke Ufa (and, for that matter, Hollywood) cinematic styles.[39] In fact, I would argue, that is what is most compelling about this film. Where this film converges and diverges with Ufa conventions is an important clue in determining what it accomplishes.

As my discussion of the function of Nelly Dreyfuss indicates, the inclusion of a Jewish woman in the film was certainly more than tokenism. Braun's script is rigorous in establishing Dreyfuss as the key to everyone's success or failure. She diverts the Gestapo from arresting Rott. Her jewelry provides both Corty and Kat with opportunities. Ebeling even uses her case to win over the lonely co-ed Annette. Narrating the persecution of a Jew in the Third Reich as an opportunity for all of the other characters is a significantly honest narrative feat in defeated Germany.[40] The tone of the rest of the film would suggest that this is not intentionally antisemitic, and perhaps is even intentionally apologetic. But it certainly reveals much about the narrative and material relationships of Germans and Jews in the wake of the Third Reich.

Narratively, Braun risks little but undertakes a lot. That is to say, like Käutner and Staudte, he is faced with finding a way to tell a contemporary history from the position of defeat. Like Käutner, he employs an object as a vessel of history. But, I would argue against his contemporary critics' dismissal of the film's historicity, at least in comparison to *In Those Days*. Braun does more than simply use the Third Reich as a backdrop for a detective story. He uses a detective story as a formula for interrogating every character's moral complicity in the crimes of the Third Reich.

If that is the film's greatest achievement, it also points to its most serious flaw. Albeit less so than in *In Those Days*, the film still turns the crimes of the Third Reich into abstractions. That is to say, it treats the problems of the past as little more than distractions from the more serious problems of the present. It is quite curious that the only character compelled to defend himself is Rott, the one who was in forced exile during the war. The film does little to question the proposition that the narrative sets up, namely that those who stayed behind are innocent bystanders now forced to struggle. Ebeling, a manager of a major hotel frequented by, among others, Nazi officials, is portrayed as Nelly's most trustworthy sympathizer. Rott is held responsible for a crime against Nelly Dreyfuss. But, once it is cleared up, we realize that the (now absent) Nazi minister and the Gestapo were at fault. There is no one present who can be held accountable.

Part of the function of star systems within a national film industry is to create believable characters in the spectator's imagination, such that the stars can be inserted into plots with a minimum of exposition. We expect action from Bruce Willis or psychosis from Jack Nicholson regardless of the films in which they are playing. In *Between Yesterday and Tomorrow* many of the stars of the Nazi cinema are recuperated for a new era. The famous German actors all play roles similar to those they played during the Third Reich. Braun uses the hotel microcosm to put together an ensemble set both in the Third Reich and in postwar Germany. In so doing, he reunites the stars of Erich Engel's *Hotel Sacher* (1939), Sybille Schmitz and Willy Birgel (here, Dreyfuss and Corty). As in the earlier film, they are lovers kept apart by the regime. This time, however, the film does not have to legitimate the interests of the regime that separate them.

We cannot understand the rubble films' treatment of the Nazi past without understanding the epistemological chain that ties that past to their displaced present. There is a tendency in both *In Those Days* and *Between Yesterday and Tomorrow* to treat the perpetrators as bad others. The Nazis are merely straw men. There is no effort to understand them or their actions or, more importantly, how ordinary Germans followed their lead. The films never place characters in situations where they make moral choices that openly confront the system. They refuse to investigate such choices. The Nazis are the bad guys. Everyone else is a victim of circumstances. Ultimately, the moral issues they *fail* to address are more important than the ones they do address.

In Those Days and *Between Yesterday and Tomorrow* reconstruct private histories of the Third Reich in which people made the right decisions that the progress of history fails to reward. Braun's film is quite a curious contrast with Capra's *It's a Wonderful Life*, the film I mentioned in comparison to Käutner's. George Bailey's morally correct decisions leave him with a troubled conscience. In an optimistic postwar America, George is not convinced that private virtue will be rewarded and therefore is not certain that it is virtuous. The German films have a much more difficult obstacle to overcome than does Capra's film: They must salvage a story of redemption from a morally defeated and humiliated nation.

Hunger, History and Hope: Liebeneiner's *Love '47*

In narrative structure, Wolfgang Liebeneiner's *Love '47* parallels Capra's Christmas classic. It is, in part, an adaptation of Wolfgang Borchert's play *The Outsiders* (*Draußen vor der Tür*), which was one of the first dramas written and performed after the war. The film begins with a shot of an old man in a top hat whose gaze directs us to a man and a woman standing on a pontoon, close to each other, supposedly preparing to jump into the river. The old man, who is later introduced as Death, is celebrating two more converts to his cause. Another old man comes stumbling through a field of dismantled bells. This is God and he is bemoaning the loss of two more souls. He can do nothing about it because no one believes in him anymore. This top half of a framed narrative that the film will never close introduces the fate of the two main characters in the film.

The split genre motif that was apparent in *The Murderers Are among Us* is taken a step further in *Love '47*. Here the two main characters, Anna and Beckmann, are portrayed through different generic codes. The whole film consists of them recounting their life stories of defeat, humiliation, and desperation. While the two characters/narrators use these stories to draw each other back from suicidal abyss, the narratives are also directed toward the audience. The characters form versions of the past that compete with each other for the sympathy of the spectator. The film solicits this along strictly gendered lines.

Liebeneiner was more than just an active filmmaker in the Third Reich. He was at the very center of power in the film industry and Goebbels's ministry. His experience with the "problem film" first came with his *Ich klage an* (*I Accuse*, 1941), a narrative appeal for euthanasia. He made a series of heroic biographical films that became useful propaganda tools for Goebbels and company. He was also chair of the artistic faculty of the German Film Academy. Klaus Kreimeier generously refers to Liebeneiner as a good example of "the divided soul of the reluctant conformist."[41] Kreimeier describes him as having been reticent to assume the job of Ufa production chief in April of 1943. And yet, his actions suggest that, at the very least, Liebeneiner was a conformist and an opportunist. Unlike Staudte, Käutner, Braun, or any of the other filmmakers discussed so far, Liebeneiner was in a position of power in the Third Reich and affected the lives and livelihoods of many other people in the industry. While there is no indication that he abused this power, and even a hint that he put it to good use, his attachment to the Nazi regime tainted his authority to tell a moral filmic tale in the wake of the war.

The initial reviews of the film failed to make note of the dueling narratives in the film. They referred to it primarily as a filmic adaptation by Wolfgang Liebeneiner and screenwriter Hans-Joachim Fischer of the Borchert play. That adaptation accounts for only half of the film. The other half is an entirely different story, written by Fischer, which gives a female counterpoint to the "coming home" story found in *The Outsiders*. In combination, the two stories provide a filmic narrative that serves as a critique of the filmmaking of the period, of which *In Those Days* and *Between Yesterday and Tomorrow* are the best, but far from the only, examples. *Love '47* answers the trend toward narratives about private innocence by showing the possibility of treating the private sphere while critiquing the attitudes within it.

The film's two main characters, who are at first strangers to each other, bemoan their torn and troubled lives. Gender marks the difference in how they construct their narrative pasts, as well as what events they speak about. Both stand on the pontoon ready to kill themselves and yet both hesitate. They look to each other for a reason not to jump.

> *Beckmann:* It is easier to die together.
>
> *Anna:* Everything is easier together.
>
> *Beckmann:* In the war we were never alone.
>
> *Anna:* Yes, but *we* were.

Anna insists on a differentiation upon which the rest of the film will be based. The teleology that will bring these two outcasts together requires reconciling their stories. The two figures will have to come to the realization that theirs are complementary rather than opposing stories.

The first half of the film consists primarily of episodes in Anna's life history. Beckmann is allowed to get in one story, if only to assure the audience that he is no longer with his wife, so that the blossoming love story between them can continue. Anna's narrative balances out the self-pitying tendencies of the Borchert play. While both characters' narratives are similar in critical tone, and both tend toward private histories rather than public ones, Anna's story goes further in its critique. Not only does she repeat the party line of blame against the political forces that caused and continued the misery, she brings it home as well. The film portrays her husband as taking pleasure in the adventures of war. This tempers her sympathy for the male coming-home story.

If not for the promise to adapt one of the most successful plays in postwar Germany, Liebeneiner might have made a compelling film about the fate of the most lasting icon of the early postwar era, the *Trümmerfrau* (the rubble woman). Anna's story moves from an innocent and youthful romance and a lovely church wedding to an idyllic honeymoon, which is interrupted by the start of a war. The film contrasts her saddened reaction to the outbreak of war with her husband's optimism about the beauty of the Caucasus Mountains. The rush of war is tempered by the attitudes of those who are left behind.

In *Between Yesterday and Tomorrow*, Annette defends her reasons for giving up hope on Michael Rott by noting that he was gone and Ebeling was there. *Love '47*'s Anna defends her own choices to be with other men similarly. While it is unclear whether her string of affairs begins before or after she receives news of the death of her husband, it is clear that it did not matter to her. Her husband left her for the war. The film posits an economy to her relations with men. As Anna puts it, "The knights let it be known how their services were to be paid for." She laments about how she has had to use her sexuality. But the film does not condemn her for her choices. On the contrary, her fate, which is portrayed as one common to many women of the era, is treated sympathetically. Instead of punishing her sexuality, the film allows for her redemption.

This compassionate treatment of gender, sexuality, and patriarchy issues is surprising this late in the rubble period (1949). There was a concerted cultural effort by 1948 to rearticulate traditional notions of family and sexuality.[42] Even this film ends up reestablishing the potential of a monogamous heterosexual partnership. Yet, Beckmann does not bemoan the loss of patriarchy, nor is he shown as capable of asserting it. In fact, in the history of Anna's men paraded onto the screen, Beckmann is the only one who does not attempt to take any control of her life. Anna and Beckmann are portrayed as equally wretched. They compete with each other for whose situation is the worst. They begin offering each other readings of their desolate environment. Anna interprets the ruins around her toward the beginning of the film in gendered terms. "The world is governed by men and that is why it looks the way it does."

Beckmann's story is *The Outsiders*, that is, the tale of a soldier returning from the war to find he has no home to come home to. His house is gone, his child is dead, his wife has forgotten him, and his parents have committed suicide. Beckmann marks the loss of his given name with the loss of his life. Plagued by guilt and responsibility for war acts, he is unable to sleep. If Anna's story breaks with the dreamlike, fairy tale histories presented in the other films in this chapter, Beckmann's projects the nightmare. The film translates the surrealist trauma manifested in the play into screen images that are similarly odd confrontations with realist tradition. An extended dream sequence representing Beckmann's plagued sleep is not a recognizable depiction of particular war experiences. Rather it is a general psychological figuration of his war trauma.

Love '47 names names. Unlike most films during and after the era, it uses words like "Nazis," "Führer" and "Hitler." We are told directly that Beckmann's father was a Nazi who committed suicide after the war. In private situations, the characters reproduce the ideological idiocies that lead to war, such as Anna's husband's desire for mountainous

Photo 6. *Love '47:* Reconciling gendered histories. (Courtesy of Stiftung Deutsche Kinemathek)

adventure. Blame for the war is not projected elsewhere. In fact, Beckmann's attempt to do so fails. The film leaves him to cope with his own anxieties about the past and offers no way out.

The first two films discussed in the chapter were fairy tale adaptations of a horrible history. The goal of restoring the (patriarchal) private sphere becomes a beacon of hope. The private realm is reconstructed as a refuge from a troubled past. *Love '47* does not offer the same hope. The private sphere remains haunted. The "love" of the title is construed as a space in which one can, at best, survive the past. Even its "happy ending" is unconvincing after the film has revealed all of the burdens with which this relationship will have to deal. This refusal to provide a fantasy space, particularly a romantic one, differentiates Liebeneiner's first postwar film from the others. It also indicates why the film was a financial and critical failure. Günter Groll wrote of the film that it was another indication of the "crisis of topical films" (*Krise des Zeitfilms*).[43] "We want out of the no-man's land, the confusion, desperation and haunted atmosphere which is reflected in this film."[44]

Love '47 premiered not only in the theaters but also in the Schleswig-Holstein parliament, where it was meant to display the potentials of the film industry to policymakers.[45] The fact that, of all of the possible films and filmmakers from which the parliament could have chosen, they chose the film made by the most historically culpable of those still making films tells us much about attitudes toward reconciliation at the moment of the birth of the new republic. Oddly enough, however, they chose a film that was morally far better than most others of the period. But the film also provided the parliamentarians another lesson: its subsequent box-office disaster showed them the economic value of leaving the troubled past behind. By 1949 audiences and critics were unified in their desire for film studios to resume their function not as moral lighthouses, but as dream factories. Alienation was out; reaffirmation was in.

Conclusion

The greatest challenge these films face is balancing the "economy of emotions," that is, balancing the need to deal with the issues facing postwar Germans with the critical need to confront the past. I have attempted to show how these films domesticated public discourse, including the questions of the Nazi past. This gesture need not necessarily lead us to dismiss the films as acritical. *Love '47* tells a private history of the Third Reich that still asks critical questions of that past. These three films comment on the way people conducted their private lives both during and after the war. They purposely situate themselves in the realm of fictions that reveal the world of personal relations and, to a lesser extent, sexuality. In some ways they represent a return of German film to the traditional world of domestic fiction, a world from which most filmmaking during the Third Reich did not stray far. More importantly, I would argue, these films stake out the only real territory left to Germans in the postwar years. It is in the realm of domestic relations and sexuality in which Germans retained a certain freedom that had been limited elsewhere. Their fantasy constructions of the most recent past remain, in these films, limited to that sphere. As the scandal over nudity in Willi Forst's *Die Sünderin* in 1950 demonstrated, even that space was being contested increasingly by the old hegemony of organized religion in Germany.

The rubble films continued to reveal and determine how people understood their present selves in relation to their past. The hide-and-seek these three films play with the difficult questions of the past at the very least established a range of possibilities for dealing with the personal implications of the Nazi years. The scope of filmic treatments of the topic in Germany hardly changed in the ensuing fifty years. Films such as *Das Boot* (dir. Wolfgang Petersen, 1981) and *Stalingrad* (dir. Josef Vilsmaier, 1993) show that filmmakers were capable of taking private innocence even into acts of war. They found a precedent in Helmut Käutner.

In the end, these films reveal the dilemma commercial filmmaking faced in the early postwar years. *In Those Days* and *Between Yesterday and Tomorrow* begin with the pretense of presenting an honest and open treatment of the Nazi past. They ultimately fall very short of doing so. But, by shying away from a direct confrontation with the past, they avoided scaring off an audience. *Love '47* does not back off from telling truths about individual choices under Nazism. It produces disquieting images of postwar trauma. And what the other directors feared would happen to their films happened to this one—it was a commercial failure. As we shall see in the next chapter, whether or not confronting the past directly was a box-office risk was not always obvious at the time. Others would try it, with mixed results.

4

The Sword That Smote You

*Jewish Filmmakers
and the Visual Reconstruction
of Jews in German Film*

The image of the Jew, in the collective and individual imagination and in historical consciousness, is of far greater and more
decisive importance as a factor over a longer period of time, in
determining the waxing and waning of antisemitic sentiment.

—Frank Stern, *The Whitewashing of the Yellow Badge*

Upon release of his film *David* in 1979, director Peter Lilienthal celebrated it as "the first German-Jewish film, that is, the first film to focus on the everyday life of the Jews during the Third Reich."[1] Lilienthal's remarks are misleading, but they bear witness to the difficulties such narratives have encountered in the face of Germany's collective memory, which was often clouded, especially in the early postwar years, by everyday material concerns. In fact, depicting the fate of Jews during the Third Reich was rarely one of the most pressing matters on the German filmmaking agenda. One set of films we might expect to give due emphasis to the horrors of the recent past are those made in Germany by Jewish directors, actors, screenwriters, and producers in the late 1940s. Contrary to the received wisdom, there were German-Jewish rubble filmmakers, but their films fulfill these expectations only partially.

National Socialism brought an ethnic population, its

cultural and collective memory, and an entire history of multicultural exchange to the brink of extinction. The chaos of postwar living conditions and control of the occupying forces exacerbated the problem. For not only had the Nazis replaced real Jews with their own phantasmagoric images of them, postwar conditions hampered the telling of the real stories of persecution, murder, and survival. The legacy of antisemitic representation of Jews, in addition to the actual genocide, threatened to consign into irretrievable oblivion the memory of the historical existence of Jews in Europe.

Some postwar filmmakers attempted to project narratives of Jews and their persecution at the hands of the Nazis into the culture that had almost eliminated them. In 1946–1949 a few films took as their subject matter the persecution of Jews in Nazi Germany and its aftermath. These films had a difficult task. For not only did they have to tell painful stories, the film language they had at their disposal was precarious, given its recent misuse during the Third Reich. These filmmakers faced the aesthetic problem of creating a new image of "the Jew" that would signify Jewishness in the wake of the vulgar filmic language of Nazi cinema.

Veit Harlan's *Jew Süss* (1940) represents the Third Reich's greatest misuse of the cinematic medium. The story is based on a real-life Frankfurt banker, Joseph Süss Oppenheimer, who is brought into the court of the Duke of Württemberg. In the film, Süss uses his sudden influence in high places to open Stuttgart up to Jews, who had theretofore been prevented from entering the city. As finance minister to the duke he establishes a toll scheme for roads and bridges that causes great unrest among the Swabian population, which swells into an uprising. Süss attempts to hire foreign soldiers to protect the duke from his own mutinous Swabian troops. The plot fails. At the same time, Süss blackmails the daughter of a powerful local politician into having sex with him by torturing her husband until she submits. Ashamed at her actions, she commits suicide, an act that turns the people against Süss for good. In rapid succession the duke dies and Süss, suddenly left without political cover, is arrested and hanged. The Jews are forced to leave Stuttgart. As the Jews retreat from the city the film fades with the entreaty: "May posterity honor this law so that much suffering to their property, life, and blood of their children and their children's children might be spared them."[2]

The film attributes to Jews every threat that the community fears, thereby making obvious the supposed need to eliminate them. In the film, Jews are depicted as threatening, filthy subhumans swarming into the city, manipulating a puppet government, and overpowering inno- cent young women. Narratively, they are shown as having no desires that are not corrupt, and taking no actions that are not wicked and unfair. Physically, Jews are depicted as dirty, long-nosed, and either humpbacked or effeminate. The actor Werner Krauss plays all of the prominent Jews except for Süss Oppenheimer, who is played by Ferdi- nand Marion. Krauss's performance provides the film with consistency in its visual stereotypification.

Jew Süss was not the only propaganda instrument to influence visual culture in the Third Reich. But, insofar as no films were available to mitigate the distorted images the film leaves behind, it can safely serve as a model of the filmic construction of "the Jew" at the close of the war. Harlan's film, for which he was tried and acquitted of war crimes, cre- ates a legacy not only of images but also of the employment of cinematic structure toward the end of identifying and isolating the figure of the Jew. The film employs the emotional mechanisms of the melodrama to inflame sentiment against Jews. It bases its narrative drive of communal harmony on the physical elimination of Jews from the region. It turns images of Jewish religious practices into scenes of decadence and cor- ruption. The figure of Süss Oppenheimer iconizes the Jewish male as excessively lascivious, ambitious, and deceitful, leaving no room for true love or honest success. It also made it difficult for subsequent German filmmakers to portray a character as recognizably Jewish without resort- ing to ugly stereotypes.

Each of the five films I discuss below inherits this representational dilemma from Harlan's film. Of course, *Jew Süss* was not the only source of xenophobic stereotypification in Nazi Germany. Antisemitism in the Third Reich was a *Gesamtkunstwerk* of all forms of public discourse.[3] But, insofar as Harlan's film utilized that collective discourse, and because it was such a wildly popular film, it remained the trauma that cinema had to confront.

Postwar filmmakers could have chosen from other preexisting ethnic stereotypes, sometimes more positively valued, albeit necessarily equally dubious. In a few cases the filmmakers discussed in this chapter aspired to dispense with stereotypification of Jewishness altogether, choosing rather to generalize the identities of those who suffered under Nazi persecution. Filmmakers of the period, both Jewish and Gentile, hesitated in representing the centrality of Jewish persecution in the Holocaust. This impulse to universalize the suffering of the Shoah lies at the heart of the current tumultuous debates about postwar German culture among historians and cultural theorists. The postwar films depict the Nazi genocide committed against the Jews in terms of related persecutions by the Nazis of other groups. This amalgamation of the victims was, among other things, an effort to attract the sympathies of an audience for a segment of the population they had learned to hate. Thus, by portraying camp inmates as a microcosm of world citizenry, or by resorting to commercial film tactics to generically transform the history of the Holocaust, these films seek ways of depicting Germany's treatment of Jews before, during, and after the Third Reich without alienating moviegoers.

Five German films appeared between 1946 and 1949 whose central themes were antisemitism and the Holocaust and its implications: *Marriage in the Shadows* (*Ehe im Schatten*, dir. Kurt Maetzig, 1948) *Morituri* (dir. Eugen York, 1948), *Long Is the Road* (*Lang ist der Weg*, dir. Marek Goldstein, 1948), *The Blum Affair* (*Die Affaire Blum*, dir. Erich Engel, 1948), and *The Last Illusion* (*Der Ruf*, dir. Josef von Báky, 1949). *Marriage in the Shadows* and *Morituri* are feature films about persecution and private fears under Nazism. *Long Is the Road*, a much more epic story that extends into the postwar years, never enjoyed full release in Germany. The narratives in *The Blum Affair* and *The Last Illusion* are organized around the existence and function of antisemitism in prewar and postwar Germany.

As public goods, films must reach out to those who have paid to see them. They must engage the desire of the spectator. This would have been most difficult for filmmakers trying to tell a story that was decidedly the antithesis of what audiences desired in defeated Germany, namely the stories of the crimes committed by Germans against Jews at a time when Germans were being punished for those crimes.[4] While Chapters 5 and 6 discuss the differences between Eastern and Western strategies for cinematic programming, it is clear that all German filmmakers faced the dilemma of balancing a critical demand to confront the transgressions of the still-recent past with a commercial demand to elide it. By 1947 DEFA officials were already beginning to fear that they had "overestimated the readiness of the viewers to confront the problems of their own past."[5] Yet DEFA had a production underway that would engage in just such a confrontation.

Marriage in the Shadows: Melodrama as Critical History

By almost all measures Kurt Maetzig's directorial debut, *Marriage in the Shadows,* was successful. It enjoyed better box office success than any other DEFA film of the era and was second only to *The Ballad of Berlin* among German films in general.[6] It was both loved and loathed by critics. The film is an adaptation of a novella by the German actor/director Hans Schweikart based on the life of the actor Joachim Gottschalk. It is a sentimental melodrama intended to attract the sympathies of a broad German public to a tragedy set against the backdrop of the Holocaust and the Third Reich.

A founding member of the collective that started DEFA out of the ruins of the Ufa studios in Babelsberg, Kurt Maetzig was the dominant director during the first twenty years of East German filmmaking.[7] Because he was the son of a Jewish mother and gentile father, that is, of mixed parentage, Maetzig escaped deportation during the war. Like many of the Jews and half-Jews who settled in eastern Germany after the war, Maetzig's identification with his Jewish cultural heritage was generally overshadowed by his commitment to communist politics.[8] Yet, he claims to have identified heavily with the story of mixed marriage at the center of *Marriage in the Shadows.* The differences between the decisions his family made and those made by the Gottschalk family impressed him. He regretted that his parents "did not steadfastly remain together till the bitter end. Rather they mutually agreed to get a pro forma divorce."[9] Later, while in flight from the Gestapo, his mother committed suicide.

Like other films of the period, critics judged *Marriage in the Shadows* by its adherence to a moralist aesthetic. The subsequent test, some critics felt, was whether the German public was ready to receive it. A young journalist named Rosmarie Knop, in a critique published three days after the film's premiere, decries the seemingly negative reviews of other critics who claim that the time is not yet right for the film.[10] Her concern is that any such deferral of the story to an indefinite later date would only encourage those who are inclined to deny the events of the recent German past. "They will nod their heads 'He's right. Why all of that again now? We know it all?' "[11]

Knop goes on to give a useful summary of the plot:

> A celebrated Jewish actress [Elisabeth Maurer] marries a gentile colleague just as the National Socialists come to power and Jews are banned from

cultural life and soon out of society as a whole. The actor, his name is Hans Wieland in the film, wants to protect his wife. Her apprehensions, still muffled and undefined, . . . appear to him senseless. He sees the beginnings of the Nazi barbarism as a passing phenomenon. . . . Thus the danger continues. Her banishment from social life is followed by his being struck from the list of those allowed to perform. One option remains open to him, divorcing his wife, thus betraying his love and human dignity. (Upon divorce nothing would stand in the way of her being deported.) He refuses and finds another path, one that they can go down together, namely suicide.[12]

Before the marriage, Maurer was an independent and successful actress. Her career was on the rise. She was the center of critical and amorous attention. Frequent use of medium-close shots throughout the film sutures the spectator emotionally into identification with her. When Wieland goes off to war, it is not his survival on the front, but hers at home upon which the film concentrates. Because the marriage coincides with the rise of the Nazis, the result of it for her is forced domestication. The Nazi removal of Jews from public life affects what was accomplished traditionally through patriarchical practice. In foregrounding her story, the film structures itself as a domestic melodrama, a gender-specific filmic code.

While *Marriage in the Shadows* and *Jew Süss* are not of the same genre, they do share some aesthetic qualities. One name that appears in both films is that of the composer, Wolfgang Zeller, who provided both films with strikingly similar musical soundtracks.[13]

Marriage in the Shadows is painfully slow in establishing the issues that are going to drive the narrative. Hans Wieland announces himself quickly as a confidant and suitor of Elisabeth Maurer, as well as being her co-star. She is also being pursued by Dr. Herbert Blohm, a publicist. To any audience member in 1947 it would have been clear that Blohm was a Nazi by the gift of Nietzsche's *Will to Power* that he presents to Elisabeth after a performance. At the very beginning of the opening sequence, a fellow actor and friend, Bernstein, and the theater director, Fehrenbach, discuss the futures of the two actors, Maurer and Wieland. The screenplay awkwardly makes sure that Fehrenbach states Bernstein's name. Thus Bernstein becomes the first character recognizable as Jewish. The dialogue makes a clumsy attempt to indicate that there is much more to Hans and Elisabeth than their appearance on the stage together. This awkward narration caught the attention of many critics who were for other reasons inclined to dislike the film.

Most of the negative criticism *Marriage in the Shadows* received was directed at the film's aesthetic shortcomings and its heavy dependence upon melodramatic coding. Bertolt Brecht was said to have referred to it as "terrible kitsch."[14] Many of the critics panned the film's half-hour long exposition, which was riddled with clichés and awkward screenwriting. Still others bemoaned the cinematography. Yet, the tone of the negative reception tells us much more about the cultural politics of the time than does it about the film. Already in 1947, Wolfdietrich Schnürre had revealed himself as Berlin's most outspoken critic of DEFA films. In his review of *Marriage in the Shadows*, under the cover of an aesthetic critique he attempts to sneak in a confrontation with the film's political implications. Although he admits that the message is "tragic and to a great extent enough to shake us and to alarm our sleeping sense of guilt," he fears that the film, which he considers aesthetically primitive, will become the standard by which German films are judged.[15] However, given Schnürre's dismissal of every DEFA production up to this point, it is likely that he was just as fearful of the idea of the Soviet-sector film company gaining legitimacy as the postwar bearer of German film culture.

In fact, Schnürre's worst anxieties about the film eventually came true. It was sent abroad and enjoyed a long and successful run in New York. Seymour Peck in the *New York Star* said the film "has the stamp of authority. This you know as you watch it is the real thing, not merely in its story and emotion, but in its craftsmanship."[16] While Peck's response indicates more of a wish projection than a close reading, it still reveals how much this DEFA product was being taken seriously in America. The American audience wanted German repentance, both so they too could put the horrors of the past behind them and so they could justify the efforts and losses caused by the war. The film was, at least to Peck, easily readable as a sign of a German recognition of collective guilt.

Schnürre was right in his suspicions that the film would also be put to domestic political use. More than just a feature film, *Marriage in the Shadows* became an event. It was seen by more than ten million viewers in its first release and attracted positive international attention. The East German Communist Party (SED), which was still trying to establish control in the not yet completely divided Germany, tried to attach itself to the popularity of the film, albeit well after its success was evident.[17] The SED response was issued in the form of a position paper that, while completely avoiding a discussion of antisemitism, praises the film's exposure of "self-devouring opportunism" and the fascinating world of the stage. The paper also shows the generally skeptical attitude toward the German population held by the SED leaders who had spent the war years in Moscow.[18] The point of the film, according to the paper, was to "expose the lethargy of the heart from which the collective guilt of an entire people arose. It tugs at the conscience of those who were silent when they should have spoken up and acted."[19] The SED reading may have overestimated the impact of the film, but the party certainly understood its proper historical political dimensions. Schnürre seems unable to accept those.

For the most part, however, *Marriage in the Shadows* received favorable reviews in the western sectors, where it was praised both for its capacity to hold the audience's attention and for its moral stance. Yet again, a film became the signifier of national virtue. As an unnamed reviewer in the *Frankfurter Rundschau* put it, "From the reaction of a German audience to this film, one will be able to discern just how far the inner transformation has come or whether it is exposed as a mere public paying of lip service. . . . From the effect of this film in Germany one will be able to measure just how much it can serve as a document of our current attitudes."[20] While the film certainly tackles the most important moral question of its day, it is hard to tell whether that is what would guide a spectator's reception of it. Viewers may be moved by the wrongness of the Nazi persecution of the Jews *or* by the sentimental tale of two lovers dying in each other's arms. The effect may well have been the same as if Elisabeth had died of cancer. It is one thing to sit passively in an audience and react to a tear-jerker. It is quite another to choose to process its moral implications and allow them to influence your behavior. The sentimental tone of the film provides many opportunities for the spectator's enjoyment without her having to concentrate specifically on the historical reasons for Elisabeth's persecution. Thus, from our historical perspective more than fifty years later, it is hard to make the claim that this narrative actually marks any ethical transformation at all.

Unlike many of the films I discuss in the next chapter, in which the message is foregrounded at the expense of simple narrative tension, *Marriage in the Shadows* attempts to integrate the historico-political narratives into its diegetic weave. The conflicts the spectator understands as ideological are embodied in believable characters. Toward the beginning of the film, this integration is a bit flat-footed. For instance, cultural difference is thematized at the cast party, as Blohm begins a diatribe against modern dramatists for their lack of the Ur-instinct that he is seeking in modernity. The battle between Blohm and Wieland for Elisabeth's affections begins. Both project their own theatrical fantasies onto her. Wieland notes that Blohm sees in her a seductress, Wedekind's Lulu, while he, Wieland, sees her in a more traditional, virtuous role. This is the awkward beginning of the cultural differentiation the film tries to portray, in which the polar opposites are modern and traditional, sexuality and virtue, Jew and German, woman and man. Wieland desexualizes her while Blohm reveals an unconscious Salome fantasy.

Under pressure as the idol of the press due to her theatrical success, Elisabeth wants to flee the city in search of dramatic nature. Elisabeth and her suitors escape to the Baltic Sea. Overwhelmed by the sublime spectacle of it all, Elisabeth recites Goethe into the violent waves of a seascape that resembles a Caspar David Friedrich painting. Hans Wieland attempts to seize the moment to kiss her, but she wards him off. She is not to be captured, and theirs remains an unpassionate love. The film overdetermines her character as pure high culture in the presence of Hans. It goes on to equate her with pure nature in relation to Blohm.

When they return to the cottage, they find that Dr. Blohm has arrived unexpectedly. The predictable struggle between Wieland and Blohm for the affections of Elisabeth turns into a *Kulturkampf* between Bernstein and Blohm. Bernstein stakes out the leftist intellectual position and argues for reason over hysteria, yet insists that the Nazis are beyond reasonable discourse. In response, Blohm gives a sort of bowdlerized Nietzschean argument, saying that the Nazis have risen because of their will to power and that they should be given a chance to show what they can do. He dismisses Nazi extremist attitudes, claiming that these were merely a tactic to achieve power and that after they get settled in office reason will take over. Bernstein counters that reason will only be abused in order to enable extremists to carry out their agenda. Wieland is relatively quiet in the exchange, remarking only that he has an uncanny sense about the Nazis. Blohm, pandering to Wieland's traditionalism, promises that the artist will finally achieve his rightful place in society under Nazism.

The argument is ultimately a dramatization of the bourgeois debate about Nazism in the early thirties. Blohm is the perfect Nazi, with the perfectly historicized attachment to Nietzsche as well as to a simplified investment in the sublime. Bernstein plays the enlightened modernist, with his arguments about the use and misuse of reason. Wieland is a traditionalist, looking to art as an autonomous entity that should be left to pursue harmony and beauty, and not be functionalized by the likes of Blohm. Thus, his position is different from but sympathetic to Bernstein's. The film removes Elisabeth from the argument; she is shown sleeping through this male exchange of political perspectives.

Blohm, who is soon to reveal himself as a Nazi, treats her as nature to his culture. He refers to her at the cast party as "glowing ice." While sailing in the wild Baltic Sea, Blohm convinces Elisabeth of his affections, saying, "My heaven and your glow, when they collide it will be like lightning that starts a fire." For Blohm, Elisabeth is exotic, dangerous and therefore titillating. The film exaggerates this difference as the sequence culminates. When they dock their boat and come ashore, a Hiddensee villager is posting a "Jews Not Wanted!" sign in front of his inn. Bernstein is visibly shaken, as the spectator would expect. It is one of the few spots where the film does not narrate what we already know. With little sympathy for Bernstein, Blohm does not understand why Elisabeth is also upset. The dialogue is awkward as Elisabeth struggles for a way to tell Blohm that she too is Jewish.

The sequence depends entirely on the build-up of the first thirty minutes to establish successfully the presumption that Elisabeth is the epitome of Teutonic beauty. When Elisabeth announces that she is Jewish, we are meant to be as surprised as Blohm is. The film has not affixed to her any of the stereotypical images of Jews. In fact, it is exactly this stealthy approach that allows the melodrama in which she is central to function. She is labeled Jewish and then the story is allowed to continue in a melodramatic fashion to which a German filmgoer in 1947 would have been accustomed. Establishing her as Jewish suspends her actions. In his desire to protect her, Hans insists that they marry. She accepts. We now can anticipate her isolation from public life. Coming simultaneously, her marriage and the shadows of the Third Reich confine her. The combination of the two moves the film from the public sphere into the domestic realm.

The fact that the filmmakers presumed they needed such heavy-handed melodrama in *Marriage in the Shadows* in order to draw the sympathies of the audience should tell us much about what they presumed of the early postwar German public. Much of the style can be explained by its being Maetzig's first film and by the residual influence of the Nazi-era film aesthetic, especially upon a director who had not yet developed a style of his own. But the screenplay, the documentary-style camera-work, and the melodrama also suggest that it was not a certain bet that a German audience would respond positively to the fate of Elisabeth Wieland, Kurt Bernstein, or any other Jewish characters in the film. But to an audience raised on Ufa products, kitschy sentimentalism was a sure thing.

The drama in *Marriage in the Shadows* ends tragically, just as the 1947 audience would expect. Once the film identifies Elisabeth as Jewish, it has little more need for that identifying marker. The dramatic tension is then centered on ways in which she either slips from her confinement or flees back to it. One of the successes of the film is its depiction of the arbitrariness of her categorization. She never feels comfortable in the role, nor is she ever believable in it. The only sign of her Jewishness is her sense of solidarity with the other Jewish characters. And, the portrayal of Jewishness in those characters is also done through language, through names such as Bernstein and Silberman or through explicit statements about their situations.

If the film's absolute dependence on the gender-specific genre of the melodrama is not clear enough, it becomes even more so when Elisabeth is contrasted to the other Jewish characters in the film. The best example is in the sequence where Elisabeth visits Dr. Silberman in his office. This gives us a chance to see how Silberman's office is becoming a clearinghouse for the Jewish underground. What the film has been trying to set up all along becomes obvious, namely that gender and ethnic background are separate categories in determining how characters are portrayed. The men are shown to be actively engaged in their fates, seeking ways to escape or help others escape, whereas the women are portrayed as dependent upon others for protection. Dr. Silberman helps a poor woman whose husband is being hunted by the Gestapo, while Elisabeth seems little more than a damsel in distress. She refuses the suggestion that she flee to Denmark, noting that having already lost her vocation, to lose her husband would be too much. The shadowed, asexual marriage is based on patriarchal protection.

Toward the end of the film, the Nazis force Hans to act on his love for Elisabeth. They plan to deport her for having broken the Nuremburg laws against Jews appearing in public. Rather than have her die lonely, tortured, and afraid in a camp, Hans decides that they will end their lives together. Unbeknownst to him, she looks on while he poisons their coffee. They die quoting the same Schiller play in which they acted together at the beginning of the film (Photo 7).

Much about this story and about the situation at DEFA in 1947 suggests that the choice of materials was not governed completely by the need to tell a moving tale about the Nazi persecution of Jews. To be sure, all indications are that that was Maetzig's motivation in pursuing the story. But the fact that Maetzig was allowed to make the film probably had as much to do with DEFA's marketing strategy as its drive to confront its audience with the sins of the recent past. In a trade press article published in October 1946, Georg Klaren, the artistic director of DEFA, discusses the kinds of films the company wanted to make and what obstacles stood in the way of making them. The greatest problem, according to Klaren, was the obsession of most screenwriters of the time with topics that were primarily of concern to men. Klaren states quite openly, "We are still looking for the ideal film that portrays the fate of the modern career woman with all of the conflicts that come from the discrepancy between a private life and a career."[21] DEFA authorities were, at the time, still hopeful that their films would play all over Germany. Since women had traditionally constituted such a large part of the film-going public, and an even larger one in the immediate postwar

Photo 7. *Marriage in the Shadows:* Hans and Elizabeth seal their fates together. (Courtesy of Stiftung Deutsche Kinemathek)

years, DEFA was looking for a move away from the typically male-oriented coming-home film.

The film sets up two models of the representation of Jews as non-threatening. The first model is created by filtering Elisabeth's experience through the melodramatic gender code. Her Jewishness functions as a means to turn the story into a struggle with which a greater part of the audience would more directly identify. It transforms a story with which spectators would have difficulty identifying into one that was an actuality in their lives. The victimization of Jews becomes identified (and therefore perhaps universalized) with the plight of women in a patriarchy struggling to assert themselves, a standard trope of the domestic melodrama. Given the postwar tendency to see women working outside the home as a threat, women may have identified most with her forced domestication. The authorities may have hoped that the audience would extend such identification to her Jewishness. The audience, however, generally consisted of the same people who, a few years earlier, expressed few objections to treating Jewishness as a crime punishable by death.

The Silberman character works with another model in the portrayal of Jews in film, namely the representation of the assimilated Jewish German. Both Silberman and Elisabeth display a devotion to the traditional ideals of German high culture. He defends German classicism and its inherent notion of *Bildung* all the more intensely as the regime tries to deny it to him. When they prohibit him from going to the concert hall, he resorts to reading all the Goethe and Schiller he never had time for before. The very culture from which his persecutors are trying to disarticulate him becomes his resistance to his oppressors. And the audience can easily identify with a person so dedicated to the cultural values that were again, in postwar Germany, suddenly under attack from within and without. Thus, they can identify with the notion that Silberman suffers persecution because of his Germanness and thereby neglect the real reasons for his persecution.

Marriage in the Shadows, despite its overdone melodramatic pitch, remains one of the most compelling attempts by postwar German filmmakers to weave a narrative of the persecution of Jews under Nazism together with the opportunism of non-Jewish Germans. Placing the film in a familiar formula allowed it to reach a much greater audience than almost any other rubble film, especially those discussed in this chapter. As we shall see regarding the other films, a clearly conceived

story did much more for the commercial success of a film than did its
ideological commitment.

Morituri: Universalism and the Ethics of Survival

Artur Brauner, a young Polish Jew who immigrated to Berlin after the
war, writes of *Morituri,* "I wanted to bring to the screen all of that which
I experienced."[22] Brauner, the film's writer and producer, escaped the
horrors of the concentration camp and went on to fight in the partisan
resistance. Many of his family members perished at Auschwitz.[23] The
film premiered at the Ninth Venice Biennale on August 28, 1948, the
same festival at which *Marriage in the Shadows* and *Long Is the Road* were
presented. The Berlin blockade prevented Brauner from holding the
film's German premiere there. Instead, it was presented in Hamburg on
September 24, 1948.

A contemporary reviewer describes the film as follows:

> People hidden in the thick Polish forests in the last years of the war hope
> that the apocalypse of human madness will pass them by. They are Poles,
> Jews, Germans, and Ukrainians. Five escaped political prisoners stumble
> upon their hideout, among them a Frenchman, a Canadian, a German and a
> Russian. A Polish doctor helps them escape and leads them to the hideout.
> Together the residents of the forest refuge live through the days and weeks
> of fear and desperation. Hunger is a constant danger. Death stands
> constantly at their side.[24]

Morituri was the first feature film in Germany to portray a concentration camp. The opening sequence of the film is full of what have since
become the primary signifiers of concentration camp representation.
The camera opens on barbed wire and then tracks quickly at chest-level
along a row of people standing at attention in striped uniforms. It then
tilts up to face-level and finally down to foot level, revealing a row of
barely clad feet. A drum roll accompanies the movement. At the end of
the row the camera tilts down to a German shepherd dog and a pair of
occupied riding boots. The camera cuts to a medium-long shot of a line
of shirtless prisoners undergoing a selective physical examination as
each number is called. The doctor decides whether or not the prisoners are fit to work. The next cut is a medium-close canted shot of the
doctor who determines their health and, consequently, their fate. Just
like the first shot, the action moves slowly at first and then increases
quickly as the inmates are all declared fit, despite obvious ailments. The

camp guard remains represented only by a shot of his boots and the dog. (As in many films, *Morituri* avoids showing actual perpetrators.) The doctor's face grows increasingly sullen and he stops looking at the prisoners at all. The shot then blends into a canted shot of the row of prisoners combined with a close-up of the doctor's face. The cuts from canted shots of prisoners shouting numbers to canted shots of the doctor's proclamations increase in rapidity with swelling music in the background. Then the doctor finally opens his eyes and resolutely declares a dozen prisoners unfit. The establishing sequence shows a random persecution based neither on health nor ethnicity.

The environment, uniforms, and process suggest that the men are Jewish. But the next sequence takes pains to show that these prisoners do not necessarily belong to the European Jewish population, as the visuals would have suggested, but to a multi-ethnic group of prisoners whose reasons for internment remain undefined. In fact, the very point of the film is that a universalist mix of *morituri*, those condemned to death, has become an ethnic category unto itself. They all state their nationality/ethnicity in one way or another. The young Klaus Kinski appears briefly as a Dutchman who is comforted by a Frenchman just before his death. A German prisoner asks each of his fellow detainees his origin, finding Poles, Serbs, Russians, and Italians as well. The deliberateness of ethnic and national construction suggests at least an intention to create a universalist model. The shots and dialogue of the opening sequence create a chaos that suggests no orderly persecution. Rather it portrays random terror held together only by the threat of imminent death. Later in the film, the same doctor who determined their fate in the opening sequence helps the prisoners escape from the camp. Only a few of the escapees make it to the forest hideout.

Much of the film takes place in this hideout, which is run by a woman who has taken in those who, for indeterminate reasons, are under threat from the Nazi regime. This forest resembles more the mystical fairy tale site of transformation than a war-ravaged region. A series of quick canted shots shows many of the hideout inhabitants to be either deranged or deformed (Photo 8). Very few of the characters are actually called by their names. Together, they form a sort of grotesque Greek chorus. The plot consists of a series of stories about survival and death in anticipation of the war's end.

The lone Jewish character plays a pivotal role in the plot at the point where the film engages the *Jew Süss* legacy. In *Jew Süss* the mob's

Photo 8. *Morituri:* The camp of the wretched and dispossessed. (Courtesy of Stiftung Deutsche Kinemathek)

demand to avenge the death of a young woman is portrayed as justified because of the identity of the person who led her to her death. *Morituri* uses a figure of a Jew as the only character with the moral authority to overcome the lynch mentality directed against a young German soldier.

The Jewish character (who, like many of the characters, remains unnamed) is one of the last to be introduced, but he is the key to the major moral trilemma set up by the film. His introduction into the story is not about his Jewishness. Instead it fixates on his status as the only obviously middle-class character and on his vocation as a defense attorney. When the refugees capture a German soldier who has stumbled upon their camp, they question whether they should kill him, set him free, or hold him prisoner. If they kill him they will share the same guilt as their persecutors. If they set him free, he could inform on them, thereby putting their own lives at risk. If they hold him prisoner he will eat a portion of their very tight food supplies, again putting their lives at risk.

The Jewish lawyer rises up to demand that they give the soldier a fair trial, and in the course of the trial he gives a long speech about metaphysical guilt and the loss of humanity. He makes a heavy-handed plea for them to transcend judgment based on hate and prejudice and admonishes them all to survive so they can bear witness to their own persecution. In a film about survival, the lawyer provides moral guidance, that is, the norms by which they should conduct their lives. If in this scene the lawyer is portrayed according to any Jewish stereotype, it is that of G. E. Lessing's enlightened humanist, Nathan the Wise. He convinces the camp's elders to let the soldier live, noting that living as they do is punishment enough. Later Eddie, the most outspoken of the escapees, sets the soldier free after extracting a promise that he will not betray them.

Claudia Dillman-Kühn refers to *Morituri* as a film that "unites false pathos, a paucity of drama, penetrating imagery, a furious black and white *mise en scène*, expressive scenes of masses and hollow dialogue. . . . The documentary gaze determines the first half of the film, while a plot oriented around clichéd ideas dominates the second half."[25] Her comments reflect both the film's grand project and its many inconsistencies. It sets out to spin a tale of universal victimhood at an understandable time for such a story. Yet, the filmmakers and the conditions under which they worked conspired to produce a mediocre film that fails to reach its rhetorical goal.

If, however, exposing the universal character of victimhood was one of the film's goals, then its work was not all for naught. In a narrative where all of the characters are under the threat of Nazism, Jews become assimilated into general victimhood. Despite the many individual fates portrayed in the film, its main character is the principle of survival. Love stories are set up, only to be truncated in the name of endurance. Survival is not a hero in *Morituri*. It is, in fact, quite humble; failing as often as it succeeds. Survival does not favor one group of those condemned to die over another. Regardless of the Nazis' motivations for taking their lives, these refugees are all *morituri*. The film ends with the soldier whom Eddie liberated informing them that the front had moved beyond them and that, at least for them, the war is over.

Survival as a central but not valiant figure was in itself a universalist theme in postwar Germany. It allowed those who lived through the carpet bombings, invasions, mass rapes, and POW camps to be equated with those who emerged from the concentration camps, work camps, death marches, and hideouts. The historiographic problem is, of course, that it ignores the causal relationships involved in victimhood. In 1948 in Germany, universalizing victimhood contributed to the project of reconciliation everyone found necessary in order to escape the miseries of the postwar era. One can even argue that it functioned as tool for Jewish survivors, reducing the paranoia that necessarily came with having been the chosen victims. At that moment, the possibility that their trauma might eventually be forgotten must have seemed much less powerful than the persistent memory that they had been singled out for persecution. It might be argued that, in order to reestablish a stable sense of self, Jews needed to presume that others had shared their experience. Thus, however inaccurate its telling of history, the film's universalizing of victimhood played an important role in post-Holocaust Central Europe.

Morituri's contribution to the construction of a collective memory of the Holocaust was mitigated by its somewhat flat ideological mission and, more importantly, by its failure to reach an audience. Not only was the film a box office failure, viewers sometimes demanded their money back after seeing it. According to press reports, this was due to the film's portrayal of Nazi victims.[26] While a viewer fifty years later would be hard pressed to find what it is that contemporary moviegoers found so offensive, the film's portrayal of a community held together by nothing more than being persecuted by Germans was a message quite unwelcome in berubbled Germany. It was far and away the least successful of the films discussed in this book, not only at the box office but with critics, who simply dismissed it as aesthetically unrefined without even addressing the ideological content. For Artur Brauner, who would go on to become one of the most successful producers in Germany for the next fifty years, it initiated the project to which he would continually return. *Morituri* failed at the box office, but succeeded as the beginning of a lifelong project that would include producing such Holocaust-related films as *Zu Freiwild verdammt* (*Damned to the Wild*, 1983), *Der Rosengarten* (*The Rose Garden*, 1990), and *Hitlerjunge Salomon* (*Europa, Europa*, 1990).

Long Is the Road:
The Return of Jewish Life to German Film

Another film that never reached nor even sought a wider audience is *Long Is the Road* (*Lang ist der Weg*, 1948). Israel Beker's Yiddish/German film was wholly intended as a public information campaign. Attempts at reconstructing the impetus for this film yield ambivalent results. One version has it that Beker, on whose life the film is based, approached IFO (the acronym for Yiddish Film Organization, later changed to International Film Organization), a group founded in 1946 with the help of the American Joint Distribution Committee.[27] Cilly Kugelmann, whose work on the film is the most thorough to date, states with certitude, however, that "the initiative for this project came from the multiregional cultural office of the self-governing group of Jewish survivors in the American occupation zone."[28]

In either case, it is certain that the cultural authorities and Beker saw that retelling Beker's real-life story could help make the case that displaced Jews should be allowed to emigrate to Palestine.[29] *Long Is the Road* is at once a film directed toward a specific audience with a specific political aim and a feature film with an easy-to-follow plot. To be sure, the sponsors of the film wanted to convince the audience, presumably concentration camp survivors then living in Displaced Person (DP) camps, that emigration to Palestine was the only possible happy ending to their long and tragic story. More importantly, the film seems designed to cultivate sympathy for their plight throughout the world, and particularly among the British, who were refusing Jews passage to Palestine. While the film's ideological purpose is clear, the filmmakers approach their aims through the common methods of historical fiction rather than through those of public relations films.

Long Is the Road promotes its own authenticity from the start. Although it will set forth a fictional narrative, the voice-over announces it as if it were a documentary. "Driven from their homes for political or racial [*sic*] reasons, over a million people are still scattered all over Europe. They are known as DPs. This is a story from the lives of these people, told just as it actually played itself out, by those who lived it." The film moves freely from documentary to a fictionalized narrative that parallels the actual experiences of many of the actors. This seamless interweaving of fact to fiction, what contemporary reviewers referred to as "semi-documentary," is a form that audiences of the time would have understood. Both *Jew Süss* and another film from the same era, *Request Concert* (*Wünschkonzert*, dir. Eduard von Borsody, 1941) attempt to provide their historical fictions with documentary veracity.

Wolfdietrich Schnürre, the writer who had polemicized against DEFA's attempts to portray the recent past in film, offered a rather belated critique of *Long Is the Road* in 1951.[30] In the Lutheran periodical *Kirche und Film,* Schnürre praises the film's conciliatory tone. The horrible events portrayed are done so, according to Schnürre, "without leaving the impression that hate and resentment, which would be understandable, determine the outcome."[31] Schnürre claims the film enjoyed a success abroad it deserves at home. He calls it a "reminder of a guilt that cannot be denied, but can only be forgiven."[32] That Schnürre would praise this film for its authenticity and fail to note in it the same sort of sentimentality that he lambasted so heftily in *Marriage in the Shadows* suggests that the stakes are different for him. To be sure, the political situation in Germany changed radically from 1948 to 1951. The more likely explanation, given Schnürre's tendency to dismiss much of the work produced at DEFA, is that *Long Is the Road* was produced in Munich and not in Berlin's Soviet sector.

While a voice-over announces the German invasion of Poland, the film's opening sequence fills the screen with signifiers of Jewish religious practice, Eastern European Jewish culture, and Yiddish dialogue. The signs of Judaism that Harlan's film had used as symbols of the decrepit underworld show up here as humble and righteous. Without exoticizing or fetishizing Jewish life, these shots establish for almost any potential viewer the film's *mise en scène* as an Eastern European Jewish household. Likewise, the first utterance of the main character, David Jelin (played by Beker), is "Ghetto," a word tied in this context specifically to the European Jewish experience. The film then dissolves from a Star of David on a tablecloth to a map of Warsaw indicating the ghetto. In this sequence, the private religious self-understanding represented by the domestic object is forcibly transformed into a politically persecuted public identity. This bold reinsertion of honest images of Jewish life into a culture that had distorted such imagery and attempted to exterminate that life enables *Long Is the Road* to function as a powerful answer to *Jew Süss.* These images strive to dispel any doubt about whom the film is portraying and in what light. As I shall argue, they succeed only partially.

That this is a Yiddish film is significant. Not only does the story contain many of the typical tropes of traditional Yiddish theater, it also marks the brief revival of Yiddish theater that took place in the DP camps after the war.[33] Much of the cast, including Beker, belonged to a professional Yiddish theater group that performed in the camps. A number of Yiddish films were made immediately after the war in Poland, but political circumstances there quickly dashed hopes of a

Photo 9. *Long Is the Road:* The Jelin family prepares to move into the Warsaw ghetto. (Courtesy of Stiftung Deutsche Kinemathek)

renewal of Yiddish culture. A Yiddish film in postwar Germany kept hopes of a Yiddish cultural renewal alive by portraying a set of experiences, painful as they were, that was common to a specific audience.

Long Is the Road provides some of the first depictions of the experience of the transports to Auschwitz. Unlike most later portrayals of the train to Auschwitz, the passengers are not all shown as passive victims. Some fight with one another for food. David, who becomes separated from his parents, jumps from the train under heavy machine-gun fire. His parents hear the fire and are left to wonder whether or not it was he who jumped and whether he is still alive. He is equally unaware of their fate.

Beginning in the 1950s and coming to a head with the discussions surrounding Steven Spielberg's *Schindler's List*, the idea and practice of representing Auschwitz has been problematized. *Long Is the Road* is the first film in the West, at least from a Jewish perspective, to present images of the infamous incinerator stacks, which arriving inmates look at in horror. The fact that there is no record of an emergent critical discourse regarding this imagery suggests that the idea of reproducing images of the Holocaust is not one that compelled serious questioning in the immediate postwar period as it did fifty years later.

In the Auschwitz arrival sequence, David's mother and father are subjected to the *Auswahl*, the moment of arrival at the camp in which the father is sent "left" to his death. While *Morituri* may have been the first feature film to depict this process in general, *Long Is the Road*, which was actually filmed a year before *Morituri* but released for limited pubic viewing at about the same time, presents an even more disturbing depiction because of the story's much more personal tone. While a viewer more than fifty years later has plenty of information to fill in the details, the cryptic portrayal of events suggests that the film was made for an audience that was fully aware of the practices of the camps and needed no further images to make meaning of the story.

Although it was conceived as a film with a specific political agenda, *Long Is the Road* often confuses matters. A typical public relations film imagines a specific intended audience that it is trying to sway. Beker's film vacillates between the audience of survivors, who would have understood Yiddish, and the audience of exiles and friends, who would have had the political and economic means to solve the DP problem. It is either trying to convince the world community, most specifically Great Britain, to allow Jewish DPs to immigrate to Palestine or it is trying to convince those DPs to do so. *Long Is the Road* was also shown in New York, where it received rave reviews from the German-Jewish community. The German-Jewish newspaper *Aufbau* proclaims, "This film must be shown to all of those who are in the position of determining the fate of those displaced persons who have been torn from their homes and communities."[34]

The trend in Germany in 1947, at least in the American sector, was a shift from viewing the Nazi-perpetrated genocide as a crime primarily against Jews to a universalized "crime against humanity." In this light, Jews having been driven from their homeland, interned, and then murdered by the millions gets conflated with the millions of Germans who had been driven from the eastern provinces, as seen in the opening sequence of the film.

When the makers of *Long Is the Road* pitched their project to the Information Control Division, they were met with a friendly reception. Not only did the screenplay eschew pointing a finger at the Germans, but the technical requirements in making a full-length feature film necessarily would involve German filmmakers. So *Long Is the Road* at least had the structural makings of a conciliatory project. The film seemed to embrace the Americans' new Cold War aims of cultivating alliances with the Germans instead of prosecuting them, and the utopia imagined by the film is projected onto faraway Palestine, requiring no reprisals toward the Germans.

Beker's narrative idea was adapted for the screen by Georg Külb, a former Ufa screenwriter. Herbert Fredersdorf, an active filmmaker in the Third Reich, began the project as co-director with camp survivor Marek Goldstein. Fredersdorf encountered acute problems with the actors and did not finish the project.[35] Kugelmann has shown the distorting effects of this combination, especially in the screenwriting. "Most astonishing is the complete lack of determination of guilt, the gestures of reconciliation that characterize the whole film, an attitude of which there is no documented evidence from the camps of Jewish survivors."[36] Although we can presume that Külb's assignment as a screenwriter for a feature film was not necessarily to stick to the facts, the location of his deviations are significant. Even the film's prologue ("Driven from their homes for political or racial reasons, over a million people are still scattered all over Europe . . .") conflates the experiences of Jewish Holocaust survivors with Europe's other refugees and arguably even foregrounds the latter. It is possible, however, that the filmmakers sought to cultivate sympathy for the fate of Displaced Persons, at least for a potential German audience, by attaching them to the sympathies being expressed in Germany toward those who had been driven from the country's former eastern provinces.

Whether or not Beker and the others intended to conflate their fates with those of the German displaced community, this seems to have been the film's effect. Its tendency to universalize the fate of the Jews within the context of greater human suffering gets picked up in its reception for years to come. It treads so lightly on the question of German–Jewish relations that even the specificity of Jewish experience—the ghettoizations, Yiddish, the postwar restrictions—are all lost in the voice-over appeals to the suffering of all humans under war. Conservative German political commentators in the 1950s would attempt to co-opt it in their call for resettlement of the refugees of Silesia and the eastern provinces.[37]

If Germans are treated mildly in the film's judgment, *Long Is the Road* does not reconcile itself as easily with the Poles, who are depicted as openly antisemitic. German antisemitism, on the other hand, is confined to institutions and never embodied in characters. The kind and patient German doctor who cares for David's mother is a contrast to the rude and greedy Polish tenants of their former apartment. The worst of the opportunistic behavior is projected onto the Poles, while Germans are portrayed as showing exemplary good will and sympathy.

Perhaps the biggest confusion created in both the screenplay and the subsequent film surrounds the character of Dora. David meets her in a missing persons office when he returns to Warsaw in search of his mother. She introduces herself to David as a Jew who, along with her family, was driven from Germany before the war, in 1938. Kugelmann suggests that historically this would have likely made her a part of the Polish-Jewish population in Germany that was forced to leave that year. Yet, she speaks neither Polish nor Yiddish and David must translate for her. Given the way her character is constructed, it is difficult to imagine that she belongs to some actual historical group of persecuted Jews.[38]

Dora does not seem to share common experiences with the rest of the DPs. She is well dressed, clean, and blonde, and she is carrying a large suitcase. "It is uncertain," Kugelmann notes, "where a young woman who has survived a concentration camp and whose parents were murdered was to have gotten a suitcase heavy with contents."[39] Why do the filmmakers have it there? This leads Kugelmann to interpret Dora as an eastern province refugee rather than a camp survivor. She suggests that the switch must have come at some point between the writing of the screenplay and the film production. If she is to be read as a German gentile, the film's conciliatory project is more plausible. "The gradual process of David's intimacy with Dora, his later love, and his marriage to her, functions as a symbol for the longed-for reconciliation between Jews and Germans."[40] And it would certainly explain why she is fleeing *with* her possessions and seems out of place among the Jewish refugees.

Was she originally conceived of as a gentile and only later made Jewish? Why would the filmmakers make that switch? To be sure, she is not a believable character. But if Dora were really a German refugee, why would she live in the DP camps for Jews, instead of those reserved for Germans who had been driven from the east? She initially refuses David's marriage proposal because she cannot get past the pain of the camps. How would that sequence fit into the reading of her as gentile?

Ultimately, the contradictions of Dora's character in an otherwise painfully genuine film are confusing. The review in *Aufbau* also bemoaned that Bettina Moissi's "inauthenticity was disturbing."[41] There is some question as to whether or not Moissi, the daughter of the famous Austrian-Jewish actor, Alexander Moissi, was treated as a Jew under Nazi rule, given that she remained employed in regional theater. But the decision to cast her affected the reception of the film. I would argue that Dora belongs to a trend of postwar film in Germany that we have already discussed. Dora is yet another contestant in the beauty pageant of camp survivors as portrayed in early postwar films. The portrayal of Susanne Wallner in Staudte's *The Murderers Are among Us* serves as another glaring example. She too arrives home from the concentration camp freshly coiffed and carrying *two* large suitcases. The fact is that these films are trying to sell their story. They compromise naturalism by finding the most attractive ingénue available so as to make the film visually compelling. As for the suitcase, in *Long Is the Road* it serves both to portray Dora as a person in transit and to provide a narrative device to initiate an exchange between David and Dora (he helps her with the suitcase), thus introducing romance into the plot.

Despite our impulse to read *Long Is the Road* as exceptional, there are many ways in which it fits well into filmmaking trends of the era. Not only does Dora adhere strictly to the beautiful victim role found in other films, but about halfway into the film David becomes a typical *Heimkehrer*, returning home to his bombed-out city after the war. His task becomes the familiar one of negotiating the chaos in order to reestablish his own subjectivity. This is, however, where the film breaks off from others of the period. He is not Hans Mertens (of *The Murderers Are among Us*) or Michael Rott (of *Between Yesterday and Tomorrow*) wrestling with his past and his identity. He holds a certain idealism that is unavailable to a gentile German character at that time.

Long Is the Road was never released widely. It was made in the summer of 1947, but enjoyed only a selected release in the cinemas in the fall of 1948. By the time it enjoyed a general German premiere, many of the questions regarding the fate of Jewish DPs had been addressed. Thus, the film that presents one of the first authentic tales of Holocaust persecution, survival, and eventual postwar reunion ended up in oblivion well before it ever found the audience it deserved. The political functions for which it was conceived prevented the emotionally powerful narrative from finding a well-deserved audience.

The Frankfurt School and the Portrayal of German Antisemitism

Scholars and filmmakers after the war grew obsessed with overcoming the Nazi's legacy of the visual distortion of Jews and Jewishness. It is difficult to portray antisemitism, however, without reproducing the hate-filled imagery that accompanies it. Thus, many creative thinkers and artists on both sides of the Atlantic dedicated their efforts to under-

standing the visual aspects of antisemitism. I digress briefly here to discuss a film project that never quite came to fruition, one that involved
some of the most important cultural theorists of their day. In their story,
we can see the problems inherent in creating a critical narrative about
antisemitism and the Holocaust, problems that will also surface for the
makers of the last two films discussed in this chapter.

In her book *Die Einstellung ist die Einstellung*, Gertrud Koch describes
an educational film project in southern California in the mid 1940s in
which T. W. Adorno, Max Horkheimer, Siegfried Kracauer, Friedrich
Pollock, and other members of the exiled Frankfurt School all took part.
The goal was to create a visual analysis of the intricacies of antisemitism.
Over several years, working in conjunction with the American Jewish
Committee, Horkheimer led an immense effort that was to scrutinize
the thesis that "hatred of Jews, despite the proclamation of human
rights during the most progressive periods and in the most progressive
of countries, has never really been vanquished and is capable of flaring
up anew at any moment."[42] This might seem like an obvious project in
the late 1930s to early 1940s, with the crimes of National Socialist Germany in full view. Yet, the Frankfurt School project transcends the
scholars' own Teutonic worries. In fact their project takes on an even
gloomier tone as they note that "while frank disgust for the anti-Semitism of the government is revealed among the German masses, the
promises of anti-Semitism are eagerly swallowed where fascist governments have never been attempted."[43] This quote suggests that these
scholars were generous in their assessment of their fellow Germans. It
also insinuates that America was not immune to similar antisemitic
actions.

Early on in the project, the financing of which supported the exiled
Frankfurt scholars, the idea for an experimental film surfaced. The goal
was to narrate the situations in which antisemitism manifests itself as a
part of the thought of average Americans. In order to do so, the film
would attempt to test the audience's antisemitism as well as that of the
characters in the film. The setting of the film was to serve the purpose
of testing nine categories, "ideal possibilities," of antisemites that the
scholars had elucidated in their "Research Project on Anti-Semitism" of
1941. The nine categories are:

  A. *The 'born' anti-Semite:* He reacts with apparent "instinct"
     against so-called Jewish racial traits. . . . He simply cannot stand
     the Jews. It can often be observed that this type appreciates so-

called "racy" women akin to the Jewish type if they are
presented to him as Gentile.

B. *The religious-philosophical antisemite:* The Jews have crucified
Christ. . . . He is the stranger who deliberately excludes himself
from the Christian community.

C. *The back-woods or sectarian anti-Semite:* . . . This type has made
anti-Semitism a substitute for religion. . . . He believes in
Jewish world domination.

D. *The vanquished competitor:* . . . His hatred does not stem from
specific characteristics of the Jews but rather from certain
economic relationships through which he suffers. Since this
type of antisemitism has some basis in reality, it also has a
certain rational character. Under certain conditions therefore, it
can disappear easily.

E. *The well-bred anti-Semite:* . . . This type of antisemitism . . . is
particularly common in the Anglo-Saxon world. . . . The Jews
are supposed to be loud, unreserved, obtrusive. . . . Jewish
intellectuals are as impossible as Jewish business men. . . . Their
intellectual conversations break the rules of the game.

F. *The 'Condottiere' anti-Semite:* . . . They are inclined to hate the
Jew partly because of his cautiousness and physical inefficacy,
partly because, being themselves unemployed, they are
economically uprooted, unusually susceptible to any
propaganda, and ready to follow any leader.

G. *The Jew-baiter:* . . . What he hates most of all is the Jew's
allegedly higher psychological faculty for "enjoying life.". . .
The relation of this type of anti-Semitism to sexual drives . . . is
comparatively unconcealed.

H. *The Fascist-political anti-Semite:* . . . He deals with anti-Semitism
as an export article. . . . To him anti-Semitism is reified. It must
function.

I. *The Jew-lover:* . . . people who stress the differences between
Jews and Christians in a way friendly to the Jews. . . . The Jews
are exceedingly sensitive to this kind of anti-Semitism. The
declaration of a man who professes to be particularly fond of
the Jews because of their "prophetic" or other qualities
discomforts them. The anti-Semitic types mentioned above can
shift by certain mechanisms into different brands of Jew-lovers
and overcompensate their hatred by a somewhat exaggerated
and therefore fundamentally unreliable adoration.[44]

These descriptions allow an ample supply of richly disgusting characters with which to make a film. In fact, Erich Engel's postwar debut film, *The Blum Affair* (1948) coincidentally exhibits a range of these typologies. While it is not difficult to see some of the weaknesses of these categories, they provide a productive starting point for a filmic discussion of anti-semitism. While the figurative portraits of antisemites proposed here draw a good picture of the perpetrator, they still present no image of the object of this hatred. This is a problem that *The Blum Affair* shares.

The Frankfurt Scholars were theoreticians who were trying to dabble in film. How would a group of critical sociologists and philosophers, all of whom harbor ambivalences about the general status and cultural function of mass-produced images, go about producing a set of such images that would be of both scientific and didactic value? The Frankfurt School theorists were trying to use a medium of whose values they were quite skeptical to set up a sociological experiment involving both control and test subjects. Their attitudes about film and its possibilities are laid out pretty clearly in their description of the use to which a filmic narrative will be put in their project.

> A film will be made, showing boys of 12 to 15 at play. An argument and a fight ensue. The relation of guilt and innocence is difficult to untangle. The scene ends, however, with one boy being thrashed by the others. Two versions of the film will be made. In one, the thrashed boy will be played by a Gentile, in the other by a Jew. Another variation will be introduced by showing each of these versions with two different dramatis personae. In one version, the thrashed boy will bear a Jewish name, and in the other a Christian name.[45]

This plan already contains the tensions that will eventually doom it. It depends upon a subtlety of visual construction, a finesse of the image that few filmmakers ever would have been able to achieve. The typologies construct such mimetic pictures of the antisemite that they seem to paralyze the scholars in a certain kind of realist dogma. At the same time that they require subtlety, in the form of the ambivalent relation of guilt and innocence, they also require almost overdetermined representations of the cultural make-up of the boys, such that they can be recognized.

The process of developing the screenplay would eventually involve not only this group of exiled Frankfurt scholars but also a wide variety of individuals residing in southern California at that time. As Koch notes, "gradually a larger number of artists, intellectuals and academics landed on the West Coast, from where they observed the events of the

1940s in Europe attentively."[46] It is under such strange/estranged conditions that these scholars, artists, filmmakers, and others were trying desperately to come to grips with both their own exile and the conditions that forced it. The opening sequence of Josef von Báky and Fritz Kortner's *The Last Illusion* (*Der Ruf*, 1949), which I discuss below, is as adept as any in depicting the intellectual and aesthetic crises of identity that must have emerged in those years.

The theorists eventually dropped their work on the project, only in part because they could not agree on how to portray Jewishness or antisemitism. Part of the project's failure was due to its success. Gradually, as the Hollywood studios became interested in the project, the narrative became more refined and commercialized. The structural approach advanced by Horkheimer, Adorno, and others necessarily gave way to the Hollywood demands of a marketable drama replete with a returning soldier love story. Jewish self-censorship and political and ethnic differences within the exiled Jewish community combined to produce an ambivalence regarding the possibility of representing Jewishness. This, coupled with the Hollywood drive toward seamless narration, transformed the project into one that was unfamiliar to those who started it.

The film that eventually, albeit indirectly, came out of these efforts was Edward Dmytryk's *Crossfire* (1947). When the war ended, however, Germany turned out to be an even more conducive environment for a film that could investigate the legacy of antisemitism. The prehistory of Nazism and its causes became tied to the political battles over the future of Germany that erupted in the early postwar years.

The Blum Affair:
Detecting Antisemitism in Liberal Democracy

When DEFA chose to produce a film about antisemitism, they chose an actual case, not from Nazi Germany, but from Germany's most democratic prior era, namely the Weimar Republic. Erich Engel and R. A. Stemmle, not members of the regular DEFA director's pool, were hired to make *The Blum Affair* (*Die Affaire Blum*, 1948). Stemmle wrote the screenplay and Engel directed. The latter, who was of German-Jewish descent, had remained an active filmmaker in the Third Reich under special dispensation by Goebbels. He directed a vast number of entertainment films in the 1930s and 1940s, including the Willy Birgel/Sybille

Schmitz vehicle *Hotel Sacher*, mentioned in the last chapter. In *The Blum Affair* Engel takes up the true story from the mid 1920s of an industrialist, Rudolf Haas, falsely accused of murder.

Hans Helm's review in the *Berliner Film-Blätter* provides both a valuable plot summary and insight into the West Berlin reception of this DEFA film.

> *The Blum Affair* is not wanting for bias. However, this bias is from the start so craftily built into the singly obvious crime story that one can drop all ideological doubt. At about the same time as the lynching trials a simple murder/robbery was committed. The murderer denies the deed and accuses a Jewish industrialist of the capital crime. Reactionary judges believe his testimony, because in believing him they are forced to indict a Jew. They help this stranded former member of the Freikorps, which attempted to prolong World War I, because they cannot believe him capable of such a deed. Against the resistance of the case's lead officer, a free-lance Berlin detective uncovers the crime. The Jew is freed. The murderer must confess.[47]

By 1948 West Berlin critics such as Helm were highly sensitized to potential political content in DEFA films. When Helms remarks that the film is still a good film despite its "bias," he is legitimating himself to his Western readership. It is a defense tactic to avoid being labeled a Soviet sympathizer. As we shall see in the chapters that follow, film reception became increasingly tied to the greater political issues of an ever more divided Germany.

The way in which the filmmakers present the crime story to the spectator is important. We see the crime first and then the investigation. Because we know who the perpetrator is, we know that the mention of a Jewish industrialist as the primary suspect is based on prejudice. Rather than speculating who the murderer is, the filmgoer is put in the position of rooting for the unjustly accused Jew and those who are trying to defend him. The suspense centers on whether or not Jakob Blum will be exonerated, not whether or not he should be.

The Blum Affair would have been a good test case for the Frankfurt School experiment. One would have to imagine the film a bit differently. Had the filmmakers organized the narrative such that the spectator had reason to believe that either Blum or Gabler (the actual murderer) could have committed the crime, the film could then have investigated the reasons why a viewer might settle on one or the other suspect. Thus, the film could have investigated the spectator's own attitudes toward Jews.

Such an experiment in postwar Germany would have been unthinkable for many reasons. First, everyone knew antisemitism was still prevalent in 1948 in Germany, and a sociological differentiation of it would have served no one's political purposes. Both the Soviets and the Western Allies were striving to attract Germans to their worldviews and were, therefore, increasingly disinclined to make themselves unpopular by confronting Germans about their racism. More importantly, directors and screenwriters in Germany would not have trusted their narrative skills to be nuanced enough at making the film such that it did not come off as itself antisemitic. Again, they feared that the legacy of Süss Oppenheimer would infiltrate their own images. Thus, the Allies, however split they were in 1948, certainly would have agreed that the time was not yet right for a film to work out the subtle distinctions that combined to create murderous antisemitism.

Engel and Stemmle did not make a mystery. They made a simple detective story where the audience is in an omniscient position occupied by none of the characters. The spectator can feel confident in her moral judgment. The film actually spends little time on Blum himself. He is an almost random figure drawn into the mess purely through the

Photo 10. *The Blum Affair:* Blum (left) faces his conspiring prosecutor. (Courtesy of Berlin Akademie der Künste)

political conniving of the antisemitic presiding officer and magistrate. *The Blum Affair* gives a brief but well-rounded picture of a Jewish businessman. He is not overdetermined as a naively innocent member of society. That is, he is indeed influential and politically connected, but he is certainly not a murderer. Dr. Blum is neither fetishized as a human ideal nor vilified as a menace to society. The film avoids constructing an anti–Süss Oppenheimer figure. Thus, the film remains much more about the machinations of the "vast right-wing conspiracies" of Weimar Germany than about "ordinary Germans and the Holocaust."

Neither the camera nor the film as a whole take the study of the individual characters very far. Instead, the film concentrates on the social phenomena of conspiracy and corruption. The shots are designed to present social interaction as it strays from due process. As such, it is not a study of antisemitism as the Frankfurt School test film proposed, namely an investigation of how personal prejudices influence an individual's judgment. This is the study of how a widely held bias is put to political use in a legal system supposedly controlled by an independent judiciary. Christiane Mückenberger sees a parallel between *The Blum Affair* and "the first scandalous rehabilitation of Nazi judges in the western sectors, which, not unlike the Haas trial, caused considerable contemporary uproar."[48] At the end of the film, when his wife expresses relief that their problems are finally over, Blum's retort that their problems "have only just begun" is underscored by the sound of marching boots.

Those marching boots could have been a clichéd reference to the coming rise of National Socialism. But, given the rising inter-German political tensions, they could also be a sonic portrayal of the continuity of the "independent judiciary" from the Weimar era through the Third Reich to the emerging West German state. The latter would be in line with the increasing tendency in East Germany in the late forties to equate a treatment of the Nazi past with a broader antifascist stance, which also included a critique of the West. It is certainly true, at least in the late forties, that the treatment of the Nazi past was a place where the two German sectors differed immensely.

The Last Illusion:
Anti-antisemitism and the Failure of Assimilation

If you were a German filmgoer in the late 1940s weary of the dismal, berubbled background of most German topical films, you would be relieved by the opening sequence of *The Last Illusion*. For a brief second the opening shot portrays a war-torn German city in ruins with melancholy non-diegetic music. But the film then cuts quickly to the bustling streets of southern California. Palm trees, large automobiles, and prosperity abound. The background jazz music suggests productive and optimistic bustle. The film thereby situates itself in a dual context that will stay central to the main character's identity crisis.

The Last Illusion is based on a screenplay by Fritz Kortner, a German-Jewish actor who had always struggled with those identity designators. It is driven by the psychological tension of assimilation. It underscores the pull between a Jewish heritage that had, before Hitler, been in danger of fading into the wash of modernity, and a German heritage that had simultaneously become more important. More than anything, the film is the story of a man's attempt to create an image of himself for himself both as a German and a Jew in post-Holocaust (West) Germany. In some ways, as we shall see, it is less an answer to Veit Harlan than a refusal to limit the terms of the debate to such simple parameters.

The opening sequence cuts to a black man, Homer, in a well-appointed servant's uniform walking to the side entrance of a small, but elegant home. A woman with a thick German accent, Emma, greets him at the door. Their exchange is a mixture of German and English. Preparations for a party are underway. The film makes light of who the "we" are who are celebrating. Homer, answering the phone, says, "We are throwing a party . . . fifteen years in this country. . . . No, no not me, it's an awful long time since *we* came." Meanwhile Emma talks about "over there" where she was "*glücklich*," noting that there is a difference between "*glücklich*" and "happy." She does not understand why one celebrates being away from home so long. "Those were the days," she says in German, "under Wilhelm . . . things went well for us while we still had him." The beverage deliverer, Ludwig, arrives. He speaks English with Homer and German with Emma. She goes on about how the Americans need a Kaiser too. Ludwig notes that his people had to look back a bit further to find a time they had it good, perhaps under David.

Thus, the dominant topic of the opening sequence is the determination of ethnic specificity. Each of these three minor figures speaks of a collective "we." For Homer, it refers to African-Americans; for Emma, the Germans; and for Ludwig, the Jews. Another man with a German accent, David, enters, seconding Ludwig's claim, noting that "ever since then, we have been in trouble."

Enter Fränkl, a German with a thick Swabian accent. He and David engage in a discussion about Goethe. Fränkl notes that all of the talk of hope in Goethe was too much for him after the Nazis and their thousand-year Reich came marching in. But now that the war is over and he is a little older, he likes the idea that Goethe slept with a nineteen-year-old at the age of seventy-four. Both men turn to Homer. "Do you know Goethe?" "Yes, sir. He was a writer I suppose. A writer for the movies." The men answer, "He would not have debased himself. Decades saved him from that humiliation." This is not only a sideswipe at Hollywood. It is an attempt to portray the situation of these intellectuals in exile, who were forced into the American system of reification, as they saw it, as an ironical reflection upon their present exercise. Goethe, according to them, was beyond this. Goethe still calls them to their Germanness.

All of the characters speak about "the Professor." When we finally see Professor Mauthner, he is sitting listening to his young student, Mary, with whom he is said to be in love. She plays piano while Homer sings a ballad about America. The whole scene is a mixture of celebration about the joys of America and the pull that *Heimat* still has on all of the exiles. Mauthner announces to David that he is considering accepting a call to his old post as a professor in Germany. David notes that Los Angeles is a place you go to, not from, and is puzzled why Mauthner would want to go back to evil Germany when he could remain in sunny California with beautiful young Mary. Mauthner replies that in both cases it is about a love affair.

Thus, the film does more than enunciate a yearning for a sense of belonging, a search for both an emotional and a physical *Heimat*, that German sense of longing for the mythic place from which one comes. The film establishes early on that it is about a German emigrant's sense of place in postwar America and Germany. The film will try to extract that feeling of belonging from all of the thorny prejudices that surround it. This is a much less utopian, much more ideologically problematic search than in *Long Is the Road*. Mauthner seeks to reestablish identity on pre-Holocaust terms of German intellectual subjectivity. *Long Is the Road* uses the Holocaust as a break from that past. Zionism, in the latter film, serves as not only a traditionalist appeal to *Heimat*, but also a modernist *caesura* from that tradition.

The Last Illusion confronts the representation of both Germanness and Jewishness. While we are sure which of the characters are Germans, there is no reason not to assume that they are all also Jews. Yet, it will still be necessary for the film eventually to secure a specific Jewish identity for Mauthner. How it goes about this task differentiates the film radically from *Marriage in the Shadows*. Mauthner never refers to himself as a Jew, and there is certainly no attempt to feminize and aestheticize Jews as in Maetzig's film. Rather, *The Last Illusion* provides a differentiated set of identificatory anchors that the spectator must be able to add up.

Perhaps the most convincing sign of Mauthner's Jewishness is the reaction of his friends to his idea of accepting the position from his old university. David, who appears to be his closest friend, is shocked and bewildered by the idea. "They are man-eaters, yes, man-eaters, cannibals over there." Mauthner's fiery response indicates that he is going to confront generalizations wherever he sees them. "There is neither a people made up entirely of criminals, nor is there one made up entirely of heroes." He even becomes conciliatory when he claims; "I do not know how I would have behaved had I been allowed to stay there." Much like his friends who reject Germany while still being called to their Germanness, Mauthner's Jewish identity is being thrust upon him by his friends to such an extent that he counters it with a veiled defense of barbarism. Photo 11 depicts one of several situations in the film where a mirror is used to signify a strong identity crisis. This is the

Photo 11. *The Last Illusion:* Mauthner goes through his own mid-life mirror stage. (Courtesy of Stiftung Deutsche Kinemathek)

battle the film will depict throughout: Mauthner tries to reclaim a German identity while others confront him with his Jewish one. When he arrives in Germany, antisemitism establishes the latter completely at the cost of the former.

The manner in which the film constructs antisemitism is noteworthy. The film is not passive, that is, it does not simply try hide from antisemitism by providing only positive images of Jews. The screenplay is similar to that of *The Blum Affair* and different from the other films in this chapter in one important aspect. It does not try to confront the truth content of antisemitic incantations. In *The Last Illusion* Kortner takes up an experiment in order to tell a story of a Jew in berubbled Germany. He gives the spectator every chance to play out his antisemitic fantasy. That is, he creates a character that fits almost all of the negative stereotypes attributed to Jewishness. Mauthner is an old man who is chasing after a young girl and who has had a history of doing so in the past. He is an outsider who has been chosen over a gentile German for a professorship. He becomes a compilation of all of the Jews around him, from David, the Jewish hysterical male, to the orthodox Jew he meets on the ship to Germany. He is Heinrich Heine, whom he quotes on the ship, and Felix Mendelssohn, whose music is played at his party. In short, he becomes the vessel for a variety of Jewish stereotypes. More important, Mauthner is rarely portrayed as affable or even tolerable. But the film insists that just because you cannot like him as an individual does not mean you are allowed to hate him as a signifier of a group.

Slavoj Žižek perhaps best describes the ideology of antisemitism. He points out that it would be useless to expose antisemitic claims to some sort of truth test to see if they hold. He imagines the message such a test would have sent: "The Nazis are condemning the Jews too hastily, without proper argument, so let us take a cool, sober look and see if they really are guilty or not."[49] Such a process would, he claims, merely serve to confirm already held prejudices. Žižek then envisages the opposite scenario, namely a gentile German during the Third Reich and how he might reconcile his everyday experience with his ideological beliefs. How was the German to overcome the contradiction of a good Jewish neighbor and the image of Jews as absolute evil embodied in official ideology? Žižek argues that insofar as the German would recognize this as a contradiction he was not fully captured by the ideology.[50]

This ideological constellation is helpful in understanding how *The Last Illusion* attempts to communicate its message. The film seeks to disclose the ugly German truths that even the terrible defeat of World War II did not change. It is not the mere existence of antisemitic tropes in the collective imagination that keeps the Nazi ghost from going away; but the fact that these old stereotypes and fantasies can, even after the defeat of Nazism, still serve as material for active Jew-baiting. And combating antisemitism cannot come from trying to disprove its premises.

The Last Illusion spends the first half-hour putting together this composite figure of the Jew, who is then hailed back to his Germanness. Mauthner is called back home to educate the young in Germany. If he were just being called back to his university position in an act of reparation, the film would not be able to sustain a compelling narrative for more than twenty minutes. Nor would Mauthner necessarily have to be a Jew. But Jewishness is, in postwar Germany, equivalent to moral authority, and the lingering existence of antisemitism is the ultimate test of moral progress.

The climax of the film is Mauthner's opening lecture at the university on "The Learnability of Virtue." The speech is Mauthner's ultimate performance of his belief in yet another German myth, in this case the traditional *Bildung*, the process by which one enters humanistic culture. Not only do his words fall on deaf ears, a hateful brawl erupts shortly thereafter, suggesting to Mauthner that his faith in humanism is misplaced. He dies soon after of heartbreak. His mortal disappointment lies not in the fact that he is not accepted as a Jew in postwar Germany, but that the place to which he has returned has lost the things for which he longed. The attacks on his Jewishness hit something even more vital in him, namely his humanist identity, which he wishes to label "German."

Visually, the film paints an entirely different picture of Germany than do the other rubble films. This Germany is filmed as dark and enclosed. The vast spaces provided by the ruins are eschewed for a claustrophobic film constructed almost entirely of medium and medium-close shots. Germany is not its buildings, countryside, city crowds, or any other location. It is effectively an institution filmed in tight studio shots. The film's frequent use of close-ups establishes its emphasis on private rather than public attitudes. The only sequence with multiple long shots is Mauthner's lecture, thus coupling his public rejection with the private ones he encounters. The rubble the film attempts to portray is emotional, and it is not only German. The ruins represented are the human remains on all sides of the war, its former soldiers, its civilian support system, the underground opposition, and those forced into exile. The film achieves this effect with facial shots used whenever a character is confronted with the contradictions of his or her past. Pans of large groups move quickly to characters in small groups. The film sutures the spectator into the narrative with conventional editing, in order to give the illusion that these disparate groups could somehow belong together.

Because the film has adhered strictly to the conventions of cinematic realism, the last sequence disrupts the narrative all the more. This transformation occurs in an almost illogical sequence shift. In one sequence Emma, the maid who has accompanied Mauthner on his return to Germany, is talking to the convalescing Mauthner about returning to America. A brightly lit medium shot from above blends into a close-up side view of Mauthner's face with his eyes closed. As the camera pulls back we see that the room is dark and the other characters are expressing concern. The film provides no explanation for this change in the state of Mauthner's health, nor does it provide any conventional clues such as jarring background music or a contemporal diegesis. The next quiet, dark sequence is a transition to the film's concluding segment. The cinematic style morphs from classical realism to a sort of psychological realism found most often in Weimar-era German film. In the end, Mauthner dies with the Oedipal image of his son in the arms of his ex-wife.

Mauthner returned to Germany in hopes of finding a country in the process of rebuilding its great humanist traditions. He subjects his homeland to an aptitude test, using the relative existence of anti-semitism as the marker of humanity's progress in Germany. Instead of finding rich belief in the fundamentals of Enlightenment thinking, he finds a land filled with the same prejudices, pettiness, and deceit he left many years before. He had hoped that he could return idealism to a defeated community. Instead the community defeats his idealism. He is called home only to realize that home is an illusory space.

Conclusion

What is the "image of the Jew" that these films offer to the collective German imagination? At the very least these films are held together as a set insofar as they all demand to have told the story of the persecution of Jews under Nazism and/or the attitudes that led to it. Each film finds

an answer to the question of the portrayal of Jewishness as well as a way
to counteract the distortions committed by Veit Harlan and others. For
Marriage in the Shadows, Jewishness becomes equated with female
domestication. In *Morituri* and *The Last Illusion*, Jewishness provides the
characters with a moral authority with which they can guide the action
of the film. The epic and partially true story in *Long Is the Road* serves
as a powerful corrective to the foul filmic language of the Nazi era,
offering images of pre-Holocaust Orthodox Jewish life carefully constructed around everyday practice. It also provided postwar German
viewers with the opportunity to identify positively with a group of people who, until a few years earlier, had been portrayed as vermin to be
exterminated.

Marriage in the Shadows* was one of the most successful films of its era,
while *Morituri* was one of the least. *Long Is the Road* did not even enjoy
a complete cinematic release. The other two were moderately successful feature films. Measured in terms of discursive impact, these films
certainly deserve more than the neglect Peter Lilienthal affords them.
These filmic attempts to rearticulate positive images of Jewishness
and/or anti-antisemitic messages in postwar Germany were important
first steps in the historical healing process. They reveal just how compromised the filmic medium had become and the magnitude of the public's expectations of it. Given that conditions set these filmmakers up for
failure, we should be amazed at their success. In retrospect, these films
can be seen as constituting a single project of recapturing the image of
Jewishness and taking control of the history-telling of the Holocaust.
The films are acts of the working-through of recent trauma as well as
attempts to categorize it in the diachronic tale of history. And, while
these films occasionally use the history of the Holocaust for purposes
other than historical edification, they do contain honest personal
attempts to think through an unthinkable catastrophe within a medium
that was used extensively to bring about that disaster. In other words,
they use film to correct the distortions created by film. It is a project that
arguably has its roots in Wagner's *Parsifal*, namely the necessity of
being healed by the sword that smote you.[51]

5

The Trouble with Rubble
DEFA's Social Problem Films

As we saw in the last chapter, DEFA leaders made a conscious effort to produce a series of films confronting the Nazi past and its historical foundations. However, the heads of the studio thought that the burden of recent German history was only one among many compelling problems that film should address. At the same time DEFA was producing the "Antifascist" films (the term the studio gave to those films that confronted the Nazi past), it also dedicated itself to making *Zeitfilme*, films set in postwar Germany that addressed the social problems of the day. Despite these intentions, *The Murderers Are among Us* was the only DEFA film produced from 1946 to 1948 that attempted to combine a discussion of current day problems—for example, housing shortages, inadequate medical care, and rampant profiteering—with a frank discussion of the Nazi past. But this film proved to be a precursor to the DEFA program of the following two years.

The very fact that we can speak of a program—that is, of a series of films that would be released during a season—indicates that filmmaking in the Soviet sector was different from that in the other Allied spheres of control. Unlike the filmmaking industry in the West, which proceeded in an ad hoc fashion until currency reform, DEFA quickly began functioning in a form not dissimilar from that of Ufa, the previous tenants in Potsdam-Babelsberg and Berlin-Johannisthal.[1] The one big difference, at least in the early years, was that directors working in the DEFA organization

116

enjoyed a much more open environment than those working under Goebbels's Ufa.

In the early years, DEFA allowed for a system of film production whereby the studio both conceived projects and accepted outside proposals. Its ability to attract funding, directors, and screenwriters allowed DEFA to plan a continuous flow of films to present to distributors. Few directors of DEFA films were under permanent contract with the studio. While the studio was run primarily by those with strong ties to the communists, most of the personnel resided in West Berlin. Its organizational structure and behavior was not unlike the Hollywood studios of the era. The studio management accepted project proposals from a variety of artists and then pursued those they thought were most viable, both commercially and ideologically. There is little evidence that, beyond acceptance of a project, they controlled the content of the films.

As Thomas Heimann notes, "many DEFA directors kept different options open. They signed contracts at the same time with film companies in the West."[2] This prevented DEFA in the early years from attempting any complete ideological or aesthetic unity. As much as some studio executives such as Hans Klering or Kurt Maetzig wanted to push DEFA toward emulation of the Soviet socialist realist model of filmmaking, their dependence upon a free market of directors and technical personnel inhibited their plans. DEFA still had designs on being the major film studio for all of Germany.

In its early years DEFA indeed showed promise of becoming a creative center for film talent from all over Germany and the rest of Europe. Roberto Rossellini worked with DEFA on his 1947 film *Germania Anno Zero*. Compared to the working conditions in the Western sectors, DEFA was a paradise. In 1947, DEFA continued to function as if the German film industry would not be affected by Cold War politics. It proved possible, at least that year, to keep this hope alive. Peter Pewas, director of the DEFA-produced *Street Acquaintance* (*Straßenbekanntschaft*, 1948), noted much later that "never before or since did I enjoy such excellent production conditions as I did with DEFA. I got everything I needed. As long as production continued, DEFA did not interfere with my artistic work. That was their principle."[3] Not only did directors enjoy artistic freedom, the DEFA studios also provided a technical capacity that facilities in the West initially found difficult to match. Full-time production staffs were able to move from one film project to the next. Thus, most of the films made at DEFA from 1946 through

1948 have the unified look of studio cinema rather than the unpre-
dictability of independent filmmaking. The only restrictions on individual artistic freedom came in the form of having to work with a studio
collective, a restriction that exists in cinematic production everywhere.

With the increasing Cold War tensions and eventual founding of the
German Democratic Republic (GDR), the freedom that DEFA enjoyed
before 1949 and that which it extended to its artistic staff were gradually curtailed. DEFA began training and developing a younger group of
directors more in tune with the political realities of East Germany. And
filmmaking itself became more and more a part of the cultural-political
matrix of the country. Therefore, the selection of projects and directors
became based as much on political as aesthetic considerations. In the
pages that follow, we will see that while this trend toward using cinema
for political ends was there from DEFA's beginning, directors still
enjoyed freedom to pursue narratives that aspired to something greater
than one set of political interests.

In this chapter I discuss four films that premiered between 1946 and
1948: Gerhard Lamprecht's *Somewhere in Berlin* (*Irgendwo in Berlin*,
1946), Werner Klingler's *Razzia* (1947), Peter Pewas's *Street Acquaintance*, and Gustav von Wangenheim's *'48 All over Again* (*Und wieder '48*,
1948). These films all fixate on stories of the postwar reconstruction of
everyday life. Aesthetically and ideologically they are bound together by
a commitment to a similar form of cinematic realism. While these are
not the only DEFA films produced in that era, they constitute a particular strand of projects to which the studio dedicated resources. The
films portray a similar range of issues, which they treat as symptomatic
of moral breakdown in postwar Germany. Each of these films puts the
berubbled *mise en scène* of Berlin to a specific purpose. As a group, they
show a progression from the initial postwar chaos to a normalized, legit-
imized, and humanized city.

Somewhere in Berlin in Year Zero

DEFA's 1946 program contained three films, Wolfgang Staudte's *The
Murderers Are among Us*, Milo Harbich's *Free Land*,[4] and Gerhard Lam-
precht's *Somewhere in Berlin*. Like most filmmakers in those early years,
Lamprecht had been active before and during the Third Reich. His
most successful film was his adaptation of Erich Kästner's *Emil und die
Detektive* (1931), for which Billy Wilder wrote the screenplay. In the

1930s Lamprecht worked on a variety of German/French coproductions. During the war, his work consisted of unnoteworthy studio productions.[5] Lamprecht was known in the 1920s for his sociocritical screenplays and portrayals of Berlin milieus. These were, as Christiane Mückenberger puts it, "stories not without melodrama and with children always at the center point."[6] Lamprecht's first postwar film certainly picks up on his earlier tendencies. As the following recap of the film's plot emphasizes, the effect of postwar conditions on the children was a central theme:

> Berlin in the zero hour. The city lies in rubble. Gangs of youths romp carefree through the landscape of ruins and play war with stolen fireworks as their munitions. Their parents are unhappy to see this mischief, but no one has time to pay attention to Gustav, Willi and the other little roughnecks. The unexpected return from the POW camp of Gustav's father should bring about the actual new beginning. . . . But hope is deceptive. The father is a physical and psychological wreck. But what the resigned parents cannot manage, the children can. Even though it takes the tragic death of Willi to tear them from their careless play and rivalries.[7]

Most contemporary critics of *Somewhere in Berlin* seem unable to separate any discussion of the plot from a discussion of real problems in Berlin's neighborhoods. The following passage is from Walter Lenning, East Berlin's most prolific film critic of the era:

> Both the first film *The Murderers Are among Us* and this new DEFA film have climbed into this reality of ruins. And they were right in doing so. For precisely that reality which we always see and have in front of us must be discovered in order to be understood. . . . This time the film is about a more collective problem, the life of our young people.[8]

Like most of the other critics, Lenning fails to differentiate the film from what it is trying to portray. Signifier and signified become one. He is also not the only critic to claim that the cinema was regaining its legitimacy by presenting reality. In fact, the tendency among critics in the Soviet occupation zone was to demand of film a narrowly mimetic stance. While all of the reviews note Lamprecht's drive toward addressing everyday life in postwar Berlin, none picks up on the broader visual and narrative themes the film lays out. The film press fixates upon the cinematic portrayal of the things, people, and places that have survived the war, without calling attention to the ways in which these aspects of the pro-filmic world have been put in constellation with one another. The readings adhere strictly to Lamprecht's realist constructs, while neglecting the ideological nature of the solutions he presents to everyday problems.

The central motif of the film is destruction. While *The Murderers Are among Us* presented a stylized version of ruins mostly created in the studio and used as a backdrop, *Somewhere in Berlin* responds to the devastation by interacting with it. I have up to now referred to rubble films as those films made between 1946 and 1949 that take as their theme the war-torn German cityscape and/or the causes of that obliteration. *Somewhere in Berlin* intensifies the berubbled *mise en scène*. Rather than a mere metonymic extension of inner discontent, rubble becomes a player. The rubble is the other, the primary external force to which the characters must respond. It will kill children and corrupt adults. In employing actual ruins, the film effaces them as an effect of another set of actions, namely the German-initiated world war.

The opening sequence of *Somewhere in Berlin* establishes the city as a destroyed *Heimat*. But, unlike any of the other opening sequences in the rubble film cycle, this one begins with a reconstruction segment. The first image is a silhouette of the Berlin cathedral in the background with a man climbing a ladder in the foreground. The dramatic orchestral score fades. There is no apparent destruction. As he reaches the top of the roof the camera tracks to the left, finally exposing a berubbled landscape as the music again swells. The camera tilts down to reveal people around a small street market. Gradually the crowd begins moving in a single direction as if in pursuit of something. One man, a pickpocket, emerges from the long shot being chased by the rest. He is climbing the rubble, coming toward the camera. The film cuts to him scrambling across screen. The tracking shot reveals a rubble landscape that is treacherous and concealing. The entire opening sequence becomes a chase scene that introduces the audience to the criminality and vice the film will portray. It also gives a disturbing picture of what has become of Berlin. The *Kiez* (roughly translatable as neighborhood), the Berlin version of *Heimat*, has become a fluid, chaotic, and corrupt place. Despite the best efforts of its citizens, it cannot maintain law and order. The inhabitants' gaze, as represented through the camera, is inadequate to control transgression.

Those in pursuit of the pickpocket are all adults, and our own bird's-eye view is that of the construction worker on the roof. When the thief escapes into a cellar, a young boy traps him there. The boy, Gustav, is master of this enclosed space. The thief has to concoct a lie to convince the boy to let him out. As soon as he is let out, the two return to the rubble field, the space the adults cannot control. Within the first three minutes, the film sets up the *mise en scène* of the ruins as both a chaotic space and a malignant agent that has come to dominate the *Kiez*. Having a thief escape and then manipulate a boy in this landscape establishes the space as menacing and in need of taming.

Masculinity arises as another, related issue in the opening sequence. While eventually the film will confront the emasculation of returning soldiers, the initial problem is that of misplaced male strength. Waldemar, the thief who befriends Gustav under false pretenses, outruns the other men on the screen. He impresses Gustav by hitting a small object at a great distance with a rock and by performing magic tricks. For the little boy, whose father has yet to return from the war, the crook possesses some impressive manly talents.[9]

The film offers a variety of male figures under whose influence and image the children circulate. The worst of them is Herr Steidel, a shell-shocked war veteran who has yet to grasp that the war has ended. At the top of the hour this middle-aged man who lives with his mother awakes from a troubled sleep, goes to the balcony, and salutes the neighborhood. His mother laments her troubles with her son to Eckmann, an artist who serves as patriarch to the *Kiez*. Eckmann has a positive ideological influence on the children and serves as a counterbalance to Birke, a black marketeer in whose house Willi, an orphan boy, lives and from whom the boys receive contraband fireworks. The police detective cannot bring any more order to the berubbled chaos than can Gustav's uncle, Kalle, the boy's self-appointed ersatz father. All of these figures are used to set the scene for the return of Gustav's father, Herr Iller, an event that is supposed to fix the social malaise of both the household and the *Kiez*.

The father's coming home sequence finally occurs over a half an hour into the film. When it does, it looks like the opening sequence of numerous rubble films. It is preceded by a compete fade to black from the previous sequence. Before the first image appears, a non-diegetic march music swells. A long shot of a destroyed building and a pile of debris appears with the diminutive figure of a man, Herr Iller, walking down the street in front of it. He is walking in rhythm with the music. His uniform is tattered and he still sports his Wehrmacht-issue cap and coat. The sequence then cuts to a medium-close shot of the former soldier taken from a lower angle. We see his distressed reaction to the destruction in his midst. It then pulls back to again reveal the war-torn *mise en scène*. This sequence is repeated twice. This rubble film, the second to be released in postwar Germany that fits such a description, provides the originary cinematic image of the traumatized German soldier returning from the war. As we shall see, this will become the most quoted and satirized image of postwar filmmaking. The length of the sequence as well as its simultaneously sad and triumphant background music give the impression of the return of the everyman soldier, the *Heimkehrer*.

The first one to notice Iller's return is crazy Herr Steidel. We finally realize that the reason he stares out the window all day is to wait for his missing comrades. The sequence then cuts to a shot of three young boys preparing to set a pyramid of bottle rockets alight in a cellar that they refer to as their bunker. When they run outside to watch the explosion, they run into the *Heimkehrer*. Not knowing that the man is Gustav's father, the boys tell him that they can do with the cellar (which is where Gustav hopes his father will re-establish his auto repair business) what they want until the father returns, if he ever does. Gustav assures the *Heimkehrer* that his father will certainly return. (Having a father return from the war appears to be a status symbol among the kids.) The kids resume their play, wondering what the dirty and defeated man wants, as he collapses in front of the cellar. Willi suggests that he might be hungry, whereupon Gustav runs back down the heap to talk to him. Next comes a medium shot where the young Gustav bends down to talk to the fatigued soldier (Photo 12). The entire sequence evokes the *Heimkehrer's* powerlessness even in the face of children who only seem to pity him. Gustav takes the stranger home only to discover that it is his father.

All of the shots of the coming home sequence are set up to dramatize the patriarch's compromised stature. Iller's tattered clothes and shoes are metonyms for his corporeal lack. When he dons his civilian suit, it is many times too large. This sequence reveals the crisis of the father's body. His diminished physical presence is a sign to him and to others of his reduced sense of identity and purpose. Unlike a similar character played by Hans Albers in *And the Heavens Above* (see Chapter 6), Iller is defeated by his surroundings. But in psychoanalytic terms, it is not a castration, that is, a permanent emasculation. Rather it is impotence, the inability to perform his masculinity. The task of rebuilding his business, which everyone, including his son, demands of him, fails to sufficiently

Photo 12. *Somewhere in Berlin:* Father and son meet on the road. (Courtesy of Stiftung Deutsche Kinemathek)

motivate him. As in *The Murderers Are among Us,* the shot/countershot combinations align him constantly with devastated surroundings.

In her work on East German literature, Julia Hell argues that the father figure is a metaphor for the party leader. This is accomplished through an overdetermining of the patriarchal body as an incarnation of the party itself.[10] Hell makes a convincing argument for how this rhetorical strategy ideologically informs early GDR literature, that is, the literature written and published in conjunction with the founding of the East German state. Her reasoning works especially well for literature because the authors were generally committed communists attempting to construct a national narrative.

It is arguable in early DEFA films, especially those discussed in this chapter, that the body of the patriarch is at stake. But given the film politics of the time, this project of reinscribing masculinity into a culture was not so much the rearticulation of the socialist man as it was the older, post–World War I project of returning masculinity to the German man. Apart from Gustav von Wangenheim, none of the directors of the films in this chapter dedicated himself to the cause of nation-building in the East. Yet, again excepting von Wangenheim, they all appear invested in the redemption and reconstruction of a traditional version of patriarchy.

Somewhere in Berlin lends itself to many comparisons with *The Murderers Are among Us*, although it is unlikely that they influenced each other much. While the directors would certainly have had contact, the films were made simultaneously in different locations. Yet both films move along similar trajectories in their initiative to recapture a troubled male subjectivity. In Staudte's film, Hans Mertens rediscovers his existential anchor, not through the love and caring of Susanne, but through a brutal yet life-saving command of a child's body. His operation to rescue the child (thereby responding to a poster that Susanne is seen painting earlier) in turn rescues him. In *Somewhere in Berlin*, Herr Iller mopes around with a similar lack of purpose, albeit without Mertens's self-destructive edge. But Iller's level of disenchantment and physical decay are overdetermined. Even the children mock his lack of strength. And, as did *The Murderers Are among Us*, this film employs a child's crisis as the catalyst for masculine rebirth.

The greatest difference between the first two rubble films lies in the enemy each film establishes. *The Murderers Are among Us* is driven by Mertens's quite literal need to master the past in the person of the war criminal, Brückner. *Somewhere in Berlin* is compelled by a need to reestablish a father figure/agent who can lead the children from their misery. The enemy is this film is the rubble itself, the threatening physical destruction in Iller's midst.

When Gustav claims that his father would regain his strength, given the proper food, Willi, the orphaned boy who lives with the corrupt Birke, intervenes. He steals from Birke's black market provisions in order to help in the task of rebuilding the father. Willi then flees his provisional home in fear of Birke's retribution. Having lost all familial anchor, Willi sets out to prove to his little buddies that he is the bravest of them all. He scales a freestanding ruin of a wall but slips and falls to the ground. His fall is visually similar to the end of Roberto Rossellini's *Germania Anno Zero* (1947), where the desperate Edmund jumps to his death. But, instead of dying on the spot, Willi is taken to Frau Steidel's apartment. There Iller visits him and promises he will rebuild his business, an auto repair garage. It is the sign that Iller will again participate in the dominant fiction of reconstruction. The next sequence has the young boys watching as Willi clings to life. In a long and sentimental death scene reminiscent of Ufa-era death kitsch, the film kills off Willi as a lesson in deterrence and the value of life for the rest of the boys.

The film cuts from Willi's deathbed to a shot of the wall from which he fell. A shot/countershot indicates that the rubble, this symbol of the enemy, is under siege—the wall is being torn down. The shot rests a while on the dust of an explosion. The next sequence has the boys hanging around together in a park. The only thing that has changed is that they have been removed from the malignant *mise en scène* of the ruins. Gustav, with the help of Uncle Kalle, then organizes all of the children of the *Kiez*. They will attack the very thing that has threatened them, and they will do so on the site of Iller's destroyed auto repair shop. The film's triumphant final sequence shows hundreds of boys pitching in to clear out the rubble, with Iller literally climbing to the top of the heap to join them. The neighborhood project and social fantasy of reinserting the patriarch at the center of community power is complete.

Somewhere in Berlin does not rely on subtlety in communicating its message. It is about the reconstitution of the real father. There is only one. The other male figures are either false fathers (Waldemar and Birke) or uncles. The women are all passive non-agents, helpless in engaging the ruined environment. This is an obvious effacement of the actual situation of the rubble women, who were often the primary breadwinners and parental authority figures. (The term *Trümmerfrau* was as recognizable in postwar German language as "soccer mom" is in current American parlance.) These women did most of the work clearing away the "concrete" signs of Germany's destruction. Hence, the film must elide this image of women in order to create the savior image of the father.

While *Somewhere in Berlin* alludes to many psychological models, it is careful to exclude the Oedipal drama from the list. Arguably, the film even goes so far as to deny this narrative by allusion to it. It sets up a sequence wherein the son does not recognize his own father. But to show that the complex has been resolved, the son takes the father to the mother. The son functions as the primary missionary in the salvation of his father. His success in the end not only redeems the father as the arbiter of moral authority, it also suggests that material reconstruction is dependent upon this model. Patriarchal restoration replaces patricide as the order of the day.

Somewhere in Berlin starts another trend in rubble film discourse, namely the eradication of discussion of the past. Ghosts of that past, in the form of militaristic, aggressive children, the war-torn landscape, missing parents, and the *Heimkehrer*, haunt the screen. But, apart from Herr Iller's small outburst at the presence of a war toy in his house, none of the characters mentions the traumatic past, any possible culpability in it, or even the causes of their current misery. The past has passed. These characters direct their attention quite firmly toward the present.

Razzia: Life with and without Father

Somewhere in Berlin and *Free Land* were, compared to *The Murderers Are among Us*, relative failures at the box office. *Free Land* was immediately pulled from circulation; *Somewhere in Berlin* was pulled and then later re-released. DEFA followed these releases with a simple romantic comedy, *No Place for Love* (*Kein Platz für Liebe*, 1947), directed by Hans Deppe. Although the story was set in postwar Germany, the film did little to engage with the important questions of the period. Deppe, basically a B-film director from the Nazi years, simply used current conditions as a background for a comedy that could have taken place at any time and place. Like most films of the era, it found an audience happy just to go to a warm cinema. But it failed to resonate either with the critics or with a wider audience.[11] In style and content, Deppe's film reveals that continuity with the studio cinematic practices of the Ufa period would be difficult to break.

Next on the DEFA schedule was *Razzia* (the title can be translated as "police raid"), postwar Germany's first attempt at a detective film. The structure of this genre presents certain difficulties for postwar sensitivities. As I will show, these problems undermine the film's narrative drive and also determine the parameters that the plot can traverse. While *Razzia* takes the black market as its primary social problem, it nevertheless continues the discourse about the restoration of patriarchal authority initiated by the first two DEFA films. Yet, whereas *Somewhere in Berlin* links the restoration of patriarchy with the country's material reconstruction, *Razzia* pursues this restoration for more political purposes, namely for reinserting the state into the father position.

Razzia hardly did any better with the critics than *No Place for Love*, but it fared quite well at the box office. As formula films, both suffered a barrage of complaints from those who were demanding not only an ideological but also an aesthetic break from Ufa cinematic practices. Unlike *Somewhere in Berlin*, *Razzia*'s close adherence to the pro-filmic world of postwar Berlin became much more a target of critique than a point in the film's favor. The trade publication *Neue Filmwoche* provides an adequate recapitulation of the plot. Police are trying to get at the heart of a Berlin smuggling ring. Their investigation leads them to a popular nightclub.

> Something is not quite right in the Ali Baba bar. A surprise evening visit by the police brings no results, but Detective Naumann is still convinced. Insiders have known it for some time. . . . The most powerful attraction at the bar is the torch singer, Yvonne, for whom even a young assistant detective falls. But when Naumann investigates things at the bar more closely, he ends up there for good. His body is found in the rubble. [He is found outside, having been shot.] The owner of the bar is preparing a big deal, peddling scarce prescription drugs. Of course the removal of these vital drugs to the black market endangers the lives of many patients. . . . Yet, this time the deal goes sour. The assistant detective, despite all the love songs, refuses to cooperate. This time the round up is a surprise and the bar owner has to put his hands over his head.[12]

The film starts with typical detective story conventions, in this case, with an arrest. Participation in the black market is the charge, and it is initially made against a little old lady who has spent a small fortune on a bottle of brandy for her husband. In a cleverly edited sequence, the film reveals that Ali Baba is the source of the brandy. This sequence also enunciates more clearly the film's ideological direction. Unlike in the films made in the Western sectors, *Razzia* promptly cites the *profits* made in the black market, not the stealing or smuggling itself, as the real sin. Were the mark-up less, the crime would be less.

In the next sequence we learn that the young police assistant, Becker, has tipped off the bar to the raid. The film sets up a tension between Becker and Lorenz, another police assistant, who is also engaged to Naumann's daughter Anna. Although the narrative is motivated by the attempt to discover both the black market source and, eventually, Naumann's murderer, the film reveals the answers to the audience much more readily than to the characters. The spectator occupies a position of privilege in which she already has all of the information. Thus, at least for the filmgoer, this is a detective story without suspense.

The black market played an active role in the everyday lives of Berliners in 1947, whether as a drain on or source of valuable commodities. Survival often depended upon some level of participation in this illegal economy. Therefore, a critical treatment of black marketeering necessarily implied an indictment of the audience's behavior. The film seems to work toward the goal of educating its public both about the harmful effects of the underground economy and of the trustworthiness of the police force. The latter, although underplayed, is the more radical gesture of 1947. The former subject matter would have been as commonplace to an average spectator in those early postwar years as news stories about e-commerce are today.

The masculinity issue that was so prevalent in *Somewhere in Berlin* also emerges in *Razzia*. Detective Naumann's murder sets loose a struggle between Lorenz, Naumann's trusted assistant and would-be son-in-law, and Paul Naumann, the detective's only living son. Paul returns from the war only to remain unemployed as a musician. Lembke, Naumann's superior, takes over the investigation, assuring a patriarchal consistency. Lorenz honors his mentor qua father (his own parents were killed in the war) by seeking to solve the case, thereby avenging Naumann's death. Paul slips into an underdeveloped Oedipal-esque situation when he recognizes that his seemingly harmless connection to the smuggling operation has made him a part of the syndicate that is responsible for his father's death. In the end, he assists in capturing Goll, the owner of Ali Baba and the head of the crime syndicate. Thus, both Paul and Lorenz share in evening the score with Goll. Lorenz will marry Anna. Paul's action to bring the case to a close redeems him of his poor choices. And the chief of police, Lembke, courts the widow Naumann, again reaffirming the state and patriarchy as one entity. The men are redeemed and the past is forgotten.

An initial perusal of the film's critical reception after its Berlin premiere suggests that, whether intentionally or not, film critics in the West were much less generous with the cinematic products of the Soviet sector than they were with films from the West. The review in the Western-sector daily *Neue Zeit* is typical: "The film's most creative moment is at the very end. . . . Unfortunately, one cannot say all's well that ends well. What comes before it is everything but good. It is sometimes blossoming kitsch, other times miserable sentimentality."[13] While not all reviews of DEFA films that appeared in East Berlin papers were positive, reviewers in *Berliner Zeitung*, *Sonntag*, *Neue Zeit*, and most predictably *Neues Deutschland*, the organ of the governing Socialist Unity Party (SED), were often more sympathetic toward the didactic projects that many DEFA films of the time were undertaking. But

Walter Lenning, generally a DEFA cheerleader, saw in *Somewhere in Berlin* and *Razzia* a trend toward simplistic studio production riddled with clichés. Just because one chooses to address current day problems, Lenning argues, "does not mean it cannot be intelligent, suspenseful and even charming . . . it does not mean that the plot could not be created such that one could at least remain in doubt about who murdered whom where why and when."[14]

The fact that the film shuns the plot tensions normally associated with a detective story in favor of a more directly communicated message appears often in the critiques. In one of the rare positive reviews, Helmut Eiseln noted in *Sonntag,* "The film dispenses brilliantly with the sparkling suspense of a real detective story—which it does not wish to be anyway."[15] Eiseln saw as innovations those aspects of the film that others saw as failings. Thus, the film's refusal to adhere to the convention of narrative tension that usually underscores the detective film is read as a break from tradition. The question, then, is why would *Razzia* do this? We can answer this question by examining the fundamental goals of DEFA at the time and by understanding some of the basic assumptions of the generic codes of the detective story.

In hiring Werner Klingler, DEFA chose an experienced director with few political burdens. His work under Nazism was confined to formula films that failed to raise anyone's ire. At the same time, DEFA acquired someone who could easily put together the needed narrative about the social ills of the black market, perhaps the most pressing everyday issue for Germans in 1947. Klingler had a record from the 1930s and 1940s of making films to fill out the studio's program. That is to say, he could simply fill in wherever needed, thus making him ideal for a production like this one, where the studio heads had ideas about what they wanted. "DEFA did not simply want a timeless crime story; they wanted a film set in the present with clear didactic and enlightening intentions."[16] DEFA certainly had a narrative goal in mind, but it appeared to be one that the studio simply entrusted to the director it hired. The goal of entertaining was, in the case of this set of films, as important as the goal of educating the audience.

As in *The Blum Affair* (see Chapter 4), the narrative problems of the film stem from a lack of trust. The makers of *Razzia* trusted neither the audience's ability to absorb the nuances necessary to sustain suspense in a detective film nor their own ability to actually render those subtleties. As such the film ends up being as much an indictment of the audience's powers of judgment as a critique of the economic structure of black marketeering.

One of the basic assumptions of the detective story is that the spectator will be able to identify with the side of justice and order. As the characters seek to solve the crime puzzle, tension is created by the degree to which the film passes out information. Occasionally tension is also created when the film undermines the reliability of the information it provides. Whatever the case, these tensions can only function if the film and the filmgoer agree on the terms of good and evil. The problem with a narrative about postwar German black marketeering is that such a consensus would have been difficult to achieve in the audience. Material necessity often weighed heavier than ideals regarding fair access to resources. Thus, the filmmakers could not assume that the audience members would line up against the black marketeer, nor that they would find the measures taken by the police just or laudable. In order to achieve their intended political message, the filmmakers had to frontload the narrative such that the audience would be sure to absorb the political message about the black market's drain on public resources. So the audience had to be shown from the start that the black marketeer, Goll, is also a cold-blooded killer.

Razzia communicates its social message through a series of preachy monologues by the chief of police, who points to children in hospitals going without medicine because medical supplies have been commandeered by smugglers. And yet, the film strives to differentiate the black market economy into macro and micro levels. Both in its plot and its ideology, the film attacks the underground macroeconomic situation, wherein supplies are tightly controlled at just under the burgeoning demand, thereby making scarce even those goods that are necessary for the survival of the population, such as medicines. On the other hand, it is careful to excuse the participation of everyday citizens in such actions. The film portrays physicians as innocent pawns bidding on prescriptions drugs for their patients. As in the rhetoric of the American "drug wars," only those on the supply side are guilty. Pursuit of the buyers would have endangered a fragile public consensus, both within the film and in the pro-filmic world.

The difference between the participants is made clear in an early sequence when Naumann is interrogating those who have been hauled in during a raid in front of the Reichstag. The old woman who has purchased a bottle of brandy for her anniversary is treated with comic respect. As subsequent market participants are dragged into the station, the number of bottles on the table increases. Each of these suspects is treated with increasing seriousness. The average consumer forced to the streets for daily purchases is given a wink and a nod, while those who capitalize on the misery are pursued with increasing intensity. The point is made at the very end of the film as well. When Lembke is asked about the source of the flowers he has brought to the widow Naumann, he is forced to admit that he got them from the black market. Thus, the film confronts the ideological problem of the black market but treats citizens' daily participation in it is as comic relief.

If the filmmakers were not sure they could trust the audience to identify with the story in the way they wished, it may also have been because of their own doubts in their ability to portray the subtle distinctions that often create suspense in a detective story. That is, often it is necessary to portray ambivalence in a character who will turn out to be the perpetrator, if only to sustain narrative tension. But allowing for this ambivalence requires filmmakers to trust in their own ability to nuance their construction of the character such that spectator is surprised when the case turns against him. The effect would fail if the spectator continued to identify with the perpetrator after the evidence had mounted against him. If the narrative drive is not merely to convict one character of specific crimes but to show how such crimes are part of an even greater social ill, then the filmmakers need to be reassured that their representation of the criminal is not burdened by mitigating positive identification by the viewer. In short, filmmakers need to be sure that they have, above all, portrayed the crime as bad and the criminal as guilty of it. When that level of certainty is required, filmmakers cannot hazard that the audience will guess wrong.

The drive toward moral certainty on the part of both the spectator and the filmic narrative creates another challenge in *Razzia*. The narrative project requires the immediate legitimation of an authoritative police force. Like the film's bald revelation of the "whodunit" aspects of the narrative, its refusal of ambiguity regarding the police would have been deemed appropriate in Germany in 1947. Unlike in Hollywood *film noir*, where the line between crime and the law always remains purposely blurred, in *Razzia* the police are on the side of the angels—with the exception of one assistant, Becker, who is punished for his transgressions.

What is even more surprising in this portrayal of the police is how little their newfound authority is problematized. The opening shot of the film shows the front of the Reichstag, symbol of national greatness and its demise. This was the most famous postwar location for the black market. It is thus interesting to note that, in order to film the realistic black market scene, the filmmakers would have to have displaced the actual black market with their staged one. With the appearance of the title, the sequence cuts to a medium close shot of Lembke, the Berlin police chief, who is lecturing the police precinct about the black market. In his speech, which serves as a voice-over for a shot/countershot sequence from a police meeting to a round up in front of the Reichstag, Lembke constructs the police force as an organization sympathetic to the people. The black market is an exploitative economy, but those who are forced to do daily business there are not necessarily bad. They are merely pawns of an underground big business.

In the film, postwar Berlin suffers from many social problems, all of which are only linked to the acts of private individuals and common crooks. These problems are not traceable to the state. Becker's complicity in the crimes implicates the police force as corrupt, but the force's ability to weed out its own corruption makes it that much further above reproach. Moreover, any culpability on the part of Becker or any other members of the force, is strictly explainable in terms of postwar conditions. The agents of the state end up impeccable. This is surely a sign that the film has no intention of addressing the Nazi past. It has constructed all of its problems in a fantasy political atmosphere of an unburdened Germany.

If DEFA leaders had hoped for an instructional film about the evils of the black market, they did not get it in *Razzia*. To be sure, it is about the black market, and it is almost pedantic in its attempts to stylize and condemn the ringleaders of that economy. But in the end, it is difficult to say what lesson a spectator should derive from the viewing experience. In both its filmic and pro-filmic incarnations, the black market simply allowed for too many relativizations to make it suitable for the didactic realism some members of the DEFA leadership were advocating. The studio heads would, however, soon find other topics more suitable to their views of the social role of cinema.

Street Acquaintance: Controlling the Rubble Women

Disease, depression, and despair flourished in postwar Berlin, as did nonmarital sexual activity. Public health officials were overwhelmed in 1946 by the number of cases of sexually transmitted diseases being reported. At its high point in the Soviet zone, the monthly average of newly reported cases was 120 for every 10,000 people.[17] Walter Lenning reports a claim that in 1948 "one of every ten seventeen-year-old girls is infected."[18] In December 1948 a new law in the Soviet sector created a police unit under the command of public health officials that could round up young women (though not men) and have them examined for venereal diseases. This ordinance also mandated a public health campaign to combat the spread of sexually transmitted infections (STIs).[19] The film *Street Acquaintance* arose out of the general public relations and police campaign, not only in the Soviet sector but in the Western sectors as well, to gain control of the STI epidemic.

In 1947, DEFA commissioned Peter Pewas, a director with experience and antifascist credentials (he had studied at the Bauhaus, worked with Erwin Piscator, and so on), to produce a feature film about venereal diseases based on an existing screenplay by Artur Pohl. Even more so than *Razzia*, the film is a bold example of DEFA's impulse to employ the cinema in the task of public education. Pewas was an apt choice for the project because of his own activism in community politics. After 1945, he became a city official in the western Berlin borough of Wilmersdorf.[20] His first project with DEFA was to have been a film about the German resistance movement, but the project fell apart over disagreements with the screenwriters. His cooperation with DEFA continued, however, as soon as he read Pohl's screenplay. In an interview he gave years later, he explained that he "quite simply felt the duty to enlighten and help quite concretely through this film."[21] The result is a multivalent narrative that develops important distinctions regarding gender construction, attitudes toward sexuality, and the relationship between the individual and the state.

The film centers on the story of a young working-class girl, Erika, and her attempts to escape the misery of her impoverished postwar life. Blaming her parents' belief in the war for her own gloom, Erika moves out and is taken in by her altruistic admirer, Walter. But he is only a beat reporter with a small income. She hungers for an exciting nightlife and plates full of real food. She accepts an invitation to a party at the home of Annemie, a prostitute at the center of a group of smugglers and thieves, all of whom will give her what she wants in return for sex.

Parallel to Erika's story is that of Marian and Herbert. Herbert finds his way home from the war to rebuild his life with Marian. Soon after his arrival, Herbert discovers that Marian had an affair in his absence. Herbert seeks solace in the arms of Erika, whom he meets at Annemie's.

Shortly thereafter, Marian discovers that she has a sexually transmitted disease that she has likely passed on to her husband, who in turn has passed it on to Erika.

Erika is taken into police custody in a round up of all single women in a café. (It is a sign of the verisimilitude of the scene that something so shocking to an audience more than fifty years later occurs in the film with little explanation necessary.) She is tested for and confirmed to have gonorrhea and is ordered to stay in the hospital for treatment. In fear and denial, she escapes to the apartment she shares (platonically) with Walter. After he refuses to protect her from being taken in again, she goes to Annemie. There she discovers that Annemie has left her own syphilis untreated for years and is beginning to suffer physical deformities. Frightened and alone, Erika runs back to the hospital, where the nurse welcomes her with open arms. The film ends happily with Walter retrieving a happily recuperated Erika from the hospital.

Once Pewas tied himself to this somewhat controversial topic, the discourse of the film then began to circulate around the ways in which the public health campaign could be transformed into a film that was aesthetically viable in its own right. The question that Pewas faced was

Photo 13. *Street Acquaintance:* Female sexuality as a public health crisis. (Courtesy of Stiftung Deutsche Kinemathek)

how to transform the pro-filmic reality into a cinematic realism that would achieve his desired effect. How should the film portray the real conditions of an epidemic in a way that would, at the same time, provide a compelling contemporary story?

This question in turn leaves us to ask what exactly the desired outcome of viewing the film should be. Is the film meant to be informative or persuasive as it dramatizes the real conditions of metropolitan life? We can better determine the film's goals by establishing what kind of cinematic realism the filmmakers attempted to create. This is often best brought into relief by investigating what kinds of choices they had to make in bringing the film to the screen.

Pewas secured Georg Bruckbauer as his cinematographer. In so doing, Pewas made a strong formal break from the screenplay he inherited. Bruckbauer, whose most impressive work during the Third Reich was on Helmut Käutner's *Romance in a Minor Key* (*Romanze im Moll*, 1943), was a stylist of a much different sort than the most active early DEFA cameraman, Friedl Behn-Grund, who had filmed, among others, *The Murderers Are among Us*, *Marriage in the Shadows*, and *Razzia*. Bruckbauer adopted many of the more innovative cinematic techniques that had circulated internationally in the 1940s. He experimented with wide-angle shots that minimized the individual in the *mise en scène*, as well as deep-focus shooting, a technique that had gained prominence since Orson Welles's *Citizen Kane* (1941).[22]

An encounter with Roberto Rossellini in 1947 during the production of *Street Acquaintance* stimulated Pewas's commitment to realist cinema. As Pewas describes it, "Rossellini invited [Count] Treuberg and me to the French sector for a screening of his *Paisa* and *Open City*. I was thrilled and so moved that I hugged Rossellini spontaneously and told him: 'You have understood how to tell the truth in a new way.' "[23] Rossellini had done what Pewas claimed he wanted to do.

It is tempting to presume that Pewas's encounter with Rossellini made him a convert to the Italian neo-realist style, one that had by then become a movement as much as it was an aesthetic. But his subsequent film work does not bear out this claim. No matter how interested Pewas was in the real issues on the street, he was and would remain a studio filmmaker. He used professional actors and had his sets built to exact specifications for certain shots, which indicates that he did not adopt the doctrine that Rossellini was advancing in 1947. Pewas did not take to the streets to make *Street Acquaintance*.

That is not to say, however, that neo-realist aesthetics and Pewas's film do not share an affinity. Stylistically it would seem that both Rossellini and Pewas were influenced by yet another national cinema, namely the 1930s French filmmaking of the likes of Jean Renoir and Marcel Carné. *Street Acquaintance* creates a stylized realism, an attention to the details of the shot and *mise en scène* that is very similar to that of the "poetic realists." The film's editing techniques are almost identical to Carné's *Le jour se lève* (*Daybreak*, 1939). Poetic realism, as Dudley Andrews so deftly derives from French film critic Jean Mitry, "models social experience by means of a cinematic experience that chemically transforms whatever facts make up its climate."[24] While the look and feel of Pewas's film transport one into the cinematic world of prewar France, the narrative and its outcome are very firmly grounded in the sociopolitical signification of postwar Germany.

Street Acquaintance takes as its primary directive the dramatization of a social problem from the pro-filmic world. While STIs figure heavily in both the film and the screenplay on which it is based, the public health concerns serve only as a starting point for an even broader debate.[25] Public health becomes a vehicle from which the film works backwards to discuss bourgeois family values, women in the public sphere, sexuality and gender relations. The mask of an informational feature film provides effective cover for the explosive set of issues that lie at the heart of the social problem that motivated the filmmakers to make *Street Acquaintance*.

Pewas claims to have been moved so much by Pohl's screenplay that he decided to make the film. Of course, as is often the case, he made a film entirely different from the screenplay with which he was presented. A perusal of the screenplay discloses a narrative of a much larger scope than the film includes. Moreover, the screenplay establishes relationships between characters much more clearly than does the film. Some of the discrepancies between the two are the inevitable result of the production process. But others represent active choices on the part of the filmmakers to diverge from Pohl's vision of the film.

The most striking difference between the two is the choice of *mise en scène* for the film as a whole. Pohl, who gave the film its title, envisioned a street film very much in the Weimar tradition. Many of the settings are outdoors, in the chaos of the urban landscape. On almost every page Pohl gives "street noise" or "car honking" as sound directions, thus making the street omnipresent even indoors. Urban anxiety is built into the script as a motivator and background. The street is the site of transgression; it is where Herbert and Erika initiate their affair. In the screenplay, Erika is rounded up off the street to be tested for STIs.[26] When, moments later, she cannot give adequate information about the possible source of her infection, she cries "I just met him on the street."[27]

Pewas removes the film from the street. To be sure, it is still a milieu film, but it is one in which there are clear ties between people. Everyone knows someone who knows someone else in the film. The affair between Herbert and Erika develops in Annemie's apartment under the watchful gaze of other smugglers. It is not a secret, illicit encounter, but rather an uncontested activity in that environment. The only contest is who will actually end up with Erika. The film depicts the inhabitants of this world as grotesque and decrepit, giving it the look of an Otto Dix painting. The primary encounters on the street, conversely, are between the domesticated couples, that is, between Herbert and Marian and Walter and Erika. The problems do not take place in the public sphere but in the private one, where individual desires ignore the public good. The public space in Pewas's film retains a positive image.

The film strives to present a narrative of redemption on many fronts. Although neither the screenplay nor the film offers much in the way of commentary about the recent German past, the screenplay does, on several occasions, raise issues tying the desperation of postwar Germany to decisions made during the war. In the screenplay, when Erika is brought in for STI screening, she decries the restrictions being put on young women: "What did we have of our youth? First the BDM[28]—there we were drilled like recruits."[29] The hospital nurse draws a connection between the girls' sexual behavior and the moral legacy of the Nazis: "You are not alone to blame. What else could become of you in a world in which respectable behavior was mocked and every good gesture was suffocated, a world in which children were forced to spy on their parents and teachers?"[30] Both of these lines were left out of the film, thereby removing most of the screenplay's attempt at showing a moral continuity between the Nazi past and the postwar present.

While both the final film version and the screenplay promote conventional forms of heterosexual domesticity, the film is more directly concerned with constructing a narrative in which the characters eventually reestablish themselves within that dominant paradigm. In order to accomplish this, the film must tone down the very forcefully articulated gender battles in the screenplay. In the script, the fact that Marian has a job and a public existence is immediately made an issue. When Marian and Herbert are first reunited on the street upon the latter's return from a POW camp, Marian cries: "I always knew you would return." Herbert responds: "Yes, but I didn't know I was married to a streetcar attendant."[31] Herbert's comment is cut from the film. Later in the screenplay, Herbert comments to a neighbor: "Yeah, the world is turned upside down. My wife goes to work and earns the money and I stay at home and scrub the floors." While he is shown doing housework in the film, Herbert's comment was not used. He shows no signs of discontentment about running around the house in an apron. In fact, he displays good humor about it. He is not shown leaving the house until he discovers that Marian betrayed him. Her betrayal, in the film version, is what breaks domestic bliss. In the screenplay, he is portrayed as emasculated and resentful of their inverted roles before the sexual issues arise.

The discourse of marriage, sexual propriety, and multiple sexual partners dominates the narrative in both versions. The point that both the film and the screenplay agree upon is that working women's sexuality and sexual options must be contained. Both versions motivate and inform a response to women's non-traditional sexual relations as morally abhorrent and, quite literally, a threat to the health and welfare of the community. In the film, financial concerns force the public health official to decide that only single women will be rounded up. Visually, the film reserves its most striking imagery, not for the scenes where the characters are diagnosed with gonorrhea, but for Herbert's discovery of Marian's affair.

Herbert discovers a letter Marian's lover has dropped off at the apartment. After he avoids reading it, framed in a medium long shot, Herbert kneels in front of the letter, which we can assume carries devastating information. He then moves forward, creating a medium shot, in which the letter remains the center of attention. As he reads it, he grows physically more distraught. The lighthearted background woodwind and strings music gradually turns into heavier, more dramatic brass. The film cuts as he moves into another room. This one is more evenly lighted and has large patterned wallpaper on the walls. The camera tracks in a medium-long shot as Herbert moves to the center of the screen, into a defined, lighted space with a solitary chair. When he finally sits in the chair, the sequence gives the most visual sign of emotional devastation found anywhere in the film: a lone man in a dark apartment, distraught at having lost control of his wife's sexuality.

The sequence that follows depicts Herbert's confrontation with

Harry, the man who sent the note to Marian. In a deep-focus long shot, Harry is playing pool in the foreground. When he steps to the side, Herbert is standing in a doorway ten feet away. The only light sources shine from the doorway behind Herbert or from over the pool table. The two sources allow the cameraman to achieve the deep-focus effect, thereby keeping the visual line of confrontation between the two men clear. It is arguably the most technically sophisticated shot in the film. After Harry mocks Herbert because the latter had been in a POW camp, Herbert strikes him and throws him out of the room.

The third sequence in Herbert's reaction to the betrayal comes shortly thereafter. It opens with an angled shot of a white brick wall. Herbert walks into a wide-angle shot from the left, preceded by his shadow. The camera moves in as he continues to walk. The lighting is such that we cannot see the expression on his face. The background dominates the *mise en scène*. He is a lonely, silent, silhouetted figure. The shot ends with a wipe edit into an evening shot of him at the same focal length, walking at the same distance, this time in a studio rubble shot.

The combination of scenes weighs the narrative heavily in Herbert's favor. Equal time is not given to Marian's tortured anticipation of his return. Nor does the film dramatize Herbert's subsequent affair as intensely as it does his anguish at having been betrayed. *Street Acquaintance* treats women's sexuality as a threat to private subjectivity and public order. The film constructs the threat to his masculinity and productivity as one of the main crises of the film, enabling it to propose the containment of women and their sexual activity as the answer. Erika's story remains the film's other crisis, but not because of her disease. Rather, her desires create the problem and therefore must be curtailed. Disease becomes the tool the film uses to force her into accepting domesticity. She must be housebroken.

The public health narrative is thus a front that opens up a discussion about private actions and communal institutions. The round up of all unmarried women is depicted as a scandalous event that provides the film the opportunity to mount a critique of, or at least a comment about, the functioning of the press, the hospitals, and the police—all institutions that, as I argued regarding *Razzia*, were experiencing legitimacy problems early postwar Germany. While *Street Acquaintance* only briefly examines the police force as an agent of the public health system, it is much more pollyannaish in its consideration of the role of the press and the public health system.

The press is represented in the character and efforts of Erika's erstwhile admirer, Walter, who is also a reporter. When he strikes up conversation with Erika on the street (they obviously know each other), she asks if he has an English cigarette. He answers, "Where should I get that with my honest work?" His behavior and words suggests that he plays everything straight and breaks no rules. When he shows Erika his apartment, his words suggest that he is both frugal and fair, a combination that has an absolutely unerotic effect on Erika.

As a reporter he strives to uncover the political truths behind the stories of grief and misery on which he reports all day. The first incident of this is when he writes a story of a mother who has murdered her children. While he and his editor agree that the event is horrible, Walter strives to convince his boss of the importance of reporting the sociopolitical context in which the murder was committed. The young woman's husband had returned to his family from the West accompanied by his new lover. The returning soldier set up house with his new girlfriend, his wife, and his children. In this situation, the wife was driven to kill the children and attempt suicide. By having Walter relay this context, the film sets the press up as a defender of underdog causes as well as a critic of the bad influences from the West.

When the public health authorities announce their sweep of all unmarried women, Walter is the first to protest the gender inequity. Why, he asks, are not all of the men being rounded up as well? The doctor retorts that, while that would be a reasonable solution, the community simply does not have the means to do so. Unsatisfied with the answer, Walter writes an article condemning the one-sided practice. Whereas in the screenplay the city decides, upon prompting, to test everyone, the film drops the issue after Walter's initial questioning of the doctor. The film leaves Walter in the less threatening position of a well-intentioned but ineffective reporter.

Both the screenplay and the film portray the doctors and the public health concerns they communicate as sympathetic and legitimate. The doctors express regret for the invasions of personal privacy their measures inflict, while insisting that they have no other choice. Their position is constructed such that to disagree would mean to turn a cold shoulder to the STI epidemic that plagues the community. This justification betrays something quite important about the function of the film.

Peter Pewas was not a Communist party member, nor did he express interest in the success of the Soviets in establishing a workers' and peasants' state on German soil. But *Street Acquaintance*, in the end, enhances the political program in the Soviet sector in its construction of the public health system as a figure in the film. In that they control the police force and the hospitals, health officials obviously wield considerable power within the governing apparatus. The film portrays them as honest, well-intentioned, and efficient. Despite having pursued what even the film recognizes to be an unjust plan of treating single women as the cause of an epidemic, the state's "big brother" utilitarian argument wins out over the claims of individual rights. If the notion of state power was still struggling for legitimacy, this film puts it on the side of the good. The state consists of well-intentioned men and women who perceive the invasion of privacy as a sad but necessary act of public protection. Individuals are portrayed, in contrast, as selfish and dangerous. The STI issue allows this to happen, because STIs undermine a commonly held set of values. The state qua health system becomes the white knight that saves the community from the disease-carrying women.

When the film sets out to educate audience members about the dangers of STIs, it is at the same time teaching them a lesson about state interference. At the end of the film Erika runs into the arms of the protecting figure of the nurse. The state will keep her and make her well. Contrastingly, Annemie, the grand dame who mentored Erika in the underworld, refuses that route. Instead, she is shown scurrying down the street in front of western Berlin's symbol of consumerist decadence, the KaDeWe department store. She wanders untreated through the moral wasteland of the West. However much the filmmakers wanted to address the local issue of sexually transmitted infections, they ended up, whether deliberately or not, conflating them with the rapidly escalating Cold War discourse.

'48 All over Again and the Rubble Woman as Revolutionary Ideal

At the same time that DEFA was preparing the "infotainment" *Street Acquaintance*, the studio was developing a film to commemorate the historical uprisings in Germany in March 1848. For the SED, the '48 revolution was a precursor to the one they wanted to bring about a century later with the help of Soviet force. The project was, from beginning to end, the work of Gustav von Wangenheim, an experienced theater director who had been in exile in the Soviet Union during the war.

Thomas Brandlmeier refers to the three films of the era with *und* (and) in the title (. . . *Und wieder '48,* . . . *Und finden dereinst wir uns wieder,* . . . *Und über uns der Himmel)* as "films that refer to a vacuum, a phantom or chimera."[32] The monster that motivates and populates Gustav von Wangenheim's . . . *Und wieder '48 ('48 All over Again)* is that of a history that must be tamed and brought in line with current political necessities. It is arguably the most politically strident German film of the era, East or West. But in working through the history of a century before, the film accidentally unveils something important about filmmaking practice in the rubble years. By including a strong, intelligent and independent woman, *'48 All over Again* highlights the weaknesses and inconsequence of almost all of the other women portrayed in the films of the era.

Given the many reasons why the history of the 1848 uprising would have been relevant to many in 1948, it is understandable that the reviews of the time concentrate on the portrayal of that historical event. An article entitled "Spiel zwischen Jahrhunderten" ("A Play between the Centuries"), published on November 14, 1948, is a good representative of the themes that were picked up in the film's early reception:

> The students are the ones who carry the plot. They are meant to serve as both the leads and extras in a film within the film about the events of 1848. This elegant and elegantly executed premise allows parallels and differences between now and then to show up surprisingly well. With all the means of a good director at his disposal, Wangenheim reveals the legacies and lessons of this history and shows the light that this history casts upon contemporary events.[33]

This praise again shows the degree to which reviewers sought and found historical realism in every film. The film's didactic mission remained in the foreground of all of the reviews, whether positive or negative. The film critic for the *Tägliche Rundschau,* Hans Ulrich Eylau, writes, "One may find one or two films with greater technical or artistic perfection, but for sure there will be none more responsibly tendentious in its purpose of educating the people, none of greater intellectual or moral depth, none with similarly decisive, while at the same time generous and open political aims."[34]

'48 All over Again muses heavily on the project of making the revolutionary impulses of March 1848 relevant a century later. The film within a film starts out treating the hundred-year-old events in a comic fashion. This attitude reflects that of the director, who says at the beginning, "Well, the events of those days were ridiculous, were they not?"

Our female protagonist, Elsa Weber, then makes it her humble goal to heighten the historical consciousness of all her fellow students working on the film. Eventually, the director comes around to her point of view, one already shared by the film's producer and set designer. Eylau claims that *'48 All over Again*'s "whats" are more important than its "hows," namely the ways in which it builds its story. I would argue the opposite. The portrayal of the 1848 events is confusing and visually disrupting in the film. How the film constructs it main protagonists, Elsa Weber and Heinz Althaus, leaves a much richer picture of the filmmaking and its struggles with historical representation than do the lessons of 1848.

A notable feature of *'48 All over Again* is how it employs the film medium itself. It is not a filmmaker's film, that is, a film that foregrounds or thematizes the sophisticated ways in which the film constructs its meaning. It does not display a mastery of many of the techniques that allow for filmic nuance. In fact, the possibilities inherent in the cinematic apparatus are barely exploited at all. Instead, Wangenheim and company appear to be staging the film much like they would have staged a play. It relies almost entirely on spoken text to relay its message. It is an amazingly wordy film, with many formal speeches. In fact, it is arguably more a series of lectures on film than a play.

The film's opening sequence creates dual images of Weber that it retains till the end. The camera's first glance in her direction shows her in nineteenth-century garb with a bonnet on her head. The image aligns itself with the visual stereotype of women in traditionally subservient heterosexual roles. Weber, played by Inge von Wangenheim, the wife of the director, appears older than a traditional student. When asked by the director of the film within the film for her opinion of his portrayal of 1848, she at first declines to answer, affecting the demeanor of a shy schoolgirl. When the director persists, Weber offers her opinion. While continually deferring to the director as well as her college history professor, Weber notes that the director's choice of making the film as he does merely reproduces the caricatures that support the "Prussian-German legend about 1848." Having anticipated a brief affirmation, the director is insulted. Weber calmly asserts that her fellow students might do well to look at this history in a different light. Although she chooses her words wisely, she favors a Marxist, class struggle interpretation of history. The camera then picks Althaus out of the crowd, who insists that the revolution warrants nothing more than the ridicule the film casts upon it. When Weber contradicts his ill-informed opinion, he demands that she leave him to his own thoughts. She declines with a smile.

The film constructs Elsa Weber out of an array of ambivalences. She is a strong-willed, intelligent student leader and a war-widow who is forced by circumstance to raise her nephew and care for a sickly sister. The film paints her as an idealist, working to enlighten her fellow students and the world, while making her a typical rubble woman forced to face the mundane difficulties of postwar German existence. In short, by attending to the multiple challenges in Weber's life, even if it is merely to contextualize her as a revolutionary female character, the film provides the most thorough development of a female character in any postwar German film to that point.

'48 All over Again insists that the characters work through their own histories as a part of working through Germany's political heritage. In back-to-back sequences, the film establishes Althaus and Weber as juxtaposed figures with similarly troubled pasts to work through. In the fourth sequence, Heinz sits at home preparing for an anatomy exam. A sewing machine rattles in the background, reproducing a sound similar to machine guns. He pushes away the picture of a brain that he is trying to study. Heinz (played by E. W. Borchert, the actor who played Hans Mertens in *The Murderers Are among Us*) notes to his father that there are some images that one cannot simply push away. His attempt to memorize aloud slips into a retelling of his own war traumas and the senseless loss of life. It is a shot almost identical to the one of Borchert in *The Murderers Are among Us* when he tells a similar story. By 1948, this had become a stock scene of the rubble film. A voice in his head reminds him of his exchange with Weber earlier in the day.

The film's fifth sequence opens with a dissolve from a medium-close shot of the face of Heinz Althaus to the same of Elsa Weber. As the camera pulls back, we realize that Weber has worked through the night on her studies. The sequence quickly sets up another comparison, that of Weber and her sister, who bemoans her wartime experiences and wonders how Elsa could possibly be interested in history after having lived through the war. The sister situates herself as a victim of circumstances, offering a litany of concerns about the uncertain status of her husband and her fears of raising a child. Her fears mount to the point where she accuses her sister of being without feelings. The film uses this exchange to show that Elsa's interest in history is a response to her own war trauma. Not only did she lose her husband to the war, she lost her son in an air raid. She has sublimated her losses into the study of history.

These two sequences establish a relationship between Althaus and Weber that can only be consummated through a common understanding of history. In fact, this relationship functions as the mechanism through which Althaus is converted to historical materialism. It is important to note that the film does not reconcile competing historiographies and ideologies. It merely portrays more and more of its characters as being convinced by the version of history that Elsa Weber propagates.

We presume that the relationship that evolves between Althaus and Weber is sexual only because cinematic convention tells us to expect as much. But the film creates much more sexual chemistry around Althaus's interaction with the wealthy art history student Lizzy, as well as in the exchanges between Weber and Herr Ring, the production designer of the film about the 1848 uprising. In fact, Althaus and Weber verbally deny any sexual attraction to one another. The film eschews the convention of the "eye match," which generally serves as the viewer's visual clue of heightening romantic interest. Weber's appearance in

Photo 14. *'48 All over Again:* The ruins of Berlin as classroom for historical materialism. (Courtesy of Stiftung Deutsche Kinemathek)

male garb in one of a series of skits at the student ball furthers an androgynous image of her that develops throughout the film. Althaus functions as a sexual figure only through the eyes of Lizzy, whose interest in him stems from her own personal rivalry with Weber. The film's drive toward creating an intellectual affinity between Althaus and Weber succeeds at the cost of any filmic cue that would suggest a sexual bond between them. Almost as if it were an answer to the discourse established in *Street Acquaintance*, this film creates a public romance, without the pitfalls of individual desire.

Weber is, from the start, an agent of historical materialism. There is nothing private about her. Even details of her life with her troubled sister become public. But her complete removal from the private sphere occurs only after the film establishes her past, one easily recognizable as common to many women of the era. Thus, as a model to female spectators, Elsa Weber devotes her life to history in order to prevent Germany from repeating its historical errors. If there were such a thing as a communist nun, Elsa would be one.

The film takes great care never to mention socialism. It may have been the last remnant of pre–Cold War naiveté to have believed that, by not mentioning it, the film might have kept viewers from noticing the ideological force behind it. There is, however, a shot of Althaus perusing a set of the collected works of Marx and Engels in the library. Eschewing communist jargon was one of the few attempts at subtlety throughout the film.

In the cabaret sequence, the film lays out its answer to the mounting Cold War pressures in the pro-filmic world. In the second skit of the evening, Weber appears as Gustav Adolph Schlöffel, the student leader of the 1848 uprising. Her performance serves as the ideological corrective to the historiography that would portray Otto von Bismarck as the unifier of Germany. With music reminiscent of Kurt Weill, Weber sings a song about Schlöffel, the refrain of which is

> Die deutsche Einheit sagte der
> kommt nicht aus Preußens Schießgewehr
> nicht aus der Knechtschaft,
> die uns gerecht schaft.
> die kommt vom freien Volke her
>
> [German unity, he said
> comes not from the guns of Prussians
> and not from the bondage

that makes us righteous
It comes from a free people]

The next skit concerns itself with a continuity between 1848 and 1948, namely the division of a supposedly single country into zones. The song (sung by Harry Hindemith, who also plays Herbert in *Street Acquaintance* and Herr Iller in *Somewhere in Berlin*) is a defiant ode to German unity, the boldest direct political statement to have emerged to date in a rubble film.

Was ist denn das
Das ist ein Pass
Ein Pass von 48, 1848
Denn alle Deutschen wohnen
In 36 zersplitterten Nationen
Man irrt sich, Man irrt sich
Ich glaube gar man irrt sich
mit der Jahreszahl, mit der Jahreszahl
1848

Was ist denn das
ein deutscher Pass?
Denn alle Deutsche wohnen
in 1, 2, 3, 4—1, 2, 3, 4
zersplitterten Nationen
'48 Deutscher Bund
Wie war Deutschland auf dem Hund?
Manchem kaeme zu gelegen
Deutschland wieder zu zersaegen
in einem foederierten Braten
wie 1848

Deutschland als ewig
*un*vereinigten Staaten
wie 1848

aber man irrt sich, man irrt sich
ich glaube gar man irrt sich
mit der Jahreszahl, mit der Jahreszahl
1948

[What is that?
It is a passport
a passport from 48, 1848
For all Germans live
in 36 splintered nations
There must be some mistake

I really think there must be some mistake
with the year, with the year
1848

What is that?
A German passport?
For all Germans live
in 1, 2, 3, 4—1, 2, 3, 4
splintered nations
'48 German federation
How had Germany gone to the dogs?
Many would find it quite opportune
to cut Germany up
into a federated roast
just like in 1848

Germany as eternally
ununited states
like 1848

But one is mistaken
I believe one is mistaken
with the year, with the year
1948]

Not only do these lyrics reveal an increasing assuredness on the part of Germans in expressing their political will, it also reveals the degree to which DEFA was gradually shifting away from a strategy of appealing to Germans in all four sectors. For while these two songs plead for German unity, the second song also set up an enemy to whom it would be advantageous for Germany to be divided. This was the rhetoric of the Soviet Union, which always claimed a desire to unite Germany under a socialist flag.

'48 All over Again's gesture insinuates that the failure of the revolution of 1848 is the failure that led to Nazism. The songs in the cabaret scene perform an ideological gesture that divides the world into those who have, since 1848, fought for a democratic German unity, and those who would adhere to the myth that Bismarck was the father of the nation. The latter, according to this worldview, are those directly responsible for the ensuing history of democratic failure, totalitarian catastrophe, and military destruction. They are also the ones who would, according to the song, keep Germany split. The students' debates about history split along these simplistic lines. As such, this film offers, by far, the least conciliatory narrative among those presented in this chapter.

Conclusion

Because I have discussed the films in this chapter chronologically, a certain trajectory in their narrative strategies becomes evident. The first film, *Somewhere in Berlin*, reconstructs the dominant fiction of the nuclear family headed by an empowered patriarch. However critically and skeptically we may view that gesture at a distance of more than fifty years, at the time it was not a very risky ideological gesture. Gradually each film attempts to expand the possible realm of discourse in Germany, from discussing the legitimacy of the family to discussing that of the police force, the state, and finally the nation. *Razzia* sets up the police as respectable social authorities capable of bringing order to the community. *Street Acquaintance* risks even more by positing the woman as symptom of postwar chaos. It effectively advocates inserting the state as an authority structure that can curb the irresponsible behavior of individuals. And finally, *'48 All over Again* dares to utter not only the word "state," but "nation," "Germany," and "Volk" as well.

However disinterested some of the DEFA heads may have been initially in enforcing an aesthetic doctrine, these films nevertheless achieve a sort of cinematic unity. They engage with the various strands of realist cinematic discourse in circulation in Europe at the time. Whether it is the expressionist realism of the classical Soviet cinema, French poetic realism, Italian neo-realism, or Stalin-era socialist realism, the DEFA realism evident in these films aspires, at the very least, to the egalitarian humanism to which these other filmmaking cycles also appeal. Unlike the Italians, the directors of these films dispense with neither professional actors nor controlled studio environments. But far from merely attempting to institute contact with contemporary social reality, these films offer scenarios designed to shape the outcome of communal questions. While this, in part, seems like a task similar to that undertaken by Soviet-style socialist realism, these films actually assume a different posture. What emerges is a non-dogmatic form of realism that is at once informed by the material order of the streets and the myth-building atmosphere of the studios.

The year 1948 marked the end of the fantasy that Germany would function under one political and economic system anytime in the near future. On June 20, the Western zones introduced a currency reform in which the East refused to participate. The Soviets responded to this move by the West with a blockade of the western sectors of Berlin, a gesture that was more a propagandistic move than a real cutting off of supplies. The West countered with an airlift, again a gesture more political than material in aim. The advent of the Cold War actually meant both an increase in the material prosperity of Germans and a gradual decrease in the discussions of guilt that had informed public discourse. Germans in all zones of occupation again had discourses of power around which dominate fictions could be organized. Rubble metaphors gradually gave way to phoenix metaphors.

Currency reform and the intensifying Cold War had a tremendous effect on the film industry, both East and West. The distribution of films from East to West became increasingly difficult, though not impossible. For DEFA this meant, however, the gradual loss of a large part of the German-speaking market. Western filmmakers did not fare much better. Currency reform meant that consumers suddenly enjoyed a retail abundance they had not seen since before the war. A visit to the cinema, which had required next to no financial commitment before the advent of the D-Mark, suddenly became only one of many consumer choices. Theater owners could no longer count on full houses merely by being the only source of affordable entertainment. A positive effect of reform was that capital for film production suddenly became available. The number and nature of films produced changed dramatically in the West in the second half of 1948.

Just days before the release of '48 All over Again, members of the cultural elite in Berlin's Soviet sector met to discuss the role of culture in the "two-year plan" that had been adopted by the Socialist Unity Party. Many of those in attendance, including DEFA's artistic director, Kurt Maetzig, tried to defend DEFA's attempt to work with filmmakers from the West. The communist could work with "a handful of primarily bourgeois artists, who were well-intentioned and attempted to dedicate themselves to the challenges of the day, even if they revealed some weaknesses."[35] Others, however, "attach themselves opportunistically to DEFA in order to make a living. Still others claim that one cannot just capitulate all points to the socialists. . . . Thus we plod along and take advantage of the bourgeois artists whom we will eventually have to repulse."[36]

The cooperation that had created a fruitful environment in DEFA's first years was collapsing. Some directors, including Wolfgang Staudte, would continue to commute between East and West well into the 1950s. By then, however, DEFA's environment had changed. The political pursuits of the fledgling German Democratic Republic demanded increasing involvement in the operations of the studio. While that involvement would ebb and flow over the next forty years, never again would DEFA be as politically and financially independent as it was from 1946 to 1949.

6

Comedic Redemption
and the End of
Rubble Film Discourse

nd the Heavens Above premiered on December 9, 1947, two days before *Between Yesterday and Tomorrow*. They were the first two films to appear in the American sector. Over a year earlier, Wolfgang Staudte's *The Murderers Are among Us* was celebrated as the first postwar German film and Helmut Weiß premiered *Sag die Wahrheit* as the first film in the western sectors. *Between Yesterday and Tomorrow* was packed with old stars whom Eric Pommer drew to the rebuilt studios of Geiselgasteig near Munich. At least at the beginning of his two-year reign, Pommer represented a singular authority in an industry torn apart by ideology, destruction, and Cold War political machinations. As Peter Pleyer reports:

> On Pommer's urging, the American military government freed up the studio facilities in Munich-Geiselgasteig. The studios were, with his support, put back in working order. And the first film projects in the American zone were approved and realized. Pommer saw to it that the Americans did not generally confiscate the former film possessions of the Reich. Rather they were used to rebuild and reequip the old studios in Geiselgasteig and Berlin-Tempelhof.[1]

Pommer showed that he held influence both with the American authorities and with the remnants of the German film industry.[2] His return also signaled a kind of redemption; the father returned to guide his prodigy gone astray.

151

Film without a Title:
Filmmaking and the Art of Diversion

If Pommer immediately began dominating film politics in the American sector, no single director influenced rubble film production more than Helmut Käutner. Although Staudte actually directed more films in the period and was instrumental in the founding of DEFA, his general influence at DEFA was limited. Käutner not only started a studio and directed and produced films, he acted in some and wrote screenplays for others. Among those screenplays was one he wrote for his long-time assistant Rudolf Jugert's directorial debut film, *Film without a Title*. It would become the most successful German film of 1948.

A contemporary review from the Berlin evening newspaper *Telegraf* reveals the layering of humor and irony built into Käutner's script:

> Three men, a film director, an actor and a screenwriter, want to write a screenplay while on holiday. They have everything required, except an idea. Then they meet an authentic couple. The screenwriter tells the other two the story of this couple. "That's the film," cries the director. "Of course, at the end there will be the requisite contemporary misery." The camera fades to a rubble ballad shot with sharp angles [à la *The Murderers Are among Us*] with a heartwrenching ending. The actor [played by Willy Fritsch, the famous German actor of the 1930s and 1940s] is of the opinion: "People want to laugh, and see me." And he royally satirizes his own acting history and much current acting as well. The screenwriter wants reality however, which serves as the basis for the end of the film.[3]

That the reviewer would see the story line with which the film ends up as "reality" imparts the success of the film's narrative project. It begins with an open, almost cynical discussion of the possibilities of filmmaking. A non-diegetic voice-over warns the audience before an image appears: "Attention audience, you will now see a light-hearted film without a title." Given the serious nature of most of the German films with which the audience had been presented to that point, this announcement must have been met by the audience with a wry smile. It is a clear confrontation with the DEFA program discussed in Chapter 5.

The camera then opens onto a scene wholly different from that of a typical rubble film. As it pulls back from a man writing at his table, the melancholic urban jazz background music mixes with an idyllic countryside. The camera pans past a cow and a line of orderly schoolgirls marching along a path. It then settles on a couple walking arm in arm. The perspective switches to that of the couple as they encounter three men sitting under a tree arguing:

Screenwriter: It just won't work. I said it from the start; you just can't make a humorous film these days.

Actor (Fritsch): One should though. People need to relax. They want to enjoy themselves a bit.

Screenwriter: Every attempt to that end would be seen as either banal or cynical against the desolate backdrop of our times.

Actor: Then set it against a different backdrop.

Director: Then I am out. I refuse to make such a film after everything that has happened. We need a comedy that has both feet on the ground. (The others laugh) What are you laughing at?

Screenwriter: I am just imagining a comedy with both feet on the ground . . .

Actor: . . . set against the desolate backdrop of our times.

Director: Okay, let's start from the top.

Screenwriter: No rubble film.

Actor: "The well-dressed citizen goes astray."

Screenwriter: No coming-home film.

Actor: "From the Black Sea to the Black Market."

Director: No fraternizing film.

Actor: No anti-Nazi film.

Screenwriter: That would be tactless, wouldn't it?

Director: No political film, no propaganda film, no film about the bombings.

Actor: No film that is for or against something.

Screenwriter: What kind of film can we make then?

Director: A contemporary comedy . . .

Actor: . . . with both feet on the ground

Screenwriter: . . . set against the desolate background of our times.

This metadiscourse on the problem of postwar screenwriting enjoys more authenticity than any other rubble film sequence. For this is exactly the dilemma in which filmmaking finds itself almost immediately after resuming production in 1946. The director wants both phantasmagoric storytelling and a film that addresses current issues. The screenwriter is skeptical of all ideas that smell of mimetic realism. Why would they want to reflect the world as it is? This statement positions the filmmaker close to Käutner himself, who, as we see later in the chapter, resorts to structures that distance the story from "the desolate background of the times."

The filmmaker agrees with Fritsch that an "anti-Nazi film" would be tactless. Why? What sort of manners would be transgressed? Is the screenwriter suggesting that it is tactless to do an anti-Nazi film because it is kicking the Nazis while they are down? Or does the comment refer to the audience, who does not need to be convinced to hate Nazism? (Given that all of their present difficulties are tied to Nazism, it would be tactless to rub their noses in it.) Or is it a direct parody of DEFA and its announced antifascist film program? It is hard to decipher the comment politically and aesthetically. Yet, it reveals the filmmaker's and moviegoers' desire for a fantasy film. In occupied Germany, one was not supposed to fantasize about denazification, one was supposed to undergo it.

Fritsch expresses hesitation toward ideological commitment. He wants to avoid a film that is for or against something. This, coupled with the rejection of an anti-Nazi film or any sort of political film, either indicts Fritsch's character as the worst apologist among them, or it reveals him as the lanceman in the struggle to create a new fantasy space. Throughout the film Fritsch's character advocates exactly those films that Fritsch himself will eventually make, namely kitschy *Heimatfilme*[4] that either ignore or distort the troubling superegoic past.

The director is ridiculed because he tries to stay contemporary. They reach consensus that they will to deal with the presence of the past, without that past being politicized, that is, without anyone being subjected to scrutiny or blame. They will portray the present conditions without asking too much about how those conditions came about. And, above all, they will entertain the audience with humor. The Nazi past becomes just one more inconvenience among many from which the film draws its humor.

With the opening sequence Käutner's screenplay humorously dismisses almost every film made in Germany to that point, including Billy Wilder's "fraternization film," *A Foreign Affair*. But the screenplay also turns its critique inward, for the filmmakers are at a loss as to how to tell a compelling "realist" story. Even as the "real" story unfolds in front of them, they supplement it with their own narrative preconceptions. The screenwriter repeatedly admonishes the other two characters for adding "unrealistic" aspects to the true story of Martin and Christine. At issue is the ability of current filmmakers to conceive or write stories as compelling as the real ones in their midst. As we shall see, however, that "real" story is the most ingeniously disguised fantasy of them all.

Like Käutner's first postwar film, Jugert's directorial debut (and Käutner's second postwar screenplay) is a framed narrative. Inside the frame of the three filmmakers is the story of a farmer's daughter, Christine, who, during the war, moves to the city as a servant to an upper-middle-class family. During a night bombing raid, Christine and Martin, the patron of the house, suddenly find themselves in each other's arms, beginning a love affair.

Photo 15. *Film without a Title:* A bomb destroys Martin's bourgeois life. (Courtesy of Stiftung Deutsche Kinemathek)

This initiates an odyssey in which the lovers try to find one another again after the war. Martin, an unlikely soldier, is conscripted into the home militia. His Berlin villa is destroyed. He shows up at Christine's parents' farm penniless. His business partner and ex-fiancée (and sometimes lover), Angelika Rösch, makes her way through postwar Germany by fraternizing with British soldiers. After giving up an attempt at restarting an antiques business with Angelika, Martin resolves to take up a profession that will be useful to his desolate postwar countrymen: He will build furniture. With that decision, Christine's reluctant and practical father agrees to consent to Martin and Christine's marriage.

The film courses through every narrative framework lampooned by the filmmakers in the opening sequence. It makes light of almost every social ill Germany faced in early 1948. More importantly, it satirizes "realist" filmmaking that would aspire to intervene in societal questions. It casts a parodic eye on unemployed youth, lazy refugees, city dwellers plundering the countryside, and farmers thriving on the black market. Despair serves as a source of humor. *Film without a Title* finally reveals itself as a direct cinematic confrontation of DEFA's topical films.

Like *Between Yesterday and Tomorrow*, the narrative of *Film without a Title* moves along various levels, at least two of which are woven together. In the process of their futile discussions, the three men trying to write the screenplay are interrupted by Christine and Martin. When the couple leaves, one of the three men tells their story. They then weave this love story into their own screenplay, as the other two men try to imagine certain scenes from Martin and Christine's life differently than they actually happened. The camera pulls back to reveal the third level of narration in which the other levels plus all of the other subordinate characters' fates are encompassed. This is the omniscient perspective granted the spectator, and it is at this level that the irony functions. From here we witness the arbitrariness of the act of writing that we are witnessing.

Film without a Title divides the narrative point of view among the three men. The one that lays out the love story splits off into two counterparts, represented by the director and the actor. The former is still serious about authenticity and inquires after the couple's actual story. The actor, Fritsch, continually emphasizes the split between the "real" story and the way it should be told. He is interested in their plight as fiction rather than biography and seeks to adorn it. Fritsch wants to alter their personal history when it is not "real" enough for him.

In both cases their embellishments, which place the spectator in an ironic perspective shared with the screenwriter, take the form of lampoons of German film history. Claiming to have his finger on the pulse of the audience, Fritsch proposes an ending to the story that reaches to the heights of filmic kitsch. The filmmakers mock the idea of this happy ending, which includes overdone traditional costumes, with the couple surmounting all odds to reach their bliss. The director proposes a serious ending that seems to mimic *The Murderers Are among Us*. With shots and lighting imitating Staudte's film, it highlights the poaching of filmic Expressionism in early postwar German film.

This sequence, in which the filmmakers try to bring closure to their project, foregrounds the fact that film is always dependent upon borrowed cinematic languages. In fact, it points out clearly what is evident in all of the films discussed in this chapter, namely the extent to which these films draw upon almost any filmmaking tradition in order to figure out a way to appeal to an audience and offend no one. The film makes light of its own project while pretending to tell the original love story of Martin and Christine. The fact that the filmmakers within the film whittle the fantasies down to a simple love story across class lines stands as the most effective ideological feat of all.

The Martin–Christine love story has all of the makings of a perfect fairy tale. A class barrier inhibits their relationship. Both have to navigate the "forest" of transformation, in this case the troubled landscape of postwar Germany, in order to find one another. Christine's village and its concomitant set of rules of interaction glow otherworldly in Martin's eyes. Likewise, his ruling-class values and tastes confuse and stimulate her. Christine's is a strange version of a Cinderella story in that the social conditions come down to meet her rather than her rising to meet them. Their happy end restores order to the social chaos around them.

Hedwig Traub–von Grolman, in her review following the premiere of *Film without a Title*, reads the film neither as a farce of filmmaking nor as a fantasy construct, but as a humorous portrayal of the real conditions of postwar Germany.

Willy Fritsch plays the prominent actor under his own name and he manages to parody himself preciously. . . . The film evidently takes nothing seriously. And yet it does not shy away from confronting contemporary questions: the black market and the refugees, the shortage of space, the world of rubble, the city dwellers in the country, and the greediness of the farmers.[5]

This is a common reaction to the film, that is, that it confronts the worst of the problems with which the spectator was faced. Thus, even this comedy retains cinema's status, at least in the press reception, as a moral beacon. Traub–von Grolman takes up the working title of the film, *Antiques*, as indicating the old values that must be eliminated. "The film holds up a mirror: look, this is what you look like, you who want to make your money from the poorest of the poor. And you, eternally unhappy refugees and envying spectators living in strange quarters without cooperating in the work. . . . These are the 'antiques' that must be thrown overboard."[6] Edith Hamann called the film "the eye and soul witness of our times."[7]

An article in Berlin's *Nachtexpress* is among the very few contemporary detractions from the film. While almost all other reviews read the film as a playful parody, the reviewer "R.K." is insulted by the jokes made of the most serious problem of postwar Germany. The film's inclusion of two disgruntled refugees and their plight strike this reviewer as offensive. "One should not have to tolerate one of Germany's deepest wounds being made light of."[8] This reviewer perceives Germany's deepest postwar wound to be, not the burden of its genocidal recent past, but the "ethnic cleansing" of Germans from the eastern provinces.

In the films discussed in Chapters 3 and 4, the refugee problem either overshadows or becomes equivocated with the German genocide of the Jews. The latter is not mentioned at all in *Film without a Title*. In *In Those Days* and *Between Yesterday and Tomorrow* both problems are dealt with in the fates of individuals rather than groups. *Long Is the Road* includes the refugees among the general displaced population of Europe. *Love '47* portrays both an individual fate and a glimpse of the scale of the problem. Viewed over a half-century later, we look at these problems as radically different, especially given our limited sympathies for wartime Germans. The expulsion of Germans from their homes in what was Silesia or Eastern Prussia seems like a brutal but perhaps understandable consequence of the violence Germans had wrought upon their neighbors. However, this trauma blinded many critics, journalists, and certainly many refugees from seeing almost everything else.

Another appropriate question to ask of *Film without a Title* is: Why resort to comedy? The filmmakers at the beginning of the film pose many possibilities about what the film should do. They question how one could make a comedy "with both feet on the ground set against the desolate background of our times." It is taken for granted that they will produce a comedy. Fritsch gives escapism as the obvious answer: "The people need something to laugh at." Comedy disarms a situation. It makes it less formidable. It neutralizes that which is being discussed.

Film without a Title seeks to neutralize recent German history and the material destruction, social upheaval, and subjective crises that came in its wake. It does so by parodying those films that try to take the past seriously as well as those that engage themselves in the present. No one could resent a film that attempts to serve as a bridge over the troubled waters of postwar Germany. But, mitigating the postwar conditions is not all the film does. It also separates the past and whatever (unmentioned) atrocities may have occurred therein, preventing the story from establishing a causal relationship between those atrocities and present conditions. By seeking to be an apolitical film, it becomes an amnesic film. Likewise, in its parody of filmmaking it attempts to neutralize the very notion of making a topical film in berubbled Germany, that is, the DEFA program.

Kirstin Burghardt identifies the moral lesson in *Film without a Title* as "building a better life."[9] This film's supposed contribution to moral rearmament is to strengthen the spectator's optimism. "The example of the successful integration of a man who lost his vocation through the war [Martin] shows the spectator that opportunities are available to combine a renewed existence with a collective use for a postwar society."[10] In none of her lessons does Burghardt discover the treatment of the past as a category for evaluating the moral worth of a film.[11] In neglecting this, Burghardt seems to reproduce the attitudes of the creators of *Film without a Title*.

Many films of the era use the commonplace trope of the love triangle to propel their narratives, though they employ it in different ways. How films apply common formulae such as this can tell us something about the time and place in which they are set. Such tropes can also be called upon to inform and influence certain choices within a film.

In *Film without a Title*, Martin Delius is confronted with a choice between his business partner and sometimes lover, Angelika, and the farmer's daughter, Christine. The former represents his prewar desire, class standing, and profession. The only war scene of the film is also the consummation of his interest in Christine. Thus, the war changes his desire. With the end of the war he must decide between his prewar self, one that is tied up with his relationship with Angelika and the representative objects of the past, and a new life with Christine and the concomitant postwar realities. His commitment to Christine reflects a choice of new over old. He decides, literally, to build new furniture with her instead of selling antiques with Angelika. It involves turning his back on his privileged class standing and its history for one where he will make more than a symbolic contribution to people's lives. The film illustrates this choice heavy-handedly when Christine cleans off the valuable patina of history from the statue of his namesake, St. Martin. Removing the patina is the final step in Martin's deliverance from his old ways.

Manhandling the Rubble: *And the Heavens Above*

Josef von Báky's *And the Heavens Above* (. . . *Und über uns der Himmel*)[12] spins a similar tale of liberation from old ways. The film's star, Hans Albers, animates and motivates this transformation. The film situates Albers's character as the vessel of almost all postwar German (male) fantasies. His presence in the film also structures its meaning and suggests how contemporary audiences may have understood it. It is the most deliberate and economical use of the star system in the rubble films.

The choice of Hans Albers as a leading man raises plenty of questions. Albers had served as German cinema's object of desire since his appearance as Lola Lola's (Marlene Dietrich) new lover in *The Blue Angel* (1929). A sequence in *Mädchen in Uniform* (dir. Leontine Sagan, 1932) in which a group of schoolgirls swoons over a photo of Albers indicates his early status as a teen idol. In the Third Reich, Albers established himself as German cinema's leading man. Despite Albers's refusal to cooperate with the Nazis or to even be photographed with them, there was little question who would play the leading role in *Münchhausen*, von Báky's film celebrating the twenty-fifth anniversary of the founding of Ufa.[13] He was Germany's answer to Clark Gable, Humphrey Bogart, and Fred Astaire wrapped into one. As Eric Rentschler has argued, "in a cinema with males often plagued by deficient egos and choleric dispositions, Albers is confident, blithe, and playful."[14] He organized feminine desire and formulated masculine self images.

Although Albers was not the only star to reemerge from the rubble of Third Reich cinema, he was one of few to do so with his dignity intact. His reputed resistance to the Nazis lent him an authority that far exceeded that of any other actor of his stature. Thus, for contemporary German viewers, Albers's first postwar film role would not be a *Heimkehrer* named Hans Richter as much as it would be *Hans Albers* dealing with the new postwar situation. While still erotically charged, his role now is of the family patriarch reorienting himself and reconstructing his family amidst the postwar moral and material destruction.

The plot, as summarized here in Friedrich Luft's review of the premiere, is quite simple:

> A man, in fact Albers, returns home from the war and finds his half-destroyed apartment. He slips into the new Berlin lifestyle, swinging between material crisis and starvation and con artistry. He falls into the thievery of the black market. His son also returns home from the war, blinded. As he regains his eyesight he sees his father on his way toward being transformed by contemporary turpitude. He rebels, leaves his paternal home and begins working. In the end, he leads his father back to poverty and righteousness.[15]

The reviews of the film in late 1947 and early 1948 concentrated heavily on Albers. Whether or not the film as a whole succeeded depended almost entirely on how the reviewer reacted to Albers's presence and the revival of star system filmmaking. In fact, most of the reviews decried von Báky's attempt to make both a rubble film and a star film. One noted that instead of making a break with old-fashioned and discredited filmmaking, filmmakers "still run on the same tracks."[16] While *And the Heavens Above* was relatively successful at the box office, among critics it was the object of the same criticism that most postwar German filmmaking has received, namely that of being too conventional and risk averse.

Perhaps more than any other film discussed in this book, *And the Heavens Above*'s obvious attempt to create commercial appeal warrants a sort of Kracauerian reading. Siegfried Kracauer argues that because commercial films endeavor to reach a large audience, they tell us much about their potential spectators. "Films address themselves, an appeal, to the anonymous multitude. Popular films—or, to be more precise, popular screen motifs—can therefore be supposed to satisfy existing mass desires."[17] Because of the many competing forces in play in rubble filmmaking, this formula cannot be applied consistently to all of the films. Political requirements and censorship, Cold War power constellations, and uncertainty about the medium as a whole all play equally important roles in the formation of most of the filmic narratives in early postwar Germany. Yet, much about the construction of von Báky's film compels a reading of it as at least an attempted projection of collective fantasy.

This type of reading demands answers to certain questions, among them, What is the fantasy to which the film appeals? As we will see, *And the Heavens Above* appeals to the two most difficult and improbable of deceptions, namely redemption and optimism. Both entreaties come off heavy-handed and obvious. Yet, the structure of the illusion tells us much about what the filmmakers thought their audiences desired. And, because the relationship works in both directions, we can presume that this film to some extent influenced their attitudes and longings as well. As Thomas Brandlmeier puts it: "Even if we take into consideration the public's preference for foreign films and films made during the Third Reich, the rubble films are just as much an essential source of contemporary self-understanding."[18]

The film exposes the spectator to its messages immediately. The opening shot is of the sky, over which the credits roll. Immediately a voice every filmgoer in 1947 would have recognized, namely Hans Albers, begins singing. The lyrics make a direct appeal to an imaginary collective:

> What has become of us?
> A small pile of sand at the sea.
> The storm blows further the grain of sand
> that sand is just like me
> . . . From every side the wind blows
> But let the wind blow on.
> For the heavens above us
> will never let us down

Fred Ritzel classifies this song as a "well-written, melancholic, mourning ballad, lifting one's feelings with a typical sixth note jump—similar to Michael Jary's war-time song of endurance, 'Ich weiß, es wird einmal ein Wunder geschehen' ('I Just Know That a Miracle Will Happen')."[19] Such melodic and thematic reference to wartime music is a typical strategy of this film. It employs a nostalgia for better days when the spectator was not at the mercy of the elements. "There are no direct references to feelings of guilt here, no account of why the Germans are in such a dismal situation. We witness only an abandoned herd, helplessly left out in the wind yet without remorse, without any apparent understanding of their situation."[20] While it is arguable that Ritzel extracts more from the lyrics than is actually there, he does describe the film's overall tone quite accurately.

However hackneyed the optimism the film's credit sequence purveys, it sets up an opening "coming home" sequence that differentiates itself from the other rubble films. As the credits clear, the camera remains fixated on a sky with clouds moving past slowly, a filmic connotation of time passing. The shot then tilts down and pans across the top of a berubbled house. The film cuts to a close-up of a man, Albers, peering around a corner, establishing the previous shot as his point of view. His tired eyes, unshaven face, and ragged clothing indicate that he is much more like the *Heimkehrer* characters of postwar films than like the Albers characters of old. But the upbeat music suggests that the spectator will encounter a less dreary film than the theme would lead her to expect.

The dialogue turns almost immediately to humor, as Albers's character, Hans Richter, makes light of the decrepit state of his apartment house. His self-deprecating style ensures the spectator that this is not a parody of rubble filmmaking as much as it is an attempt to bring levity to the scene. As much as the film will include vignettes of the desperate situation of postwar Germany, it skirts them in the opening sequence, emphasizing news of survival and renewal instead. Hans learns that his

Photo 16. *And the Heavens Above:* Hans returns to find a world just waiting to be saved. (Courtesy of Stiftung Deutsche Kinemathek)

son, Werner, will also return soon from the war. He meets an attractive young widow (Edith Schroeder) and her daughter, who have moved in next door, and he discovers that his horse, Florian, has avoided slaughter.

The second sequence constructs a romantic reminiscence of Hans's past, one predating and not including the Third Reich. As he leafs through a photo album, each photo becomes a brief scene of familial bliss. The film provides no explanation as to the fate of Hans's wife, but it is clear she is no longer around, thus leaving him free to pursue Edith. The sequence's evocation of pre-Nazi nostalgia creates a sense of innocence and purity the characters long to recapture.

The modern realities of collapse interrupt his reverie as Hans is awakened by something falling off the wall. His gaze falls upon a young couple in the courtyard whose conversation indicates longing for the joys of youth, of which they have been deprived by the war and the destruction it caused. He then observes the desperation of an older couple who have no butter for their bread. Each time the film cuts back to a medium-close shot of Hans, taken from below, giving him an omniscient presence. As a baby cries and music swells, the film cuts to an overcrowded apartment and finally back to Hans, who takes his hat and exits.

The first thirty minutes of the film continue a pattern found in many of the rubble films, namely a visual exposition of the narrative with minimal use of dialogue. That exposition grounds Hans as a provider to the neighborhood, as he immediately assumes leadership in a smuggling enterprise and rises in prosperity. The spectator's ability to find this exposition plausible comes, not from the screenplay or the *mise en scène*, but only from her having been accustomed to the charisma of Albers the actor.

The visual organization of most of the films discussed in this book so far has been non-hierarchical. That is to say, the shots and sequence montages are composed such that they juxtapose a variety of images, all of which share equally in importance. In *The Murderers Are among Us*, either the shots of the main characters are constructed in such a way that rubble and destruction share the space, or the sequence moves quickly from one character to the other. In all of the films discussed in Chapter 2, as well as *The Blum Affair* and *Morituri*, depiction of time and place share priority with the characters in the construction of the *mise en scène*.

And the Heavens Above differentiates itself from these films in that it organizes its visual hierarchy almost entirely around one figure, in this case, Hans Albers. In the opening sequence, when we see the standard expository rubble shot, it is immediately tied to Albers's point of view, as are the following sequences of nostalgia and misery. Along the way the film includes some of the most extensive shots of destroyed Berlin presented in a feature film.

The epiphany sequence, where Hans Richter decides to return to the virtues of hard work, depicts some of the more miserable conditions of the period. And yet because of the prominence of the looming figure of Albers combined with the non-diegetic optimistic song, these scenes communicate an entirely different attitude. The film juxtaposes each shot of the agonizing labor of Berlin's *Trümmerfrauen* with a counter-shot of Albers's patriarchic supervision. The narrative of Hans Richter gone astray is marginalized by the story of Hans Albers cheering on German reconstruction. Having cast Albers, the distinction between the star and the character was muddled to begin with. Thus, *And the Heavens Above* accomplishes its preachy optimism almost extradiegetically.

If the semiotics of the star system preach blind optimism, the story line pursues another project. While its narrative depends upon Albers's presence, it has other filmic tricks at its disposal as well. Tension in the first third of the film is built around Hans Richter's son Werner's return from the war. All of Hans's activities in the black market are justified as means of restoring his son's eyesight and material comforts. Werner's homecoming is the engine that will drive the rest of the film, namely the challenge to the father's carefully constructed point of view. Werner literally cannot see the world in the same way as his father.

The film plays most dramatically with both real and filmic memory in the sequence in which the newly reconstructed family, completed by the ersatz mother Edith Schroeder, drives through Berlin on their way to the clinic where Werner's blindness is to be treated. A shot directed towards Hans's eyes tells us that we are seeing Berlin as he does. This Berlin is in ruins, its former grandeur reduced to rock piles, its once active streets now all but deserted. Werner asks where they are. The answer of "Potsdamer Straße" invokes for him images of a bustling Berlin at what was once one of Europe's busiest squares. He does not perceive the harsh realities of the present, only the opulence of the past.

The return of Werner's eyesight does not reunite him with his father's worldview. Hans Richter sees the material hardships as a challenge to be overcome at all costs. When Werner views the berubbled city and its decrepit inhabitants he sees the injustice of having a wealthy few among a struggling, impoverished majority. The film aids in this construction by depicting the bar where Hans does his black market business differently from Werner's point of view than it does when we see it from Hans's. Where Hans sees opportunity, Werner sees only decadence, signified by a series of canted shots, most notably of dogs being fed food that most humans in Berlin could not afford.

The plot summary above reveals a curious tension, if not complete contradiction, in the film's ideology. Among the films discussed so far, *And the Heavens Above* is most dedicated to marketability. Its narrative offers the black market as the only form of market capitalist enterprise and juxtaposes it against hard work, which is supposedly its own reward. The film's critique is essentially that the reproduction of capital comes at the expense of the worker. The film employs a fundamentally Marxist message as an agent in the enterprise of selling itself to the widest possible audience.

When Werner returns home the shots have straightened out, although his attitude toward them has not changed. He takes up zero sum argument, insisting that the food Edith has prepared in order to celebrate his regained eyesight has been taken from the mouths of those whose toil goes unrewarded. His father counters that one has little to do with the other. While the confrontation is clearly designed to give Werner the moral upper hand, the screenplay contradicts itself by providing Hans with the better argument. Again the star system takes precedence over the moral message and realist conventions. Hans argues that honest hard work has little virtue, since all those engaged in it still seem to be starving. However confused this may leave the spectator, the sequence leads into the previously discussed epiphany.

This sequence puts the film on course toward a "prodigal father" narrative. Werner contests the depiction of the black market as a necessary evil of the times. We look for Hans to fall so that he can be forgiven. But Hans does not plummet and therefore does not have very far to go to be redeemed. Only at the point where father and son join forces (in a stock Albers-film barroom fight) is there a threat of legal consequences. At that point the police suddenly see Albers on their side as he is invited to join them in pursuit of the "real" criminals. His own change of heart goes unspoken.

The real redemption narrative portrayed by this film is one that is not shown at all. Hans and Werner Richter come home from the war to a bombed out city and yet the war, their actions in it, or any culpability of Hans and his generation for the causes of it go undiscussed. These men have no past to hide, no guilt to process, no ghosts to slay. The war is over. Their only battle concerns how to negotiate present conditions. This battle, presented with saccharin optimism, was a powerful fantasy to present to a guilt-ridden and demoralized audience.

The final question to be asked then is: How does the film affect the contemporary spectator's self-understanding? The centrality of Albers to the film, both visually and narratively, invites the viewer to identify heavily with him and his perspective. Thus, Werner's indictment of his father's corrupt behavior appears as more of a transgression than the vague business dealings in which Hans is involved. The reconciliation is understandable because the spectator desires it. The redemption lies merely in the father choosing to protect his son's honor by ceasing his role in black market scheming. The fact that father and son are reunited is redemption enough. These transgressions are much more easily explainable than, say, war crimes would have been. The latter would only force unpleasantries to the surface, something the film avoids quite well.

Redemption for Hans is a relatively easy matter at the end of the film. He is never forced to accept the moral consequences of his actions. All he needs to do to redeem himself from the crimes of black marketeering is just stop doing it. He does inform the law about other marketeers, but without confessing his own participation. At most, he must own up to having alienated himself from those he loves. The happy ending creates a fantasy space radically different from the lives of the film's spectators. Of course, his easy redemption also lies in the nature of the crime. Black marketeering has no clearly distinguishable victim, and is therefore an easy crime to walk away from as long as one is never caught.

The choice of black marketeering as Richter's trespass might also offer something in the way of an explanation for why the more troubling Nazi era goes completely unmentioned in the film. In the latter, redemption is not so easy. One does not simply stop warring and pretend that everything can go back to normal. That would be a *deus ex machina* too preposterous even for the director and star of *Münchhausen* to employ in berubbled Germany.

The Apple Is Off!: The Church Picks a Role for Itself

If von Báky's *And the Heavens Above* was astute in using Hans Albers as an antidote to berubbled misery, 1948 saw two films that would exploit

the contours of Germany's postwar culture even further. Helmut Käutner's second postwar film, *The Apple Is Off!*, and R. A. Stemmle's *The
Ballad of Berlin* exaggerated the trend started by *Film without a Title* of
turning the discourse of filmmaking in berubbled Germany in on itself.
And yet, these films are not just lampoons. They engage in the process
of creating a grand narrative of redemption, one that goes beyond a
mere redemption of the medium.

   The Apple Is Off! was part of the first big series of scandals in postwar
German cinema. Even before the project went into the studios, Munich
Bishop Johannes Neuhäusler registered his objections to the film's content. It was, he claimed after reading a smuggled copy of the screenplay,
a mockery of the biblical story of original sin and therefore ought to be
censored.[21] The Americans allowed the project to continue. When
shooting for the film commenced, the plot thickened. Not only did the
church view Käutner's film as sacrilegious for its screenplay treatment
of Adam and Eve, the costumes of paradise's inhabitants consisted of
cellophane. While nudity and sexually explicit content had been common in films of the Weimar era, they had all but disappeared from the
silver screen under the Third Reich. Thus, the phenomenon of the
film's genesis effaced the actual cinematic experience. Heide Fehrenbach has given a thorough account of the attempts by both the Catholic
and Lutheran churches to establish a cultural hegemony in the rebuilding of German national cultures during the reconstruction. "The pas-
sionate and unrelenting nature of their quest," Fehrenbach claims,
"revealed the fact that these elites considered the regulation of culture
to be crucial to the establishment of a healthy, stable German nation."[22]
The Catholic Church's rapid response to Käutner's film confirms
Fehrenbach's assertion, while at the same time suggesting that the conservative Christian front in Germany was not as unified as she argues.
In the case of *The Apple Is Off!*, the Lutheran and Catholic hierarchy
divided in their response.

   The film fell into an argument between the churches and the film
industry that had already been brewing for months. In fact, it began with
the re-release of Käutner's *Freedom Street No. 7*, a film starring Hans
Albers that takes as its background the red light district of Hamburg during the war. The film, which was made in 1944 but censored by
Goebbels's ministry and then distributed in 1948, motivated broad-
based protests among both Protestant and Catholic youth groups.
Beyond an attempt to keep Käutner's earlier film from being shown, the

controversy represented a struggle on the part of conservative forces in Germany to assert their influence over the newly forming organization of the public sphere. The churches were skeptical of an American-style democracy that would encourage people to make moral choices without appeal to the traditional societal structures of church and government.

The controversy surrounding *Freedom Street No. 7* shows that both Catholic and Lutheran churches saw themselves not only as defenders of cultural chastity, but also as active youth organizers and cultural mediators. In the case of *Freedom Street No. 7*, they could use the fact that the film was made during the Third Reich to mount an after-the-fact resistance to the regime. Käutner's Adam and Eve spoof seemed to present another grand opportunity for the churches to continue to define new societal roles for themselves. But, as the struggle between the state-supported churches and the film industry continued, the churches themselves were forced to answer to charges of intolerance.

The reviews of the film assumed a basic familiarity with the plot, namely Adam and Eve's fall from grace. But the script, written by Käutner and Bobby Todd in the mid-1930s, diverges from the biblical story from the start. In fact, the divergences are ultimately the motivators of the plot.

Adam Schmidt, owner of Adam's Apple Juice manufacturers, is having marital problems that are driving him to suicide. Adam is having an asexual affair with his secretary, Eva, while his wife, Lilith, is torn between him and Schmidt's junior partner, Dr. Lutz. Adam stumbles into the psychological practice and sanitarium of Dr. Petri. While waiting to leave Petri's institute, Adam has a dream in which he becomes his biblical namesake. The other characters fall into line, with Petri ruling the gates to heaven and Lutz becoming the fallen angel Lucifer. Adam's banishment from paradise is a result of his betraying Eva with Lilith, who demands of him the apple (Photo 17). Eva awakes to find herself alone in paradise and goes in search of Adam. Unable to decide between Eva and Lilith (the virgin/vamp dichotomy), Adam fantasizes an amalgam of the two. As he awakes from his dream and runs to catch a streetcar, he encounters just such a woman.

Like the many plot summaries I have presented in this book that stemmed from original reviews of the films, this one only reveals a portion of what is happening in the film. In fact, in this film, the *mise en scène*, music, set design, cinematography, and special effects compete with the heavy dialogue to weave the film's narrative. The film orga-

Photo 17. *The Apple Is Off!*: Eve forgoes her biblical role. (Courtesy of Stiftung Deutsche Kinemathek)

nizes its visual constructs in a baroque fashion. Unlike *And the Heavens Above*, Käutner's film presents a non-hierarchical, confusing ocular structure in which no single figure, image, or setting dominates. While Adam remains the film's primary fixation, his story is embellished to such an extent that he is almost effaced.

Reconstructing exactly what the Catholic Church objected to in the film is difficult because Bishop Neuhäusler never articulated his dissatisfaction clearly. On June 4, 1948, Käutner and Curt Oertel, one of his producers, met with representatives of the Catholic and Lutheran churches, the Information Control Division in the American sector, the Bavarian military government, and the press. The outcome was a communiqué in which Käutner assured the public that he had no intention of blaspheming the churches. The churches, for their part, promised to reserve all further comment on the film until it premiered.

Five months later, when the film finally made it to the cinemas, the churches removed their complaints. Pastor Werner Hess's article in the Lutheran journal *Kirche und Film* reveals the basis of the misunderstanding between the clergy and the filmmakers.[23] They apparently did not understand how to read a filmscript. All of the incidences that they picked out as blatantly offensive in the screenplay were such minimal parts of the film that, when they appeared on screen, the clergy barely noticed them. As Hess notes, "The scene of a witch burning that had been discussed so much is hardly noticeable as such."[24] The images in question are part of a scene of excess in a torture chamber. A casual viewer would not even have noticed it. Pastor Hess goes on to write an aesthetic critique of the film, noting its technical accomplishments, style, and acting.

In the end, however, the film's irreverence toward the biblical story of creation and its meaning for Christianity (its meaning for Judaism is elided) is too much for even this preacher of tolerance. Hess refers to the film as "areligious." He also notes that its failure to account for Christian sensibilities damages the film industry's credibility regarding its own ability to censor itself. Hess attempts to justify the church's invasiveness as an attempt to protect honest Christians from being unduly influenced by erroneous imagery. "The danger that the imaginations of the filmgoers are given an entirely false concept of the context of this important dogmatic foundation of the church's belief is not to be dismissed."[25] As has always been the case, the churches expect no competition in the proper interpretation of the biblical text. Käutner's interpretation confronted church dogma both by adapting a biblical narrative and by resorting to allegory.

The church's reaction to Käutner and to the film exposes the move by clerics to reestablish themselves as the moral authority in postwar Germany. While that attempt became more and more deplorable in subsequent years, in this particular case, the film itself did much to create the confusion. In fact, given the allegorical make-up of the film, the reaction on the part of organized Christianity in Germany is at least understandable if still objectionable.

The Apple Is Off! uses allegory as an excuse for ambiguity. This notion of allegory as a systematic multiplicity of meaning opens the gate for any possible reading. The film, which experiments with the telling of the Judeo-Christian originary narrative without committing itself to a singular view of that narrative, relativizes both the story and its lesson. Thus, the film exposes itself both to clerical criticism regarding its portrayal of Adam and Eve and to questions about the relevance of this fable for a postwar German audience. The film aggravates the situation by failing to endorse any singular reading. The original sin, symbolized in the picking of the apple, just happens. Neither Adam nor Eve is to blame. Rather the biblical character of Lilith qua snake is transplanted into the story as the original disturber of domestic peace.

Helmut Käutner regarded *The Apple Is Off!* as a misadventure. He later referred to it as a surrealistic film that failed as such in part because of his audience's demand for psychological realism. "The psychology of the dream and the psychology of the audience are two irreconcilable things. If something is photographed, people want to believe it."[26] Here Käutner makes excuses for having failed to engage the audience's fantasy. But he goes on to note that the reason that this piece worked well on stage but blundered on screen was that it was emotionally incredible. "There are things that an audience simply cannot follow, despite the blind faith that one can do everything in film."[27] In short, Käutner tries to pass the film's shortcomings off either on his choice of medium or on the audience's failure to understand him. He refuses the possibility that he simply failed to produce a text around which they could organize meaning or fantasy.

Insofar as Käutner resorts to ambiguity in storytelling, especially in those parts of the diegesis that might confront ideologically delicate subjects, he embraces allegory arduously. He even resorts to lavish excess, especially in the sequence in which Adam and Eve visit hell. Here all the semiotic excesses of a baroque church are indulged. Each framed act is punctuated with a single-shot message. The first of hell's nightclub entertainment acts is a can-can dance that ends with a shot of one of the dancers' garter being held up with a detached human hand. The second act is a round of boxing that ends with the black boxer being knocked into a starry-eyed close-up. The third act, a fashion show, ends with a woman's plumed hat revealing itself to be a crowing cock. A Wagnerian scene constitutes the fourth act and ends with a close-up of a Nazi party emblem on Siegfried's cloak. The next act ends with a marching band trampling flowers. The torture chamber is punctuated by a little girl sawing the head off of her doll. The final act, from a Weimar-era jazz club, ends with a close-up of the face of one of the dancers, who wears a pig mask.

The sequence focuses heavily on images of vulgar, everyday brutality. The film attempts to put together the excesses of baroque allegory. But it comes up short insofar as the characters themselves do not display the requisite melancholy that theorists of allegory, such as Walter Benjamin, would expect from an allegorical play.[28] To be sure, Adam attempts suicide, but not out of the metaphysically grounded alienation Benjamin reads in baroque allegory. Rather he does so because of his childish desire to have everything his way.

In fact, if we follow Benjamin, Käutner misunderstands allegorical principle insofar as he perceives allegory to be mere relativism and ambiguity rather than a dialectical system of value representation. Had he followed a Benjaminian model, he would necessarily have created a much more complex moral tale, one the church may well have protested to for other reasons. For as Benjamin shows, the play of mourning achieves a moral and semiotic sophistication adequate to the bourgeois task of replacing religion. As it was, the church could be satisfied with a film that displays mild biblical irreverence and cellophaned nudity.

Not only does the film not function according to dialectical principles that would strive toward human edification, it seems to mock those principles. In the penultimate sequence of the film, Lucifer and Petri call a summit of heaven and hell (a thinly veiled reference to the Cold War is included) to force Adam to decide between the vampish Lilith, who comes to him as a serpent sent by Lucifer, and the virginal creation of a bureaucratic heaven, Eve. Adam refuses them both and leaves. Heaven and hell are distraught at the possibility that they will not be able to achieve procreation on Earth. Only the literal intervention of the *deus ex machina* can save them. It comes in the form of a hand holding an apple that engulfs both women and synthesizes them into the perfect object of Adam's fantasy. The film ends under the pretense that the audience should wonder if this is the solution, although, in actuality, it may be the only question the film answers adequately.

The critics panned Käutner's film and it failed miserably at the box office. I would suggest that its biggest failure was not the misunderstood narrative as Käutner viewed it, nor the sacrilege decried by the Church. The key to its failure lies in its ignorance of the gender politics of 1948 Germany. The film adheres to one of the dominant trends of the rubble-era filmmaking (especially among those films that bombed at the box office) of projecting societal woes on feminine sexuality and/or moral inadequacy. This trend, as I discussed last chapter, transcended the increasing Cold War divide in Germany. The tendency to portray women as both unscrupulous and dependent upon men must have affronted an audience consisting largely of women, most of whom were single and independent.

It is worth repeating that the most commercially successful film of the era, *Marriage in the Shadows*, was also the film that constructed, both aesthetically and thematically, identificatory structures for a primarily female spectatorship. It is hard to know whether or not this convergence was coincidence. The only other film to rival its commercial success was R. A. Stemmle's satire of postwar German culture and the Cold War, *The Ballad of Berlin*, to which we now turn.

The Ballad of Berlin: Capital Satire and the End of Rubble Film Discourse

The opening frame of *The Ballad of Berlin* reveals an entirely different attitude toward the contemporary malaise and troubled past in Germany. The film opens with a reproduction of sound and audio waves filling the screen, upbeat jazz background music, and an authoritative voice commanding "Achtung" of the owners of "Telecinemas" (a prediction of television, as well as the broadcasting of films to cinemas, a technology still in the making more than fifty years later). As the voice-over gives the specifications for how the film is to be viewed, we realize that we have been transported one hundred years into the future.

The first recognizable shot to appear on the screen is that of a street full of high-rise apartment buildings. Words come zooming toward us informing us that we are seeing pictures of contemporary Berlin, that is, Berlin of 2048. (The city looks surprisingly like the Berlin of 2001.) The voice-over changes to a calm, gentle male voice addressing the Berlin spectators: "Dear Berliners, this is the Berlin you know, the Berlin you see daily from your helicopters. All day long planes take off and land at the new Berlin airport, as the middle point of the main route from New York to Moscow. The airport occupies that space where the so-called Gruenewald is said to have stood." The introduction goes on to describe how Berlin has changed and grown in the 100 years since 1948. It is a dream of a vital and important metropolis, an almost pure fantasy construct for a spectator of 1948.

The opening sequence immediately refers to the blockade of Berlin. The rhyming of the German title, *Berliner Ballade*, with "*Berliner Blockade*," as well as the reference to Berlin as the air-traffic center between Moscow and New York are easily readable as responses to the main topic of interest in the minds of Berliners. Stemmle began shooting the film at the start of the airlift in June 1948.

The film then cuts to a sequence of shots from Berlin 1948. The contrast, and thus the film, offers the viewer of 2048 a sense of accomplishment, which translates to the actual 1948 viewer as a sense of hope. And, while many films of the era pretend to the same pollyannaism, this film constructs its optimism differently. *The Ballad of Berlin* seeks to reclaim and revitalize the account of Berlin for Berliners. As a narrative redemption of the *Reichshauptstadt* it also marks an end to the discourse of misery, self-pity, and absolute subjective uncertainty that defined the rubble film. Instead it employs the well-known and popular images of suffering to begin to produce a memory of them.

The Ballad of Berlin holds out the collective memory of the hardships of the postwar years as a foundation upon which a new postwar community can be founded. Despite the unlikely political conditions that surrounded its genesis, Stemmle's script does not give up on the idea of a unified Germany. In fact, as Photo 18 shows, the film uses German disunity as a source of humor. And it does so by shifting the discourse from Germany's past to its position at the center of the increasing rift between East and West.

The Ballad of Berlin starts out mimicking documentary form. The narrator introduces a rubble film as artifact to his futuristic audience. Its

Photo 18. *The Ballad of Berlin:* The Cold War lampoon. (Courtesy of Stiftung Deutsche Kinemathek)

"archival material from 1948" shows the bombed out Berlin landscape. When the sequence finally lands on a returning soldier, the film again highlights its lampooning intentions. The sequence cuts from a panoramic to a close-up shot of the main character, Otto Normalverbraucher. (The name translates literally as Otto Average-Consumer.) The voice-over anticipates the attitude of the 1948 audience. " 'Oh no,' the filmgoer of 1948 will have said as they saw these pictures, 'not another *Heimkehrerfilm.*' Such footage of bombed Berlin was well-known back then." In preempting this critique, the film buys itself a bit more time to convince the audience that it will not become the thing it pretends to satirize. That is to say, the most difficult project of this film is to prevent itself from becoming a rubble film.

In its first five minutes, *The Ballad of Berlin* speaks much to the changes that had occurred in filmic discourse. The film takes on, as one of its secondary tasks, contrasting itself with the earliest rubble films, namely *The Murderers Are among Us* and the DEFA social realist films discussed in Chapter 5. In fact, this attitudinal divergence from those earlier films moves *The Ballad of Berlin* toward its project of rearticulating a new Berlin.

Rubble film discourse begins with *The Murderers Are among Us* and that film's engagement with metacinematic questions. It approaches the answers to those questions through recourse to generic narrative formulae. Visually, the film sets up Berlin as a threatening and contested space, the metaphor for the berubbled inner psyche of the film's characters. The cityscape is both uncannily threatening and absent. The DEFA problem films then transform this site of metaphysical despair into one of moral turpitude. Berlin is not only the site of unhappiness, it becomes the stage for black market corruption, intrigue, murder, and promiscuity. The unstated presumption is that the city's moral failures explain the failures of the regime that was headquartered there.

The opening shot of *The Murderers Are among Us* (see Chapter 2) started with the caption "Berlin 1945, The City has Capitulated." After a small sound wave sequence that announces the futuristic intent of *The Ballad of Berlin*, the film cuts to the caption "Berlin 2048." Instead of a camera rising from a grave to depict a bombed-out city, *The Ballad of Berlin* begins with an animated crane shot of a thriving Berlin. The opening shot of destruction that had become a fixture of rubble films is here replaced by a metropolis that is whole again. Not only is it no longer a threatening place, Berlin is, according to the narrator, the center of the world. It serves as the nexus between America and the Soviet Union. All in all, this is a power fantasy that a film two years earlier would not have allowed itself.

However unlikely it might have seemed in 1948, this fantasy of the importance of Berlin is critical to understanding this film, whose first shooting day was the first day of the Berlin airlift. The fantasy speaks to Berliners who were still under siege by the time the film premiered on New Year's Eve 1948. And although the film contains insider humor for inhabitants of the blockaded city, it also speaks to filmgoers in the rest of what would become West Germany. The films tell them that the city is worth saving, a message contrary to that found in postwar filmic discourse to that point. Even *And the Heavens Above* redeems its characters by opposing them to the Berlin milieu. *The Ballad of Berlin* takes the final step of popularizing and validating the struggles of Berliners, making the residents worthy of support and praise. The film attempts to locate the fate of Berlin at the center of the fate of Germany and the Cold War disputes. In so doing, it tells us that the city is to be forgiven its trespasses.

Redemption is only a promise at the beginning of the film. Stemmle approaches the task of projecting a new image of Berlin into the spectator's imagination slowly and methodically. The film claims to be a projection back to 1948, but actually seems to progress in time from 1946 to 1948. Each sequence takes the viewer one step further through a history of postwar Berlin told, not as a lament, but rather as gradual progress. The spectator is made to trust from the start that the procession of pictures not dissimilar to the rubble films will lead to an entirely different conclusion. Humor is used to distract the viewer from the film's ideological task.

Although Otto Normalverbraucher's story dominates the first third of the film, his role diminishes as the film continues. *The Ballad of Berlin* eventually establishes its critical stance by making him a side act to the main character, which is the city itself. By the end of the film, historical events climb to the top of the film's visual hierarchy, while the individual character becomes ever more effaced. In this way, the film reveals its actual origins as a cabaret act. Otto remains merely an undeveloped character in a series of skits that are separated by vignettes. While we do watch him progress, his actions and circumstances are accompanied by very little causality. The spectator need not identify with his fate; she must only recognize it. The film does, however, interpolate the spectator into the fate of the city.

The Soviets' blockade challenged the Western Allies' position in the

Photo 19. *The Ballad of Berlin:* A satire of rubble films and of the new economic miracle. (Courtesy of Stiftung Deutsche Kinemathek)

city. The Cold War struggle subsequently changed the city's status within the imagination of both Germany's occupiers and West German citizens. As a metropolis in a provincial country, Berlin continued in its role as the source of all things bad in Germany. But an important shift did occur, one that is visible in and facilitated by *The Ballad of Berlin*.

The film begins with Berlin as the fallen *Reichshauptstadt*. The third sequence of the film depicts the city's Prussian militaristic past as having been literally decapitated. Otto wanders through the Boulevard of Victory viewing the decrepit statues of the great Prussian warriors. In another sequence, which Rainer Werner Fassbinder later quoted in the opening sequence of *The Marriage of Maria Braun*, a picture of Hitler falls from the wall during a bombing raid. But the symbolic zero hour of Hitler's fall soon gives way to the rest of early postwar German history. Soon the city is the symbol of political struggle among parties and factions. It is the site not only of black marketeering, but also of reconstruction economics. Rationing gives way to currency reform. And finally, Berlin becomes the battleground of the Cold War, a victim of political uncertainty. Otto Normalverbraucher, the Ur-Berliner, dies in a dispute between East and West, only to come back to life with the claim that he refuses to allow his adversaries to have it that easy. At his funeral, Otto requires them all to renounce their stubborn ways. It is the only time when Otto speaks more than one sentence in a row. Berlin and the Berliner are transformed from perpetrators to victims of international disputes.

Is *The Ballad of Berlin* a *Heimkehrerfilm* or a lampoon of one? If it is a meant to be a caricature of its postwar predecessors, especially the DEFA films, does that necessarily signal the end of rubble films as meaningful film code? The line between this film and an actual rubble film is slight. All of the images of suffering and the moans of lament expected in rubble films appear here as well. The difference lies in the use of a voice-over to guide the spectator's expectations of the film. The voice-over literally pulls the spectator up into the position of a survivor of the spectacle that he is witnessing.

There have been parodies of films almost as long as there have been films. Parodies serves an important function in metafilmic discourse: they act as forms of critique that often discern the vital elements of certain narrative practices. The question remains, however, whether or not a cinematic code can continue once its inner workings have been disclosed or subjected to parodic critique. For instance, when John Ford made his critical Western, *The Man Who Shot Liberty Valance*, critics called it the end of the Western. By making John Wayne a murderer, Ford's film shook the very filmic practices that he himself had established decades earlier. In the 1990s, a whole series of comedies took the *Godfather* films as the object of their spoof. While serious Westerns were made after Ford's film (or, even more relevantly, after Mel Brooks's *Blazing Saddles* [1972]), and certainly the gangster genre is strong enough to overcome *Analyze This* (1998), parodies do make it difficult to continue certain film practices unabated.

Conclusion

After Stemmle's wildly popular film, little remained for the rubble film to say or reveal. The discourse of commiseration no longer served a function in a culture that had found consumer therapy for its problems.

Not only does Stemmle's film make light of almost every filmic practice of the previous three years, including the long pan shots of rubble, the shocked soldier returning home defeated from war, and the sexual promiscuity of the *Trümmerfrau*, he also put on film the critiques against rubble filmmaking that had been printed and spoken since October 1946. By 1948, such images were already *passé* in German filmmaking. Moreover, they had become almost wholly identified with DEFA. After *The Ballad of Berlin*, rubble films ran the danger of becoming pathetic. This may well explain why *Love '47*, which premiered five months later, was, despite its much more critically astute sensibilities, both a critical failure and a box-office bust.

As *The Ballad of Berlin* shows, the world of rubble no longer held the imaginative sway it had before. Necessary for the months and years immediately following the war, the solemn images of a defeated population did not contribute to the current collective desires in the West in 1948. Currency reform promised those living in the Western zone and in the western sectors of Berlin a new level of consumerism and productivity. The film industry soon responded with images that appealed to that desired affluence. The filmic *mise en scènes* of the 1950s in Germany filled the silver screen with consumer frenzy and plenty.

However problematic Berlin may have remained in the minds of those who would soon be West Germans, the former capital remained the symbol of a unified, sovereign nation, a concept that was out of reach of the political realities of the late 1940s in Germany. Beginning with *The Murderers Are among Us* and continuing through the DEFA problem films and into von Báky's *And the Heavens Above*, rubble films had projected Berlin as the epitome of postwar German chaos. In yet another gesture of fighting fire with fire, *The Ballad of Berlin* is the most powerful example of the attempt to redeem the city by portraying it as the victim of Germany's defeat and the bellwether of Germany's postwar progress. In filmic discourse and beyond, the city had transformed itself from the defeated *Reichshauptstadt* to the symbol of the fight for freedom, a place it would hold for fifty years.

Conclusion

The Vanishing Rubble Film in Postwar Historiography

Much of the energy of the New German Cinema of the 1960s and 1970s was powered by its angry critique of the previous generation. These young filmmakers complained that the film industry in the early sixties continued to be dominated by the same people who had staffed the Nazi Dream Factory. They charged that these older filmmakers, and the older generation as a whole, had failed to face up to their own complicity in the Nazi crimes. They then used this alleged failure on the part of their predecessors and parents as a rhetorical foil against which they posited their own cinematic project. The signatories of the Oberhausen Manifesto[1] declared a new era of German filmmaking that would be, among other things, a cinema of confrontation.

My reading of the rubble films has been animated by the need to correct an oversight that flourishes most specifically in German studies scholarship in America. The received wisdom is that Germans, German film, and/or German culture failed to confront the Nazi past until the 1960s. It is a story that lives on as a part of the mythological structure that surrounds the 1968 student movement and its presumed uncovering of the truth. This dominant fiction of the 1960s is propagated most frequently by scholars who are accomplished at debunking other dangerous cultural myths. By now it should be clear to the reader that this claim by the New German filmmakers was little more than myth. The rubble films do address the Nazi past. While we might find that their efforts are often morally and ideologically problematic, it does no service to the pursuit of historical truth to ignore the accomplishments or even the failed attempts of the previous generation.

The historiographic legacy of the rubble film project offers an interesting comparison with that of the New German Cinema. I consider the latter a project only insofar as it represented, for the most part, a generational shift in the filmmaking personnel. Rather than the false dichotomy of willingness versus unwillingness to come to terms with the past, which informs the rhetoric of the New German Cinema and its historians, we see between the generations an important disagreement about what it means to investigate the personal and political connections of the Nazi past in narrative film.

Although the rubble filmmakers differed among themselves rather widely in terms of the degree of skill, perceptiveness, and honesty they brought to the task, they shared a common understanding of the project of putting the issues of the recent German past on the screen. Their conception of the task of filmmaking in the aftermath of Nazism can be summarized in what I would call the "Seven Rs of Rubble Films," namely:

Redemption

Reconciliation

Redefinition

Restabilization

Reintegration

Reconstruction

Reprivatization

The sum of these metanarrative tendencies roughly defines the distinctive project of rubble filmmaking. With the exception of Wolfgang Staudte, it is clear that all of the filmmakers perceived these tasks as a finite project. Once they felt they had addressed these particular topics, they took up something else. Judging by the difference in reception of the earlier versus the later rubble films, critics and moviegoers were quick to let the filmmakers know when they thought the project had been completed.

The creation of a culture of redemption was the initial and perhaps primary work of cinema in the early postwar years. The filmmakers, as well as many of the characters they constructed, were motivated by the desire to be told that they had been forgiven. The redemption narratives offer a space where the characters can change their attitudes and behaviors without atoning fully. The characters must often win back each other's trust, but never the trust of a victim. Some of the films work through this gesture in a postwar setting, while others try to redeem the postwar period by casting the war in a less condemnatory light. Often, as in *Razzia*, *Street Acquaintance*, or even *'48 All over Again*, the transgression (be it the black market, sexual promiscuity, or exhibiting an inappropriate historical-material consciousness) for which the character is eventually redeemed takes place entirely within a postwar context. *The Last Illusion*, a film relentlessly condemnatory of postwar German attitudes, nevertheless leaves room for some of the antagonists to change their ways. Chapter 6 presented films from throughout the period that, in one way or another, thematize persons, generations, social classes, and even, in the case of *The Ballad of Berlin*, geographic regions proving themselves to be trustworthy again.

On the metafilmic level, redemption refers to the need to relegitimate a medium that, at least in the eyes of the conquerors, had fallen into criminal hands. Filmmaking in the early postwar years adhered strictly to realist codes as a reaction to restrictions, both real and perceived, by the Allied forces. The Allies regarded the film industry as the purveyor of some of the worst Nazi fantasies and therefore were skeptical of anything but the most literal of moral tales. Cinema was both a contributing factor to the National Socialists' consolidation of power and an economic competitor to be eliminated. In relatively quick succession, the Allies went from a complete ban, to conditioned acceptance of German filmmaking, and finally to handing over sovereignty, along with many other powers, to the respective German governments in 1949. Thus, redemption gave way to other, more pressing narrative demands.

The rubble films had to compete with American and European cinematic products for space in the theaters. One of the few competitive advantages they had was the ability to alter, however slightly, the dominant image of Germany and Germans that quickly became a part of the international culture of the postwar years. They needed to create stories that recast the protagonists in a more favorable light. They did this through a rearticulation of who Germans were under Hitler.

Far more than mere redemption, redefinition is the process by which these films portray Germans as either passive spectators or actual victims of the atrocities for which the nation stood accused. *The Murderers Are among Us* sets the tone for this narrative task by defining the war and the atrocities as having taken place far away and having been committed by others. *Between Yesterday and Tomorrow* portrays the choice of not participating in life in the Third Reich as a transgression, while holding out in Germany appears as a virtue. With *In Those Days*, Helmut Käutner even goes so far as to base a film solely on the stories of good people in bad times. Redefinition offers the audience a tale in which their own private histories are retold as constructive events. It differs from redemption in that the stories unfold in such a way that the characters we might today view as morally suspect are portrayed such that redemption is not even necessary. The Nazi past becomes merely the cause of the inconveniences of war-torn Germany, rather than a trauma that demands continued personal scrutiny.

Before embracing the aspects covered in the last four metanarratives, rubble films had one more bit of historical ground to cover. Reconciliation in rubble films becomes in berubbled Germany the reestablishment of interpersonal discourse, what Karl Jaspers refers to in his 1946 lectures on guilt as the lost art of *Miteinanderreden*, talking with one another.[2] Jaspers argues convincingly that one of the effects of living under a violent, totalitarian regime was that it created tremendous interpersonal distrust, even among those who were politically likeminded. Overcoming this lack of trust in the other is the form of reconciliation that rubble films attempt to enunciate.

Significantly, however, the rubble films only rarely initiate a reconciliation of the perpetrators and the victims. They avoid direct narratives of reconciliation with the country's former enemies, none of whom appear in any of the films. Certain DEFA films, such as *Marriage in the Shadows* and *The Blum Affair*, work to push the audience toward a reckoning with the truths of their ugliest past. They are thus the German films of the era that most directly confront the pervasive attitudes that led to the *Shoah*. *Morituri*'s universalizing message attempts to create a narrative of unity in the shadow of a violent history. *Long Is the Road*, despite its main narrative of the persecution of Polish Jews at the hands of Nazis, also offers a humane picture of the former German enemy. It is, however, significant that all four of these films were products of Jewish directors or producers.

The rest of the films concentrate on reconciliation among gentile Germans. *Between Yesterday and Tomorrow* sets up a conciliatory scenario between those who left Germany during the Nazi regime and those who stayed. *And the Heavens Above* constructs an intergenerational reconciliation, while *Love '47* performs a similar task between men and women. However, *The Last Illusion* counters this tendency by suggesting the difficulties of such conciliatory narratives in the face of behavior that has failed to change radically.

Throughout the book we have seen how rubble films become obsessed with the problems of postwar existence at the cost of confrontations with the past. Restabilizing social relations rapidly took precedence over reflection about Nazism. (It is noteworthy that neither reflection nor remorse is among the "Rs.") In the early postwar years, the treatment of history became secondary to the portrayal of the troubled present. Sometimes, as in *Love '47*, the two are intertwined, whereas in others, such as *Razzia*, the problems of the postwar present are almost entirely closed off from those of the pre-1945 years. From *The Murderers Are among Us* to *Love '47*, the reestablishment of stable societal norms permeates the organization of the stories. *Razzia* focuses heavily on the restabilization of the rule of law and the state, whereas *The Murderers Are among Us* merely refers to it in the ending. Staudte's film does recognize, however, that the reestablishment of a functional bourgeois order too quickly enables the glossing over of a troubled past. *And the Heavens Above* skips over the disturbing past to a pre-Nazi ideal of normalcy, while presuming that stable familial and social relations and even legal order can be reestablished without the state apparatus. Often, the resolution of the plot in rubble films consists of a restoration of material security, which parallels the overcoming of the traumatic past. Even *Long Is the Road*, an exceptional film in many ways, allows that the past will be overcome once the problem of displaced persons, most specifically Jewish camp survivors, is confronted.

Reintegration refers to the reinstallation of men and women into the dominant fiction of conventional gender roles, which the war had disrupted in various ways. *And the Heavens Above* and *Somewhere in Berlin* provide the best examples of the tendency to organize film narratives around the reinterpolation of males into presumably traditional functions in the social machine. In the latter film, the resolution of the plot tension depends upon the father's eventual decision to reassume his patriarchal function. *Film without a Title* shifts the direction only slightly by insisting that intellectual work will not suffice in reasserting masculine dominance. The working motto at the end of the film is that "real men build things."

Reasserting masculinity appears across many cultures as a standard reaction to the combinations of male castration anxieties and female emancipation that often occur during wartime.[3] In her important monograph, *Male Subjectivity at the Margins*,[4] Kaja Silverman uses, among others, examples from early postwar Hollywood film to demonstrate how the construction of masculinity in late 1940s America became a site of volatile contention. She refers to "historical trauma as a force capable of unbinding the coherence of the male ego."[5] The tenuous nature of male subjectivity, Silverman argues, emerges in films such as William Wyler's *The Best Years of Our Lives* and Frank Capra's *It's a Wonderful Life*. She reads these films as revealing ambivalence about traditional masculine codes.

Having contributed to the winning side of the war, Hollywood enjoyed both an increasing hegemony in the developing cinematic discourse and, more importantly, an increasing percentage of the film exhibition space throughout most of the world. Germany, on the other hand, had been soundly defeated, and the once mighty German film industry had to fight conditions of poverty while accounting for its complicity in a criminal system. Rather than question the very foundations of subjectivity upon which Germans' understandings of themselves were based, rubble filmmakers attempted to rapidly recoup traditional gender positions. *Somewhere in Berlin* serves as the best example of a film that takes as its project the recovery of the phallic male who could eventually become the hero of the reconstruction saga.[6]

Women, too, had to be reintegrated into the dominant fictions of the postwar era. In many films, this entails reprojecting women into the domestic sphere. The most enduring image of the era is that of rubble women lined up unpiling the bricks from bombed-out buildings. It is an image of solidarity and strength, one that many of the era's films depict as coming at the cost of male defeat. In *Street Acquaintance*, the husband comes home to find his wife gainfully employed as a streetcar conductor. While she goes off to work, he stays at home wearing an apron. Many of the films, therefore, transform this strength into a social woe. *Street Acquaintance* does this by representing public women as a public health hazard. It equates any female activity outside the home with prostitution. The situation is not dissimilar in *Love '47* or *Razzia*. Other films, such as *The Murderers Are among Us* or *And the Heavens Above*, simply model the ideal woman as one whose labor is confined to a domestic sphere and who patiently awaits the reestablishment of the protective patriarchy. This trope is taken to an extreme in *The Apple Is Off!* when the film literally creates the perfect woman to free Adam from the liberated ones with whom he is confined. The only film that eschews this entire gender economy is *'48 All over Again*. There men and women are integrated into a system through their intellectual stances, that is, their engagement in a dialectical approach to history and to their own community.

Every film discussed in this book contains at least one love story. Love stories are one of the most common tropes for integrating people, usually men, into the social order. With its parallels to the Western, *The Murderers Are among Us* sutures Hans Mertens into a bourgeois family just when his desperado attitudes threatened to condemn him completely. Likewise, in *And the Heavens Above*, Hans Richter sees the error of his ways through the eyes of his new lover. *Love '47* depends upon the love trope to pull together the disparate and desperate narratives of the film. *The Apple Is Off!*, as a parody of the biblical Garden of Eden story, presumes that a male-dominated heterosexual union will provide the answer to its allegorical problems. All of the films treat single protagonists as frozen assets that cannot fully function without first being inserted into a heterosexual bond.

Reconstruction is the most famous metaphor of the early postwar period. It takes on varied and complicated forms in the cinematic discourse of rubble films. The most obvious and clichéd form is that of a phoenix rising from the ashes, a social fantasy that becomes the eventual founding narrative of both German states.[7] Some films, such as *Somewhere in Berlin* and *Film without a Title*, project reconstruction as pure promise. Still others, including *The Murderers Are among Us* and *Love '47* dwell on personal rather than material rehabilitation. Reconstruction shows up in other films as a dialectical process that is wrought with pitfalls such as corruption, decadence, and abuse, but also offers the potential for material security and renewal. In all cases, the discourse of *Aufbau* (reconstruction) is a public narrative, a metaphor for reestablishing domestic tranquility and the common good. Insofar as filmic discourse addresses this social trope, it does so with the assumption that cinema must still necessarily engage in public discussions.

The final step in the rubble film project is the attempt to separate film discourse from political discourse by reprivatizing the narrative itself. This is visible in *The Ballad of Berlin*, the film that satirizes all of the dominant fictions of the rubble film. The film's hero, Otto Normalverbraucher, is created by, married off through, and finally all but killed off by the escalating public rhetoric of the Cold War. Just when these combative exchanges seem to have put him in his grave, he rises up, berates all sides, and then claims victory through a retreat to his private sphere, vowing to ignore those forces bent on destroying him.

From the very start, the narrative drive of postwar German filmmaking was to present political discourse as a disruption of a sacred private realm. Yet even those films that attend to public historical dramas do so with reservations. The particulars of the political question, whether it involved the traumatic Nazi history or the hardships of postwar life, were formulated in such a limited sense that they could be resolved by the end of the film. *In Those Days*, a film that constructs an epic tale of the twelve years of the Third Reich, concludes with the war ending and an allegorical Holy Family having been established. Even *Marriage in the Shadows* and *The Blum Affair*, films with highly charged political messages, treat the public sphere solely as an intrusion. The tendency of all of the films is to bring the story to the point where the characters can return to ideally constructed private, apolitical lives. The satire *Film without a Title*, while lampooning all other narrative possibilities, presents the story line of the intact family as the natural order of things that films must strive to construct.

Germany from the end of the war till the founding of the two Cold War German states was a site of complex hegemonic contention. The Nazi regime, around which everyday life in Germany had been so intimately organized, had been demolished and a new state of bipolar "normalcy" had yet to establish itself. Thus, rubble films, as influential participants in public discourse, marked a path through the pitfalls of recent German history and the contentious postwar political landscape. That path led straight toward a reprivatization of narrative. Quite simply, the stories move from the arena of public history and events to the realm of private dramas and relations, presuming that the two spheres are necessary opposites. This is then the final move of the rubble film project. Filmic discourse moves out of the realm of the destroyed urban landscape into the realm of the intact rural scenery, which serves as the backdrop for the *Heimatfilme* that follow in their wake. In so doing, the rubble films all but erase their own ideological traces.

The "Re-" in all of these categories refers to a return to an original, better state of existence. Even redefinition relies upon the myth of an actual *Urmensch* who was better than the Allied accusations would have it.

Redemption, Reconciliation, Redefinition, Restabilization, Reintegration, Reconstruction, and Reprivatization are all ideological rather than aesthetic concerns. As critics have noted for more than fifty years, rubble films are, on the whole, long on ideological assertions and short on aesthetic ingenuity. Thus, viewing them as an ideological rather than aesthetic project is not only constructive, but also inevitable. As ideological films, then, their success is arguably to be seen in their disappearance. They are, to use a term employed by Slavoj Žižek, vanishing mediators designed to disappear from the collective imagination as soon as they have served their purpose.[8] A vanishing mediator is defined by Žižek as "an intermediate figure between two 'normal' states of things."[9] In other words, during turbulent times it offers a way of seeing a historical force that will necessarily disappear once a new hegemony emerges. (Žižek calls the *Neues Forum* democratic movement at the end of the German Democratic Movement such a force.)

The trouble with the rubble film project and its function as a vanishing mediator is that it serves the same historiographic impulse in Germany that continually calls for a *Schlußstrich* (literally, a line drawn beneath), that is, the resolution of public discussion about World War II and the *Shoah*. This demand for closure often rears its head in Germany during the public debates that erupt periodically around the history and memory of the Holocaust.

The attempt to shut down discussion about the Nazi past neglects some basic tenets of responsible *Vergangenheitsbewältigung*, that is, of coming to terms with the past. The primary motivator for this project ought to be to prevent the crimes of the past from ever happening again. What follows from this directive, regardless of which historical trauma we are talking about, is that the truth must not only be told, it must become part of our understanding of history, of the stories we tell ourselves about ourselves and others. We must recite that history continually, insisting that it become a part of the moral foundation of our communities.

The telling of this history is not a one-time project to be completed and left behind. Rather, it requires continual work. It also requires something that is missing in these films and the discussions around them, namely a keenly developed sense of responsibility to others. In fact, one of the biggest shortcomings of rubble films is their relative self-centeredness. The rubble film project often avoids the most difficult but necessary aspects of honest reckoning with the past. Rubble films avoid portraying real victims and perpetrators, as well as the causes of the tragedies they depict; they universalize suffering, conflating the German suffering in the aftermath of the war with that of the Nazis' victims.

What is true of an era is not always necessarily true of each film in it. Many of the films, such as *The Murderers Are among Us* and *Between Yesterday and Tomorrow*, refer to a sense of responsibility toward the past without displaying what that would entail. Others, such as the films discussed in Chapter 4, are quite successful in their confrontation with the varied issues regarding the history and memory of the Holocaust.

Furthermore, directors such as Wolfgang Staudte and Wolfgang Liebeneiner make a wholesale rejection of their generation of filmmakers problematic. While Staudte performed as an actor in the infamous *Jew Süß* and made numerous films under the Nazis, he was also the only director to return consistently to narratives about the Nazi past throughout his work in the 1950s. Liebeneiner presents an even more complicated case. Not only did he remain an active filmmaker under Nazism, he rose to the rank of artistic director of the combined Ufa operation and thus was implicated heavily in the criminal actions of the state. Nevertheless, his *Love '47*, while a critical and commercial flop, is one of the most honest and reflective attempts at making the problems of the past relevant to those of the present. Despite, or even perhaps because of, their ties to Nazism, both Staudte and Liebeneiner, as well as Kurt Maetzig, Israel Beker, Artur Brauner, Erich Engel, and Fritz Kortner, establish an important legacy of earnest historical filmmaking during the rubble years.

The rage of the Oberhausen Manifesto was fueled by what became of the German film industry and of critical filmmaking after the founding of the Federal Republic and the German Democratic Republic. Helmut Käutner continued in the apolitical vein of his work during the 1940s and even made an unsuccessful bid at a Hollywood career. Harald Braun became an advocate of Christian censorship of the industry and a producer of musicals and entertainment films. Artur Brauner continued for the next fifty years to produce commercial films, a few of which are narrative confrontations with the history and memory of the Holocaust. *Love '47* remained Wolfgang Liebeneiner's only real engagement with his and his country's Nazi past. He went on to make the film *Die Familie Trapp* (1956), upon which the story for *The Sound of Music* is based. Rudolf Jugert and Willi Fritsch went on to make *Heimatfilme* and family dramas. Kurt Maetzig was the only director of the early DEFA years to stay with the film company, becoming its artistic director. He became famous for directing a party-line biopic of the communist leader, Ernst Thälmann. Erich Engels returned to making entertainment features. Veit Harlan, director of *Jew Süß* and *Kolberg*, was rehabilitated in the early fifties and continued his career throughout the decade. His most infamous film of the era is *Different Than You and Me* (*Anders als du und ich*, 1956), about a teenage boy who is "cured" of his homosexuality through heterosexual contact.

A few of the directors of the rubble era went on to engage in critical filmmaking. Wolfgang Staudte subsequently made at least three films, *Rotation* (1949), *Roses for the District Attorney* (*Rosen für den Staatsanwalt*, 1959), and *Kirmes* (1960), that return to dark tales of the Nazi regime. R. A. Stemmle made two politically charged films in the early 1950s, *Wicked Borders* (*Sündige Grenzen*, 1951), about juvenile delinquency, and *Toxi* (1952), about a young mixed-race girl who is the offspring of a German woman and an American soldier. Josef von Báky continued in the 1950s to make a variety of adult and children's feature films worthy of critical attention. Nevertheless, this generation as a whole can be said to have left behind the task of working through the Nazi past after 1949. As I have suggested, their work in the rubble years made them feel that this was a reasonable choice. They are the first wave of cultural and scholarly figures who thought it proper to attempt to draw a line under the past.

But as the fury of the Oberhausen generation shows, the burdens of history are not, nor should they be, so easily contained. While the accusation by the Oberhausen signators that the elder generation of filmmakers had never addressed the past is simply false, it is instructive. The rubble filmmakers' choice to account briefly for the horrors of the recent past before moving on left those who followed with the impression that the older generation was singularly uncritical of the past.

Since World War II, Germany (and the world) has had to explore what *Vergangenheitsbewältigung* means, that is, what relationship one must have to the burdens of history. It has been a learning process. The lessons contributed by the rubble films have been largely (though not completely) negative: that redemption cannot be won simply through a return to earlier patterns of life; that *Vergangenheitsbewältigung* is not a finite task but rather one that requires repetition and sustained vigilance; that the only way to keep the mistakes of the past from recurring is to make them an integral part of a dynamic collective memory.

The rubble era's model for dealing with the past failed, but that failure is part of the legacy upon which the New German Cinema would build. Much of the West German filmmaking from the mid-1960s through the mid-1980s displays a more critical understanding of the process of writing and filming history. Likewise, DEFA's next wave of directors, most notably Konrad Wolf, found ways to return to the topic. The very fact that later filmmakers saw the need to take up the questions of culpability and the cultural legacy of Nazism shows that they saw *Vergangenheitsbewältigung* to be an ongoing task. And, since then, other groups of filmmakers have found innovative and productive ways to make meaning cinematically out of the troubled German past. It remains the responsibility of the critic to interrogate their efforts, valuing their successes and understanding their failures. This task is made easier if we understand the full history of cinematic treatment of the Nazi past that begins with the rubble films.

Notes

Introduction

1. Klaus Kreimeier, "Die Ökonomie der Gefühle: Aspekte des westdeutschen Nachkriegsfilms," in Hilmar Hoffmann and Walter Schobert, eds., *Zwischen Gestern und Morgen: Westdeutscher Nachkriegsfilme 1945–1961* (Frankfurt am Main: Deutsches Filmmuseum, 1989), 8. Unless otherwise noted, all translations are mine.

2. Thomas Brandlmeier, "Von Hitler zu Adenauer," in Hoffmann and Schobert, eds., *Zwischen Gestern und Morgen*, 34.

3. See Eric Rentschler, *Ministry of Illusion: Nazi Cinema and Its Afterlife* (Cambridge: Harvard University Press, 1996); and Linda Schulte-Sasse, *Entertaining the Third Reich: Illusions of Wholeness in Nazi Cinema* (Durham: Duke University Press, 1996).

4. Peter Pleyer, *Deutscher Nachtkriegsfilm 1946–1948* (Münster: Fahle, 1965); Bettina Greffrath, *Gesellschaftsbilder der Nachkriegszeit:Deutsche Spielfilme 1945–1949* (Pfaffenweiler: Centaurus, 1995).

5. Heide Fehrenbach, *Cinema in Democratizing Germany: Reconstructing National Identity after Hitler* (Chapel Hill: University of North Carolina Press, 1995).

6. See John Davidson, *Deterritorializing the New German Cinema* (Minneapolis: University of Minnesota Press, 1999); Richard McCormick, *The Politics of the Self: Feminism and Postmodernism in West German Literature and Film* (Princeton: Princeton University Press, 1991); and Thomas Elsaesser, *New German Cinema: A History* (New Brunswick: Rutgers University Press, 1989).

7. See Sean Allan and John Sandford, eds., *Defa: East German Cinema 1946–1992* (New York: Berghahn Books, 1999).

8. Among the directors, Kurt Maetzig was underground, Marek Goldstein was in a concentration camp, and Gustav von Wangenheim and Fritz Kortner were in exile. Artur Brauner, producer of *Morituri*, was in the Lodz ghetto.

9. Hayden White, *The Content of the Form* (Baltimore: Johns Hopkins University Press, 1987), 1.

10. Anton Kaes, *From Hitler to Heimat: The Return of History as Film* (Cambridge: Harvard University Press, 1989).

11. Eric Santner, *Stranded Objects: Mourning, Memory and Film in Postwar Germany* (Ithaca: Cornell University Press, 1990).

12. Alexander Mitscherlich and Margaret Mitscherlich, *The Inability to Mourn: Principles of Collective Behavior*, trans. Beverly Placzek (New York: Grove Press, 1975).

13. See Greffrath, *Gesellschaftsbilder der Nachkriegszeit*.

14. Maurice Halbwachs, *On Collective Memory*, ed. and trans. Lewis A. Coser (Chicago: University of Chicago Press, 1992).

Chapter 1

1. Eric Rentschler, *The Ministry of Illusion: Nazi Cinema and Its Afterlife* (Cambridge: Harvard University Press, 1996), 1.

2. Ibid., 13.

3. Peter Pleyer, *Deutscher Nachtkriegsfilm 1946–1948* (Münster: Fahle, 1965), 196.

4. Ibid., 25.

5. See Johannes Hauser, *Neuaufbau der westdeutschen Filmwirtschaft 1945–1955 und der Einfluß der US-Amerikanischen Filmpolitik* (Pfaffenweiler: Centaurus, 1985), 430.

6. For more information see Norbert Grob, ed., *Das Jahr 1945 und das Kino* (Berlin: Stiftung Deutsche Kinemathek, 1995), 87.

7. Ibid., 86.

8. Ibid., 86–89.

9. Thomas Guback, "Hollywood's International Market," in Tino Balio, ed., *The American Film Industry* (Madison: University of Wisconsin Press, 1976), 395.

10. Hauser, *Neuaufbau der westdeutschen Filmwirtschaft*, 148.

11. Ibid., 153.

12. Pleyer, *Deutscher Nachtkriegsfilm*, 26.

13. Ibid., 428–458.

14. Thomas Heimann, *DEFA, Künstler und SED-Kulturpolitik: Zum Verhältnis von Kulturpolitik und Filmproduktion in der SBZ/DDR 1945 bis 1959* (Potsdam-Babelsberg: VISTAS, 1994).

15. Christiane Mückenberger, "The Anti-Fascist Past in DEFA Films," in Sean Allan and John Sandford, eds., *DEFA: East German Cinema, 1946–1992* (New York: Berghahn Press, 1999), 60.

16. See Christiane Mückenberger, "Zeit der Hoffnung," in Ralf Schenk, ed., *Das zweite Leben der Filmstadt Babelsberg: DEFA Spielfilme, 1946–1992* (Berlin: Henschel Verlag, 1994), 9–48. See also Heimann, *DEFA, Künstler, und SED-Kulturpolitik*.

17. Hauser, *Neuaufbau der westdeutschen Filmwirtschaft*, 431.

18. Holger Theuerkauf, *Goebbels Filmerbe: Das Geschäft mit unveröffentlichten Ufa-Filmen* (Berlin: Ullstein, 1998), 12.

19. Pleyer, *Deutscher Nachtkriegsfilm*, 154.

20. Thomas Brandlmeier, "Von Hitler zu Adenauer: Deutsche Trümmer-filme," in Hilmar Hoffmann and Walter Schobert, eds., *Zwischen Gestern und Morgen: Westdeutscher Nachkriegsfilme 1945–1961* (Frankfurt am Main: Deutsches Filmmuseum, 1989), 34.

21. Christiane Mückenberg and Günter Jordan, *"Sie sehen selbst, sie hören selbs . . . ": Die DEFA von ihren Anfängen bis 1949* (Marburg: Hitzeroth, 1994).

22. See Wolfgang Staudte, "Ein Brief and die Zentral-Kommandatur der sowjetischen Besatzungszone," in Egon Netenjakob, Eva Orbanz, Hans Helmut Prinzler, eds., *Staudte* (Berlin: Edition Filme, 1991), 152.

23. Ibid., 153.

24. Harald Braun, "Die Bedeutung der Filmpause," in Norbert Grob, ed., *Das Jahr 1945 und das Kino* (Berlin: Stiftung Deutsche Kinemathek, 1995), 118.

25. Ibid.

26. Ibid.

27. Ibid., 119.

28. Helmut Käutner, "Demontage der Traumfabrik," *Film Echo* no. 5 (June 1947).

29. Georg Klaren, "Zeitgemäße Filmstoffe: Film, die wir drehen möchten," *Die neue Filmwoche* no. 28 (1946).

Chapter 2

1. André Bazin, "The Western: Or the American Film Par Excellence," in *What Is Cinema?*, vol. 2, trans. Hugh Gray (Berkeley: University of California Press, 1971), 140.

2. Patrick Phillips, "Genre, Star, and Auteur: An Approach to Hollywood Cinema," in Jill Nelmes, ed., *An Introduction to Film Studies* (New York: Routledge, 1996), 127.

3. Thomas Schatz, *Hollywood Genres: Formulas, Filmmaking, and the Studio System* (Philadelphia: Temple University Press, 1980), 16.

4. Ibid., 26.

5. Ibid., 29.

6. Thomas Brandlmeier, "Von Hitler zu Adenauer," in Hilmar Hoffmann and Walter Schobert, eds., *Zwischen Gestern und Morgen: Westdeutscher Nachkriegsfilme 1945–1961* (Frankfurt am Main: Deutsches Filmmuseum, 1989), 56.

7. Alfred Hitchcock, who comes from the same generation of filmmakers, exploited this anxiety-producing tactic to the fullest.

8. Hilde Lest, "Erster DEFA-Film im Atelier 'Die Mörder sind unter uns,'" *Die französische Wochenschau* no. 25 (1946).

9. Robert Warshow, "Movie Chronicle: The Westerner," in Jim Kitses and Gregg Rickman, eds., *The Western Reader* (New York: Limelight Editions, 1998), 37.

10. Ibid., 38.

11. Ibid., 40.

12. See Bazin, "The Western," 146.

13. Lutz Koepnick, "Unsettling America: German Westerns and Modernity," *MODERNISM/modernity* 2, no. 3 (1995): 6.

14. Peter Pleyer, *Deutscher Nachkriegsfilm 1946–1948* (Münster: Fahle, 1965), 453–458.

15. Koepnick, "Unsettling America," 1.

16. Tag Gallagher, *John Ford: The Man and His Films* (Berkeley: University of California Press, 1986), 50.

17. Ibid., 53.

18. Ibid., 139.

19. Mertens is constructed around the classical norms of Weimar male subjectivity, for example, frequent close-up shots of a starkly lighted emasculated figure. These norms are just as easily found in Ford films from the late twenties onward.

20. Schatz, *Hollywood Genres*, 35.

21. Although the Germany in which this film was produced consisted primarily of heaps of rubble, Staudte created his own ruins in a studio.

22. *The Man Who Shot Liberty Valance* (dir. John Ford, 1962).

23. *My Darling Clementine* (dir. John Ford, 1946), *Gunfight at the OK Corral* (dir. John Sturges, 1957), *Tombstone* (dir. George P. Cosmatos, 1993).

24. Christiane Mückenberger and Günter Jordan, "*Sie sehen selbst, Sie hören selbst . . .*": *Die DEFA von Ihren Anfängen bis 1949* (Berlin: Hitzeroth, 1994), 41.

25. Egon Netenjakob, Eva Orbanz, and Hans Helmut Prinzler, eds., *Staudte* (Berlin: Edition Filme, 1991), 155–157.

26. This is a curiosity for the psychoanalytically inclined. That which Lacanians have come to understand as the big Other or the symbolic order is exactly what is in chaos.

27. See Lutz P. Koepnick, "Siegfried Rides Again: Westerns, Technology, and the Third Reich," *Cultural Studies* 11, no. 3 (1997): 428.

28. Koepnick, "Unsettling America," 11.

29. Koepnick, "Siegfried Rides Again," 429.

30. According to Uta Poiger, East German authorities would, after 1949, attempt to prevent American Westerns from reaching their citizens, claiming that they encouraged youth gang movements. See her "A New 'Western' Hero? Reconstructing German Masculinity in the 1950s," *Signs: Journal of Women in Culture and Society* 24, no. 1 (1998): 147–169.

31. It is arguable that a haggard heroine and/or a Jewish woman would not have been interested in redeeming the German man. It would have to be an entirely different film and filmic genre, one with different gender codes (perhaps *film noir*), to have allowed her a past.

32. Mückenberger and Jordan, "*Sie sehen selbst, Sie hören selbst,*" 58.

33. Schatz, *Hollywood Genres*, 35.

34. Jürgen Habermas, "Goldhagen and the Public Use of History," in Robert R. Shandley, ed., *Unwilling Germans: The Goldhagen Debate.* (Minneapolis: University of Minnesota Press, 1998), 272.

35. See Karl Jaspers, *Die Schuldfrage* (Heidelberg: Lambert Schneider, 1946). Published in English as *The Question of German Guilt*, trans. E. B. Ashton (New York: Capricorn Books, 1961).

Chapter 3

1. See Millicent Marcus, *Italian Film in the Light of Neorealism* (Princeton: Princeton University Press, 1986).

2. Klaus Kreimeier, "Die Ökonomie der Gefühle: Aspekte des westdeutschen Nachkriegsfilms," in Hilmar Hoffmann, ed., *Zwischen Gestern und Morgen: Westdeutscher Nachkriegsfilme 1945–1961* (Frankfurt am Main: Deutsches Filmmuseum, 1989), 8.

3. Peter Pleyer, *Deutscher Nachtkriegsfilm 1946–1948* (Münster: Fahle, 1965), 45.

4. Ibid.

5. *Heimat*, meaning "homeland" or "the place from which one comes," also contains much more ideological connotations regarding a sense of belonging.

6. In the British Zone, where the film was made, the ration allowance had, by 1947, been reduced to 850 calories daily. For a discussion of the rations policy of the British, see Dagmar Barnouw, *Germany 1945: Views of War and Violence* (Bloomington: University of Indiana Press, 1996), 150.

7. See Micaela Jary's highly anecdotal and yet informative *Traumfabriken Made in Germany: Die Geschichte des deutschen Nachkriegfilms 1945–1980* (Berlin: edition q, 1993), 30–31.

8. See *Weltbild* no. 7 (1946). This report celebrates every step of progress the film made.

9. The sixth episode is a story about a servant girl who tries to save her former mistress, an old aristocratic woman, whose family is implicated in the attempted assassination of Hitler on July 20, 1944.

10. In Wolfgang Jacobsen and Hans Helmut Prinzler, eds., *Käutner* (Berlin: Edition Film, 1992), 202.

11. Ibid., 201.

12. Quoted from the *Tagesanzeiger*, Zürich, in "Ein Film im Spiegel der Kritik," *Neue Filmwoche*, September 5, 1947, 148.

13. See ibid.

14. R.B., *Die Welt*, March 2, 1961.

15. Siegfried Zielinski, "Faschismusbewältigung im frühen deutschen Nachkriegsfilm," *Sammlung 2: Jahrbuch für antifaschistische Literatur und Kunst* (1979): 129.

16. Eric Rentschler, *The Ministry of Illusion: Nazi Cinema and Its Afterlife* (Cambridge: Harvard University Press, 1996) 19.

17. R.B., *Die Welt*, March 2, 1961.

18. Jacobsen and Prinzler, *Käutner*, 197.

19. See Karsten Witte, "Ästhetische Opposition: Käutners Filme im Faschismus," in *Sammlung 2: Jahrbuch für antifaschistische Literatur und Kunst* (1979): 113–123.

20. Kirsten Burghardt, "Moralische Wiederaufrüstung im frühen deutschen Nachkriegsfilm," *Discurs Film 8: Münchener Beiträge zur Filmphilologie*, 241–276.

21. Ibid., 244–245.

22. Ibid., 252.

23. Wolfgang Becker and Norbert Schöll, *In jenen Tagen . . . Wie der deutsche Nachkriegsfilm die Vergangenheit bewältigte* (Opladen: Leske & Budrich, 1995), 53.

24. Ibid.

25. Ibid.

26. Ibid., 54.

27. Benedict Anderson, *Imagined Communities: Reflections on the Origins and Spread of Nationalism*, rev. ed. (New York: Verso, 1991).

28. "WTS," *Westdeutsches Tageblatt*, February 18, 1948.

29. As in *The Murderers Are among Us*, the character played by Hildegard Knef is presented as the bearer of historical problems, which go unaddressed. The fact that Knef plays this role is appropriate in that, over the first five years of filmmaking in Germany after the war, she comes to embody the problem of postwar Germany in a way that Nelly Dreyfuss represents the *Judenfrage* of the wartime German Reich.

30. *Westdeutsches Tageblatt*, February 18, 1948.

31. Ibid.

32. Herbert Schlömann, *Frankfurter Rundschau*, December 18, 1947.

33. Ibid.

34. Günter Groll, *Süddeutsche Zeitung*, December 16, 1947.

35. Luiselotte Enderle, *Die Neue Zeitung*, December 15, 1947.

36. Ibid.

37. *Der Abend*, March 30, 1948.

38. Ibid.

39. For a thorough discussion of the relationship between Hollywood conventions and German film in the Third Reich, see Rentschler, *The Ministry of Illusion*.

40. The Dreyfuss subplot is based on a true story of a woman of the same name, who died at the hands of the Nazis.

41. Klaus Kreimeier, *The Ufa Story: A History of Germany's Greatest Film Company, 1918–1945* (New York: Hill & Wang, 1996), 345.

42. For a thorough discussion of the changing views on sexuality and cinema, see Heide Fehrenbach's chapter on *Die Sünderin* in *Cinema in a Democratizing Germany* (Chapel Hill: University of North Carolina Press, 1995).

43. Günter Groll, *Süddeutsche Zeitung*, May 28, 1949.

44. Ibid.

45. *Film Echo*, March 1, 1949.

Chapter 4

1. Quoted in Lynne Layton, "Peter Lillienthal: Decisions before Twelve," in Klaus Phillips, ed., *New German Filmmakers: From Oberhausen through the 1970s* (New York: Frederick Ungar, 1984), 230–245.

2. Quoted in Eric Rentschler, *The Ministry of Illusion: Nazi Cinema and Its Afterlife* (Cambridge: Harvard University Press, 1996), 152

3. *Gesamtkunstwerk* refers to the Wagnerian ideal of a work of art that contains all possible modes of expression.

4. Presumably these filmmakers would also have feared that a certain segment of the audience might enjoy seeing depictions of this persecution.

5. See Christiane Mückenberger and Günter Jordan, *"Sie sehen selbst, Sie hören selbst . . ."*: *Die DEFA von ihren Anfängen bis 1949* (Marburg: Hitzeroth, 1994), 70.

6. Bettina Greffrath, *Gesellschaftsbilder der Nachkriegszeit: Deutsche Spielfilme 1945–1949* (Pfaffenweiler: Centaurus Verlagsgesellschaft, 1995), 431.

7. By the 1960s Konrad Wolf would assume that role both symbolically and in practice, but not until after Maetzig had made dozens of films and nourished generations of talent.

8. See Robert R. Shandley, "Peter Lilienthal makes *David*," in *Yale Companion to Jewish Writing and Thought in German Culture 1096–1996* (New Haven: Yale University Press, 1997), 790–796.

9. Agde Günter, ed., *Kurt Maetzig: Filmarbeit, Gespräche, Reden, Schriften* (Berlin: Henschelvertrag, 1987), 35.

10. Rosmarie Knop, *Start*, October 10, 1947.

11. Ibid.

12. Ibid.

13. Coincidentally, it was at the Hamburg premiere of the film that an uninvited Veit Harlan made a public spectacle regarding his initial ban from filmmaking. *Hamburger Volkszeitung*, April 21, 1948.

14. Günter Agde, ed., *Kurt Maetzig, Filmarbeit: Gespräche, Reden, Schriften* (Berlin: Henschelverlag, 1987), 37.

15. Wolfdietrich Schnürre, *Deutsche Rundschau*, November 1947.

16. Seymour Peck, *New York Star*, November 17, 1948.

17. Zentralsekretariat der SED, Abt. Parteischulung, Kultur, Erziehung, "Stellungnahme zum DEFA-Film "Ehe im Schatten," in the Kurt Maetzig file of the Akademie der Künste, Berlin.

18. For a thorough accounting of the East German leaders' attitude toward German guilt, see Jeffrey Herf, *Divided Memory: The Nazi Past in the Two Germanys* (Cambridge: Harvard University Press, 1997).

19. Ibid.

20. *Frankfurter Rundschau*, April 20, 1948.

21. Georg C. Klaren, "Zeitgemäße Filmstoffe: Filme, die wir drehen möchten," in *Die Neue Filmwoche*, no. 28 (October 1946).

22. Claudia Dillmann-Kühn, *Artur Brauner und die CCC: Filmgeschäft, Produktionsalltag, Studiogeschichte 1946–1990* (Frankfurt: Schriftenreihe des Deutschen Filmmuseums, 1990), 27.

23. Micaela Jary, *Traumfabriken made in Germany: Die Geschichte des deutschen Nachkriegsfilms 1945–1960* (Berlin: edition q, 1993), 37.

24. "Helm," *Berliner Filmblätter*, October 12, 1948.

25. Dillman-Kühn, *Artur Brauner*, 34.

26. "Proteste gegen *Morituri*" in the *Abendpost*, Frankfurt, August 29, 1948. Reprinted in Dillman-Kühn, *Artur Brauner*, 38.

27. See Eric A. Goldman, *Vision, Images, and Dreams: Yiddish Film Past and Present* (Ann Arbor: UMI Research Press, 1983), 144.

28. Cilly Kugelmann, "*Lang ist der Weg*: Eine jüdisch-deutsche Film-Koopera-

tion," in Fritz Bauer Institut, eds., *Auschwitz: Geschichte, Rezeption und Wirkung* (Frankfurt: Fritz Bauer Institut, 1996), 358.

29. Two other films of that year, Fred Zinneman's *The Search* and Aleksander Ford's *Border Street*, had already portrayed some of the conditions of Holocaust survivors.

30. Although the journal only gives the initials "W. Sch," Schnürre was the only film critic with those initials whose work was frequently published. These reviews appeared to be taken from another source.

31. Wolfdietrich Schnürre, *Kirche und Film*, June 15, 1951.

32. Ibid.

33. See Kugelmann, "*Lang ist der Weg*," 358.

34. "O.M.G.," *Aufbau*, November 19, 1948.

35. See Kugelmann, "*Lang ist der Weg*," 358.

36. Ibid., 364.

37. See ibid., 365.

38. Ibid., 366.

39. Ibid.

40. Ibid., 367.

41. "O.M.G.," *Aufbau*, November 19, 1948.

42. Max Horkheimer et al., "Research Project on Anti-Semitism," *Studies in Philosophy and Social Science* 9 (1941): 124.

43. Quoted in Gertrud Koch, *Die Einstellung ist die Einstellung: Visuelle Konstruktionen des Judentums* (Frankfurt am Main: Suhrkamp, 1992), 57.

44. Horkheimer et al., "Research Project on Anti-Semitism," 134–37.

45. Ibid., 142.

46. Koch, *Die Einstellung ist die Einstellung*, 54.

47. Hans Helm, "Ein Mörder unter uns," *Berliner Film-Blätter*, July 12, 1948.

48. Christiane Mückenberger and Günter Jordan, "*Sie sehen selbst, Sie hören selbst . . .*": *Eine Geschichte der DEFA von ihren Anfaengen bis 1949* (Marburg: Hitzeroth, 1994), 105.

49. Slavoj Žižek, *The Sublime Object of Ideology* (London: Verso, 1989), 48.

50. Ibid.

51. This is also a reference to Žižek's equation of the logic of perpetration being the same as that for overcoming that crime. Ibid., 3.

Chapter 5

1. Other attempts at singular studio systems, such as the Junge Film Union in Hamburg and Artur Brauner's CCC (Central Cinema Company), began around the same time. The former went bankrupt in the early 1950s; the latter is still in operation today. In 1946, however, neither were yet major factors in the German film industry. For a thorough account of the Junge Film Union, see Peter Stettner, *Vom Trümmerfilm zur Traumfabrik: Die "Junge Film Union" 1947–1952* (Hildesheim: Olms Verlag, 1992). For a history of the CCC, see Claudia Dillmann-Kühn, *Artur*

Brauner und die CCC: Filmgeschäft, Produktionsalltag, Studiogeschichte 1946–1990 (Frankfurt: Schriftenreihe des Deutschen Filmmuseums, 1990).

2. Thomas Heimann, *DEFA, Künstler und SED-Kulturpolitik: Zum Verhältnis von Kulturpolitik und Filmproduktion in der SBZ/DDR 1945–1959* (Potsdam-Babelsberg: VISTAS, 1994), 57.

3. "Peter Pewas im Gespräch," in Ulrich Kurowski and Andreas Meyer, eds., *Peter Pewas: Materiellen und Dokumente* (Berlin: Verlag Volker Spiess, 1981), 47.

4. The film ran for one night and was regarded universally as a cinematic and political failure, such that the daily newspapers' regular reviewer avoided comment on it. Christiane Mückenberger and Günter Jordan, *"Sie sehen selbst, Sie hören selbst . . .": Die DEFA von Ihren Anfängen bis 1949* (Marburg: Hitzeroth, 1994), 59.

5. For a discussion of Lamprecht's *Diesel* (1942), see Linda Schulte-Sasse, *Entertaining the Third Reich: Illusions of Wholeness in Nazi Cinema* (Durham: Duke University Press, 1996), 274–301.

6. Christiane Mückenberger, "Zeit der Hoffnung, 1946–1949," in Ralf Schenk, ed., *Das zweite Leben der Filmstadt Babelsberg: DEFA Spielfilme 1946–1992* (Berlin: Henschel Verlag, 1994), 31.

7. In Ingelore König et al., eds., *Vergangenen Zeiten: Arbeiten mit DEFA-Kinderfilmen* (Munich: KoPäd Verlag, 1998), 21.

8. Walter Lenning, *"Irgendwo in Berlin:* Uraufführung des neuen DEFA-Films in der Staatsoper," *Berliner Zeitung*, December 20, 1946.

9. See Jaimey Fischer, "Deleuze in a Ruinous Context: German Rubble-Film and Italian Neo-Realism," *iris* 23 (*Special Issue: Gilles Deleuze, Philosopher of Cinema*) (Spring 1997): 53–74.

10. See Julia Hell, *Post-Fascist Fantasies: Psychoanalysis, History and Literature of East Germany* (Durham: Duke University Press, 1997).

11. For further description and discussion of the film, see Mückenberger and Jordan *"Sie sehen selbst, Sie hören selbst,"* 126–130.

12. *Neue Filmwoche*, August 23, 1947

13. *Neue Zeit* (Berlin), May 4, 1947.

14. Walter Lenning, "Schieberkulisse und Gartenlaube: Der neue Defa-film *Razzia* in her Staatsoper uraufgeführt," *Berliner Zeitung*, May 5, 1947.

15. *Sonntag*, May 11, 1947.

16. Mückenberger and Jordan, *"Sie sehen selbst, Sie hören selbst,"* 157.

17. Udo Benzenhöfer and Gunnar Klatt, "Der DEFA-Film *Strassenbekanntschaft* (1948): Mit Bemerkungen zu seinem Einsatz bei der Geschlechtskrankheitbekämpfung in der Sowjetischen Besatzungszone und in Niedersachsen," in Udo Bezenhöfer, ed., *Medizin im Spielfilm der fünfziger Jahre* (Pfaffenweiler: Centaurus Verlagsgesellschaft, 1993), 17.

18. Walter Lenning, "Strassenbekanntschaft: Ein DEFA-Film im Dienste der Volksgesundheit," *Berliner Zeitung*, April 16, 1948.

19. See Benzenhöfer and Klatt, "Der DEFA-Film *Strassenbekanntschaft*," 18.

20. Mückenberger and Jordan, *"Sie sehen selbst, Sie hören selbst,"* 160.

21. "Peter Pewas im Gespräch," 46.

22. Ibid., 48.

23. Ibid., 49.

24. Dudley Andrew, *Mists of Regret: Culture and Sensibility in Classic French Film* (Princeton: Princeton University Press, 1996), 15.

25. The screenplay of *Straßenbekanntschaft* can be found in the library of the Hochschule für Film und Fernsehen Konrad Wolf in Potsdam-Babelsberg. It will be cited hereafter simply as "Screenplay."

26. Screenplay, 120.

27. Screenplay, 142.

28. Bund deutscher Mädchen, the Nazi Party youth group for girls.

29. Screenplay, 134.

30. Screenplay, 157.

31. Screenplay, 37.

32. Thomas Brandlmeier, "Von Hitler zu Adenauer," in Hilmar Hoffmann and Walter Schobert, eds., *Zwischen Gestern und Morgen: Westdeutscher Nach kriegsfilme 1945–1961* (Frankfurt am Main: Deutsches Filmmuseum, 1989), 33.

33. Attributed to "-es," *Sonntag*, November 14, 1948.

34. Hans-Ulrich Eylau, in *Tägliche Rundschau*, November 9, 1948. 35. Quoted in Heimann, *DEFA, Künstler und SED-Kulturpolitik*, 101.

36. Quoted in ibid.

Chapter 6

1. Peter Pleyer, *Deutscher Nachtkriegsfilm 1946–1948* (Münster: Fahle, 1965), 42.

2. Johannes Hauser, *Neuaufbau der westdeutschen Filmwirtschaft 1945–1955 und der Einfluß der US-Amerikanischen Filmpolitik* (Pfaffenweiler: Centaurus Verlags-gesellschaft, 1985), 446.

3. Dora Fehling, *Telegraf* (Berlin), January 27, 1948.

4. *Heimatfilme*, or "hometown films," are sentimental melodramas that depict small-town life, thus moving the *mise en scène* from the war-torn urban squalor to the idyllic, uncorrupted landscape. The genre was most popular in the 1950s, but has its roots in other similar formulaic narratives of the 1920s and 1930s.

5. Hedwig Traub–von Grolman, *Rheinischer Merkur*, February 7, 1948.

6. Ibid.

7. Edith Hamann, *Der neue Film*, February 7, 1948.

8. R.K, *Nachtexpress*, February 2, 1948.

9. Kirsten Burghardt, "Moralische Wiederaufrüstung im frühen deutschen Nachkriegsfilm," *Discurs Film 8: Münchener Beiträge zur Filmphilologie*, 259.

10. Ibid., 260.

11. In fact, it is hard to imagine a film that would not provide a moral lesson. *Jew Süß* could thus be read as "maintaining solidarity in the face of hardship."

12. This is my translation of the title. Another translation, *And the Sky above Us*, was used when the film was circulated in Britain through the Goethe Institute. My translation represents an attempt to capture the rhyme of the song lyrics from which it is derived.

13. Eric Rentschler, *The Ministry of Illusion: Nazi Cinema and Its Afterlife* (Cambridge: Harvard University Press, 1996), 198.

14. Ibid., 200.

15. Friedrich Luft, *Die Neue Zeitung*, 1947, quoted in Hilmar Hoffmann and Walter Schobert, eds., *Zwischen Gestern und Morgen: Westdeutscher Nachkriegsfilm 1946–1962* (Frankfurt am Main: Deutsches Filmmuseum, 1989), 346.

16. In "Hans Albers in Trümmern: Bedenken zur deutschen Filmsituation," *Die Neue Zeitung*, December 13, 1947.

17. Siegfried Kracauer, *From Caligari to Hitler: A Psychological History of the German Film* (Princeton: Princeton University Press, 1947), 5.

18. Thomas Brandlmeier, "Von Hitler zu Adenauer," in Hoffmann and Schobert, eds., *Zwischen Gestern und Morgen*, 34.

19. Fred Ritzel, "Was ist aus uns geworden?—Ein Häufchen Sand am Meer: Emotions of Post-War Germany as Extracted from Examples from Popular Music," *Popular Music* 17, no. 3 (1998): 295–296.

20. Ibid., 297.

21. H.G.F., *Der Neue Film*, June 21, 1948.

22. Heide Fehrenbach, *Cinema in Democratizing Germany: Reconstructing National Identity after Hitler* (Chapel Hill: University of North Carolina Press, 1995), 6.

23. Werner Hess, "Der Apfel ist wirklich ab," *Kirche und Film* no. 9 (1948): 1–3.

24. Ibid., 2.

25. Ibid., 3.

26. "Kunst im Film ist Schmuggelware: Helmut Käutner im Gespräch mit Edmund Luft," in Wolfgang Jacobsen and Hans Helmut Prinzler, eds., *Käutner* (Berlin: Edition Filme, 1992), 137.

27. Ibid.

28. See Walter Benjamin, *The Origin of German Tragic Drama* (London: Verso, 1998).

Conclusion

1. This is the 1962 West German document with which a group of young filmmakers, including Edgar Reitz and Alexander Kluge, declared their independence from "Papa's Cinema."

2. Karl Jaspers, *The Question of German Guilt*, trans. E. B. Ashton (New York: Capricorn Books, 1961).

3. See Klaus Theweleit, *Male Fantasies*, vol. 1, *Women, Floods, Bodies, History*, trans. Stephen Conway (Minneapolis: University of Minnesota Press, 1987), for a reading of these problems within the post–World War I German context.

4. Kaja Silverman, *Male Subjectivity at the Margins* (New York: Routledge, 1992).

5. Ibid., 121.

6. DEFA later explored "the hero of reconstruction" in a series of construction site films, the most famous of which was the banned *Traces of Stones* (*Spur der Steine*, dir. Frank Beyer, 1964).

7. It is the theme of the eventual GDR National Anthem written by Johannes R. Becher at about this time, the text of which begins "Aufbau aus Ruinen . . . "

8. Žižek picks up the term from Fredric Jameson in the latter's essay "The Vanishing Mediator; or, Max Weber as Storyteller," in *The Ideologies of Theory: Essays 1971–1986*, vol. 2, *Syntax of History* (Minneapolis: University of Minnesota Press, 1988), 3–34. Žižek lays out his theory of the vanishing mediator in *For They Know Not What They Do: Enjoyment as a Political Factor* (London: Verso, 1991).

9. Žižek, *For They Know Not What They Do*, 188.

Selected Bibliography

Adorno, Theodor W. "Auferstehung der Kultur in Deutschland." *Frankfurter Hefte*, 5 Jahrgang, Heft 4, April 1950.

Agde, Günter, ed. *Kurt Maetzig, Filmarbeit: Gespräche, Reden, Schriften*. Berlin: Henschelverlag, 1987.

Allan, Sean, and John Sandford, eds. *DEFA: East German Cinema, 1946–1992*. New York: Berghahn Books, 1999.

Anderson, Benedict. *Imagined Communities: Reflections on the Origin and Spread of Nationalism*. Rev. ed. London: Verso, 1991.

Barnouw, Dagmar. *Germany 1945: Views of War and Violence*. Bloomington: Indiana University Press, 1996.

Barthel, Manfred *So war es wirklich: Der deutsche Nachkriegsfilm*. Munich: Herbig, 1986.

Bartov, Omer. *Murder in Our Midst: The Holocaust, Industrial Killing, and Representation*. Oxford: Oxford University Press, 1996.

Becker, Wolfgang, and Norbert Schöll. *In jenen Tagen ... Wie der deutsche Nachkriegsfilm die Vergangenheit bewüaltigte*. Opladen: Leske and Budrich, 1995.

Benjamin, Walter. *The Origin of the German Tragic Drama*. Trans. John Osborne. London: Verso, 1998.

Bessen, Ursula. *Trümmer und Träume: Nachkriegszeit und fünfziger Jahre auf Zelluloid: Deutsche Spielfilme als zeugnisse ihrer Zeit*. Bochum: Studienverlag Dr. N. Brockmeyer, 1989.

Bongartz, Barbara. *Von Caligari zu Hitler— von Hitler zu Dr. Mabuse? Eine "psychologische" Geschichte des deutschen Films von 1946 bis 1960*. Muenster: MakS, 1992.

Browning, Christopher R. *Ordinary Men: Reserve Police Battalion 101 and the Final Solution in Poland*. New York: HarperPerennial, 1993.

Brunette, Peter. *Roberto Rossellini*. Oxford: Oxford University Press, 1987.

Corrigan, Timothy. *New German Film: The Displaced Image*. Austin: University of Texas Press, 1983.

Dillmann-Kühn, Claudia. *Artur Brauner und die CCC: Filmgeschäft, Produktionsalltag, Studiogeschichte 1946–1990*. Frankfurt am Main: Filmmuseum Frankfurt am Main, 1990.

Faultisch, Werner, and Helmut Korte, eds. *Fischer Filmgeschichte Band 3: Auf der Suche nach Werten 1945–1960*. Frankfurt am Main: Fischer Verlag, 1990.

Fehrenbach, Heide. *Cinema in Democratizing Germany: Reconstructing National Identity after Hitler.* Chapel Hill: University of North Carolina Press, 1995.

———. "Rehabilitating Father*land:* Race and German Remasculinization" *Signs* 24, no. 1 (Autumn 1998): 107–128.

Friedlaender, Saul. *Nazi Germany and the Jews.* Vol. 1, *The Years of Persecution, 1933–1939.* New York: HarperCollins, 1997.

———, ed. *Probing the Limits of Representation: Nazism and the "Final Solution."* Cambridge: Harvard University Press, 1992.

Gemünden, Gerd. *Framed Visions: Popular Culture, Americanization, and the Contemporary German and Austrian Imagination.* Ann Arbor: University of Michigan Press, 1998.

Gleber, Anke. *The Art of Taking a Walk: Flanerie, Literature, and Film in Weimar Culture.* Princeton: Princeton University Press, 1999.

Greffrath, Bettina. *Gesellschaftsbilder der Nachkriegszeit: Deutsche Spielfilme 1945–1949.* Pfaffenweiler: Centaurus Verlagsgesellschaft, 1995.

Grob, Norbert. *Das Jahr 1945 im Kino.* Berlin: Stiftung Deutsche Kinemathek, 1995.

Halbwachs, Maurice. *On Collective Memory.* Ed. and trans. Lewis A. Coser. Chicago: University of Chicago Press, 1992.

Hallam, Julia, with Margaret Marshment. *Realism and popular cinema.* Manchester: Manchester University Press, 2000.

Hardt, Ursula. *From Caligari to California: Eric Pommer's Life in the International Film Wars.* Providence: Berghahn Books, 1996.

Hauser, Johannes. *Neuaufbau der westdeutschen Filmwirtschaft 1945–1955 und der Einfluss der US amerikanischen Filmpolitik.* Pfaffenweiler: Centaurus Verlagsgesellschaft, 1989.

Heimann, Thomas. *DEFA, Kuenstler, und SED-Kulturpolitik: Zum Verhaeltnis von Kulturpolitik und Filmproduktion in der SBZ/DDR 1945 bis 1959.* Potsdam-Babelsberg: VISTAS, 1994.

Heinzlmeier, Adolph. *Nachkriegsfilm und Nazifilm: Anmerkungen zu einem deutschen Thema.* Frankfurt am Main: Frankfurter Bund für Volksbildung GmbH, 1988.

Hell, Julia. *Post-Fascist Fantasies: Psychoanalysis, History, and the Literature of East Germany.* Durham: Duke University Press, 1997.

Hembus, Joe. *Der deutsche Film kann gar nicht besser sein.* Munich: Rogner and Bernhard, 1961.

Herf, Jeffrey. *Divided Memory: The Nazi Past in the Two Germanys.* Cambridge: Harvard University Press, 1997.

Hillier, Jim, ed. *Cahiers du Cinema: The 1950's: Neo-Realism, Hollywood, New Wave.* Cambridge: Harvard University Press, 1985.

Hoberman, J. *The Red Atlantis: Communist Culture in the Absence of Communism.* Philadelphia: Temple University Press, 1998.

Hoffmann, Hillmar, and Walter Schobert, eds. *Zwischen Gestern und Morgen: Westdeutscher Nachkriegsfilm 1946–1962.* Frankfurt am Main: Deutsches Filmmuseum, 1989.

Hull, David Stewart. *Film in the Third Reich 1933–1945.* Berkeley: University of California Press, 1969. Reprint, Ithaca: University of California Press, 1997.

Jacobsen, Wolfgang, et al. *Geschichte des deutschen Films* Stuttgart: Metzler Verlag, 1993.

Jacobsen, Wolfgang, and Hans Helmut Prinzler, eds. *Käutner*. Berlin: Edition Filme, 1992.

Jaeger, Klaus, and Helmut Regel, eds. *Deutschland in Trümmern: Filmdokument der Jahre, 1945–1949*. Oberhausen: Verlag Karl Maria Laufen, 1976.

Jameson, Fredric. *The Ideologies of Theory: Essays 1971–1986*. Vol. 2, *Syntax of History*. Minneapolis: University of Minnesota Press, 1988.

Jary, Micaela. *Traumfabriken Made in Germany: Die Geschichte des deutschen Nachkriegsfilms 1945–1960*. Berlin: edition q, 1993.

Jaspers, Karl. *Die Schuldfrage: Von der politischen Haftung Deutschlands*. Munich: Piper, 1965.

Jordan, Günter, and Christiane Mückenberger. *"Sie sehen selbst, sie hören selbst . . .": Die DEFA von ihren Anfängen bis 1949*. Marburg: Hitzeroth, 1994.

Jüngling, Irma. "Jugendproblemmatik in der Periode der antifaschistisch-demokratisch Umgestaltung von 1946 bis 1949 und ihre Widerspiegelung im Schaffen des VEB DEFA-Studios für Spielfilme (dargestellt am Beispiel der Filme *Razzia, Strassenbekanntschaft* und *Unser täglich Brot*." Fachschuleabschlußarbeit (B.A. thesis). Hochschule für Film und Fernsehen der DDR "Konrad Wolf," 1961.

Kaes, Anton. *From Hitler to Heimat: The Return of History as Film*. Cambridge: Harvard University Press, 1989.

Kannapin, Detlef. *Antifaschismus im Film der DDR: DEFA-Spielfilme 1945–1955/56*. Cologne: PapyRossa, 1997.

Kenez, Peter. *Cinema and Soviet Society, 1917–1953*. Cambridge: Cambridge University Press, 1992.

Kitses, Jim, and Gregg Rickman, eds. *The Western Reader*. New York: Proscenium, 1998.

Knef, Hildegard. *Der geschenkte Gaul: Bericht aus einem Leben*. Berlin: Ullstein, 1999.

Knilli, Friedrich, and Siegfried Zielinski, eds. *Holocaust zur Unterhaltung: Anatomie eines internationalen Bestsellers*. Berlin: Elefanten Press, 1982.

Koch, Gertrud. *Die Einstellung ist die Einstellung: Visuelle Konstruktionen des Judentums*. Frankfurt am Main: Suhrkamp, 1992.

Koepnick, Lutz P. "Siegfried Rides Again: Westerns, Technology, and the Third Reich." *Cultural Studies* 11, no. 3 (1997): 418–442.

König, Ingelore, Dieter Wiedermann, and Lothar Wolf, eds. *Vergangene Zeiten: Arbeiten mir DEFA Kinderfilmen*. Munich: Köpad Verlag, 1998.

Kracauer, Siegfried. *From Caligari to Hitler: A Psychological Study of the German Film*. Princeton: Princeton University Press, 1947.

———. *Theory of Film: The Redemption of Physical Reality*. Princeton: Princeton University Press, 1997.

Kramer, Thomas, ed. *Reclams Lexikon des deutschen Films*. Stuttgart: Reclam, 1995.

Kreimeier, Klaus. *Kino und Filmindustrie in der BRD: Ideologieproduktion und Klassenwirklichkeit*. Kronberg: Scriptor, 1973.

———. *The Ufa Story: A History of Germany's Greatest Film Company 1918–1945*. Trans. Robert Kimber and Rita Kimber. New York: Hill and Wang, 1996.

Kugelmann, Cilly. "Lang ist der Weg: Eine jüdisch-deutsche Film Kooperation." In *Auschwitz: Geschichte, Rezeption und Wirkung*, ed. Fritz Bauer Institute. Frankfurt: Campus Verlag, 1996.

Kurowski, Ulrich, ed. *Peter Pewas: Materiellen und Dokumente*. Berlin: Verlag Volker Spiess, 1981.

LaCapra, Dominick. *Representing the Holocaust: History, Theory, Trauma*. Ithaca: Cornell University Press, 1994.

Landy, Marcia. *Cinematic Uses of the Past*. Minneapolis: University of Minnesota Press, 1996.

Lange, Gabriele. *Das Kino als moralische Anstalt: Soziale Leitbilder und die Darstellung gesellschaftlicher Realität im Spielfilm des Dritten Reiches*. Frankfurt am Main: Peter Lang Verlag, 1994.

Leyda, Jay. *Kino: A History of the Russian and Soviet Film*. 3d ed. Princeton: Princeton University Press, 1983.

Linville, Susan E. *Feminism, Film, Fascism: Women's Auto/Biographical Film in Postwar Germany*. Austin: University of Texas Press, 1998.

Manwell, Roger, and Heinrich Fraenkel. *The German Cinema*. London: J. M. Dent and Sons, 1971.

Marcus, Millicent. *Italian Film in the Light of Neorealism*. Princeton: Princeton University Press, 1986.

Markovits, Andrei S., and Simon Reich. *The German Predicament: Memory and Power in the New Europe*. Ithaca: Cornell University Press, 1997.

McCormick, Richard W. *Politics of the Self: Feminism and the Postmodern in West German Literature and Film*. Princeton: Princeton University Press, 1991.

Merritt, Anna J., and Richard L. Merritt, eds. *Public Opinion in Occupied Germany: The OMGUS Surveys, 1945–1949*. Urbana: University of Illinois Press, 1970.

Mitscherlich, Alexander, and Margarete Mitscherlich. *The Inability to Mourn: Principles of Collective Behavior*. New York: Grove Press, 1975.

Moeller, Robert G. " 'The Last Soldiers of the Great War' and Tales of Family Reunions in the Federal Republic of Germany." *Signs* 24, no. 1 (Autumn 1998): 129–146.

Moeller, Robert G. "War Stories: The Search for a Usable Past in the Federal Republic of Germany" *American Historical Review*, October 1996, 1008–1048.

Mückenberger, Christiane, and Günter Jordan. *"Sie sehen selbst, Sie hören selbst . . ."*: *Eine Geschichte der DEFA von ihren Anfaengen bis 1949*. Marburg: Hitzeroth, 1994.

Mulvey, Laura. *Visual and Other Pleasures*. Bloomington: Indiana University Press, 1989.

Murray, Bruce A., and Christopher J. Wickham, eds. *Framing the Past: The Historiography of German Cinema and Television*. Carbondale: Southern Illinois University Press, 1992.

Netenjakob, Egon, Eva Orbanz, and Hans Helmut Prinzler, eds. *Staudte*. Berlin: Edition Filme, 1991.

Perinnelli, Massimo. *Liebe '47–Gesellschaft '49: Geschlecterverhältnisse in der deutschen Nachkriegszeit, eine Analyse des Films Liebe 47*. Hamburg: Lit Verlag, 1999.

Petro, Patrice. *Joyless Streets: Women and Melodramatic Representation in Weimar Germany*. Princeton: Princeton University Press, 1989.

Pilgert, Henry P. *Press, Radio and Film in West Germany, 1945–1953.* Washington, DC: Historical Division Office of the Executive Secretary Office of the U.S. High Commissioner for Germany, 1953.

Pleyer, Peter. "Aufbau und Entwicklung der deutschen Filmproduktion nach 1945." In *Film und Gesellschaft in Deutschland,* ed. Wilfried von Bredow und Rulf Zurek. Hamburg: Hoffmann und Campe, 1975.

———. *Deutscher Nachkriegsfilm* Münster: C. J. Fahle, 1965.

Poiger, Uta G. "A New 'Western' Hero? Reconstructing German Masculinity in the 1950s." *Signs* 24 no. 1 (Autumn 1998): 147–162.

Reimer, Robert C., and Carol J. Reimer. *Nazi-Retro Film: How German Narrative Cinema Remembers the Past.* New York, Twayne, 1992.

Rentschler, Eric. *The Ministry of Illusion: Nazi Cinema and Its Afterlife.* Cambridge: Harvard University Press, 1996.

———. *West German Film in the Course of Time: Reflections on the Twenty Years since Oberhausen.* Bedford Hills, NY: Redford Publishing Co., 1984.

Riess, Curt. *Das Gibt's Nur Einmal: Das Buch des deutschen Films nach 1945.* Hamburg: Henri Nannen Verlag, 1958.

Ritzel, Fred. " 'Was ist aus uns geworden?—Ein Häufchen Sand am Meer': Emotions of Post-War Germany as Extracted from Examples of Popular Music." *Popular Music* 17, no. 3 (1998): 293–309.

Saltzman, Lisa. *Anselm Kiefer and Art after Auschwitz.* Cambridge: Cambridge University Press, 1999.

Schaudig, Michael, ed. *Positionen deutscher Filmgeschichte: 100 Jahre Kinematographie: Strukturen, Diskurse, Kontexte.* Munich: diskurs film, 1996.

Schivelbusch, Wolfgang. *In a Cold Crater: Cultural and Intellectual Life in Berlin, 1945–1948.* Trans. Kelly Barry. Berkeley: University of California Press, 1998

Schnurre, Wolfdietrich. *Rettung des Deutschen Films: Eine Streitschrift.* Stuttgart: Deutsche Verlags-Anstalt, 1950.

Schulte-Sasse, Linda. *Entertaining the Third Reich: Illusions of Wholeness in Nazi Cinema.* Durham: Duke University Press, 1996.

Shandley, Robert, ed. *Unwilling Germans? The Goldhagen Debate.* Minneapolis: University of Minnesota Press, 1998.

Silberman, Marc. *German Cinema: Texts in Context.* Detroit: Wayne State University Press, 1995.

Silverman, Kaja. *Male Subjectivity at the Margins.* New York: Routledge, 1992.

Sloterdijk, Peter. *Kritik der zynischen Vernunft.* 2 vols. Frankfurt am Main: Suhrkamp, 1983.

Stern, Frank. *The Whitewashing of the Yellow Badge: Antisemitism and Philosemitism in Postwar Germany.* Trans. William Templer. Oxford: Pergamon Press, 1992.

Stettner, Peter. *Vom Trümmerfilm zur Traumfabrik: Die "Junge Film-Union" 1947–1952.* Hildesheim: Georg Olms Verlag, 1992.

Theuerkauf, Holger. *Goebbels Filmerbe: Das Geschäft mit unveröffentlichten Ufa-Filmen.* Berlin: Ullstein, 1998.

Weckel, Ulrike. "*Die Mörder sind unter uns:* Vom Verschwinden der Opfer." In *Werkstatt Geschichte* 25 (2000).

Welch, David. *Propaganda and the German Cinema 1933–1945*. Oxford: Oxford University Press, 1983.

White, Hayden. *The Content of the Form: Narrative Discourse and Historical Representation*. Baltimore: Johns Hopkins University Press, 1987.

————. *Metahistory: The Historical Imagination in Nineteenth-Century Europe*. Baltimore: Johns Hopkins University Press, 1973.

Wulf, Joseph. *Kultur im Dritten Reich: Theater und Film*. Frankfurt am Main: Ullstein, 1989.

Žižek, Slavoj. "Eastern Europe's Republic of Gilead." *New Left Review* 183 (1990): 50–62.

————. *Enjoy Your Symptom: Jacques Lacan in Hollywood and Out*. New York: Routledge, 1992.

————. *The Sublime Object of Ideology*. London: Verso, 1989.

Zorkaya, Neya. *The Illustrated History of the Soviet Cinema*. New York: Hippocrene Books, 1989.

Filmography

And the Heavens Above (. . . Und über uns der Himmel)

Premiere: 1947
Also Known As: . . . *And the Sky Above Us* (1947); *City of Torment* (1947)
Running Time: 88 minutes
Director: Josef von Báky
Production Company: Objektiv-Film
Screenplay: Gerhard Grindel

Cast:
Hans Albers (as Hans Richter)
Paul Edwin Roth (as Werner Richter)
Lotte Koch (as Edith Schröder)
Annemarie Haase (as Frau Burghardt)
Heidi Scharf (as Mizzi Burghardt)
Ralph Lothar (as Heise, the teacher)

Elsa Wagner (as Frau Heise)
Ursula Barlen (as Frau Roland)
Ludwig Linkmann (as Georg)
Hellmuth Helsig (as Harry)
Reinhold Bernt
Erwin Biegel
Erich Dunskus
Karl Hannemann
Marianne Lutz
Alfred Maack
Richard Miersch
Gustav Püttjer
Walter Strasen

The Apple Is Off! (Der Apfel ist ab!)

Premiere: 1948
Also Known As: *The Apple Fell*
Running Time: 105 minutes
Director: Helmut Käutner
Production Company: Camera, Hamburg
Writing Credits: Kurd E. Heyne, Helmut Käutner, Bobby Todd
Producer: Helmut Beck-Herzog
Original Music: Bernhard Eichhorn
Cinematography: Igor Oberberg
Film Editing: Wolfgang Wehrum
Costume Design: Edith Kindler
Sound: Walter Rühland

Cast:
Bobby Todd (as Adam Schmidt/Adam)
Bettina Moissi (as Eva Meier-Eden/Eve)
Joana Maria Gorvin (as Lilly Schmith/Lilith)
Arno Assmann (as Dr. Lutz/Lucifer)
Helmut Käutner (as Prof. Petri/Petrus)
Irene von Meyendorff
Margarete Haagen
Thea Thiele
Gerda Corbett
Willy Maertens
Nicolas Koline

211

Carl Voscherau
Bum Krüger
Rudolf Vogel
Sigfrid Brandl

Paul Amende
Horst Hächler
Jürgen Wulf

The Ballad of Berlin (Berliner Ballade)

Premiere: 1948
Also Known As: *Berlin Ballad* (1948)
Running Time: 89 minutes
Director: Robert A. Stemmle
Production Company: Comedia,
  Munich
Writing Credits: Günter Neumann
Producer: Alf Teichs
Original Music: Werner Eisbrenner,
  Günter Neumann
Cinematography: Georg Krause
Film Editing: Walter Wischniewsky
Production Design: Gabriel Pellon
Costume Design: Gertraud Recke
Sound: Hans Löhmer

Cast:
Gert Fröbe (as Otto Normalver-
  braucher)
Tatjana Sais
Ute Sielisch
Aribert Wäscher
O. E. Hasse
Hans Deppe
Werner Oehlschlaeger (as himself)
Erik Ode (German voiceover)
Karl Schönböck
Herbert Hübner

Alfred Schieske
Herbert Weissbach
Kurt Weitkamp
Franz-Otto Krüger
Valy Arnheim
Walter Bechmann
Reinhold Bernt
Albert Bessler
Erwin Biegel (as Herr vom Bezirksamt)
Walter Bluhm
Siegfrid Dornbusch
Erich Dunskus
Joe Furtner
Herwart Grosse
Karl Hannemann
Hugo Kalthoff
Georgia Lind
Otto Matthies
Brigitte Mira
Rita Paul
Walter Strasen
Michael Symo
Otz Tollen
Ilse Trautschold
Theodor Vogeler
Eduard Wenck
Ewald Wenck
Erik von Loewis

Between Yesterday and Tomorrow (Zwischen Gestern und Morgen)

Premiere: 1947
Running Time: 107 minutes
Director: Harald Braun
Production Company: Neue Deutsche
  Filmgesellschaft, Munich
Writing Credits: Harald Braun, Jacob
  Geis (story), Herbert Witt
Executive Producer: Walter Bolz

Original Music: Werner Eisbrenner
Cinematography: Günther Anders
Film Editing: Alfred Schlyssleder
Production Design: Robert Herlth
Costume Design: Irmgard Becker
Sound: Walter Rühland

Cast:
Hildegard Knef (as Kat)

Winnie Markus (as Annette Rodenwald)
Sybille Schmitz (as Nelly Dreyfuss)
Willy Birgel (as Alexander Corty)
Viktor de Kowa (as Michael Rott)
Viktor Staal (as Rolf Ebeling)
Carsta Löck (as Frau Gertie)
Adolf Gondrell (as Dr. Weber)
Walter Kiaulehn (as Managing
    Director Kesser)
Erich Ponto (as Professor von Walther)

Erhard Siedel (as Herr Hummel)
Otto Wernicke (as Minister Trunk)
Alfons Kiechle
Rudolf Vogel
Axel Scholtz
Karl Hanft
Alice Verden
Willi Schneider
Werner Peters

The Blum Affair (Die Affaire Blum)

Premiere: 1948
Also Known As: *Blum Affair* (1948;
    U.K.)
Running Time: 109 minutes
Director: Erich Engel
Studio: DEFA
Writing Credits: Robert A. Stemmle
Original Music: Herbert Trantow
Cinematography: Friedl Behn-Grund,
    Karl Plintzner
Film Editing: Lilian Seng
Art Direction: Emil Hasler
Sound: Erich Schmidt

Cast:
Hans Christian Blech (as Karlheinz
    Gabler)
Ernst Waldow (as Commissioner
    Schwerdtfeger)
Paul Bildt (as Magistrate Konrat)
Alfred Schieske (as Commissioner
    Otto Bonte)
Kurt Ehrhardt (as Dr. Jakob Blum)
Karin Evans (as Sabine Blum)
Helmuth Rudolph (as Wilschinsky)
Gisela Trowe (as Christina Burman)
Friedrich Maurer (as attorney Dr. Ger-
    hard Wormser)

Arno Paulsen (as Wilhelm Platzer)
Maly Delschaft (as Anna Platzer)
Gerhard Bienert (as Karl Bremer)
Hugo Kalthoff (as Detective Lorenz)
Reinhard Kolldehoff (as Max Tisch-
    bein)
Emmy Burg (as weapon dealer's wife)
Renée Stobrawa (as Frieda Bremer)
Herbert Hübner (as State Magistrate
    Hecht)
Jean Brahn (as Fritz Merkel)
Albert Venohr (as weapons dealer)
Gertrud Boll (as maid)
Otto Matthies (as reporter)
Herbert Maisbender (as editor)
Werner Peters (as Egon Konrad)
Margarethe Schön (as Sophie Konrad)
Eva Bodden (as secretary)
Arthur Schröder (as state legislator von
    Hinkeldey)
Richard Drosten (as dentist)
Lili Schoenborn-Anspach (as patient)
Margarete Salbach (as Ruth Tischbein)
Blandine Ebinger (as Lucie Schmer-
    schneider)
Chloe Adolphi (as Alma, little girl)
Anita Hinzman

Film without a Title (Film ohne Titel)

Premiere: 1948
Also Known As: *Film without a Name*
    (1950; USA)

Running Time: 99 minutes
Director: Rudolf Jugert

Production Company: Camera,
Hamburg
Writing Credits: Helmut Käutner,
Ellen Fechner, Rudolf Jugert
Producer: Erwin Gitt
Original Music: Bernhard Eichhorn
Cinematography: Igor Oberberg
Film Editing: Luise Dreyer-Sachsen-
berg, Wolfgang Wehrum
Production Design: Robert Herlth,
Gerhard Ladner, Max Seefelder
Costume Design: Irmgard Becker,
Irmgard Bibernell
Sound: Walter Rühland

Cast:
Hans Söhnker (as Martin Delius)
Hildegard Knef (as Christine Fleming)
Irene von Meyendorff (as Angelika
Rösch)

Erich Ponto (as Herr Schichtholz)
Carl Voscherau (as Farmer Fleming)
Carsta Löck (as Frau Schichtholz)
Fritz Wagner (as Jochen Fleming)
Käte Pontow (as Helene)
Willy Fritsch (as himself/actor)
Fritz Odemar (as writer)
Peter Hamel (as himself/director)
Annemarie Holtz (as Viktoria Luise
Winkler)
Hildegard Grethe (as Farmer Fleming)
Margarete Haagen (as the maid
Emma)
Werner Finck (as Hubert)
Nikolai Kolin (as Kaminsky)
Hannes Brackebusch (as privy council
Pöschmann)
Bum Krüger (as Dancke)

'48 All over Again (Und wieder '48)

Premiere: 1948
Running Time: 100 minutes
Director: Gustav von Wangenheim
Production Company: DEFA
Cinematography: Bruno Mondi
Production Design: Willy Schiller

Costume Design: Walter Schulze-
Mittendorf

Cast:
Agnes Windeck
Eduard von Winterstein

In Those Days (In jenen Tagen)

Premiere: 1947
Also Known As: *Seven Journeys* (1947;
USA)
Running Time: 99 minutes
Director: Helmut Käutner
Production Company: Camera,
Hamburg
Writing Credits: Helmut Käutner,
Ernst Schnabel
Cinematography: Igor Oberberg
Original Music: Bernhard Eichhorn

Cast:
Gert E. Schäfer (as Willi)
Erich Schellow (as Karl)

Winnie Markus (as Sybille, first
episode)
Werner Hinz (as Steffen, first episode)
Karl John (as Peter Keyser, first
episode)
Erich Weiher (as Monteur, first episode)
Alice Treff (as Eliesabeth Buschen-
hagen, second episode)
Franz Schafheitlin (as Dr. W.
Buschhagen, second episode)
Hans Nielsen (as Wolfgang Grunelius,
second episode)
Gisela Tantau (as Angela, second
episode)

Ida Ehre (as Frau S. Bienert, third episode)
Willy Maertens (as Wilhelm Bienert, third episode)
Erica Balqué (as Dorothea, fourth episode)
Eva Gotthardt (as Ruth, fourth episode)
Hermann Schomberg (as Dr. Ansbach, fourth episode)
Kurt Meister (as policeman, fourth episode)
Hermann Speelmans (as August Hintze, fifth episode)
Fritz Wagner (as lieutenant, fifth episode)

Hans Mahnke (as Niginski, fifth episode)
Isa Vermehren (as Erna, sixth episode)
Margarete Haagen (as Baronin von Thorn, seventh episode)
Franz Weber (as policeman, sixth episode)
Erwin Geschonneck (as Schmitt, sixth episode)
Carl Raddatz (as Josef, seventh episode)
Bettina Moissi (as Marie, seventh episode)

The Last Illusion (Der Ruf)

Premiere: 1949
Running Time: 100 minutes
Director: Josef von Báky
Producer: Richard König
Production Company: Objectiv, Munich
Original Music: Georg Haentzschel
Cinematography: Werner Krien

Cast:
Fritz Kortner (as Professor Mauthner)
Johanna Hofer (as Lina)
Rosemary Murphy (as Mary)
Lina Carstens (as Emma)
William Sinnigen (as Elliot)
Michael Murphy (as Spencer)
Ernst Schröder (as Walter)

Paul Hoffmann (as Fechner)
Arno Assmann (as Kurt)
Charles Régnier (as Bertram)
Alwin Edwards (as Homer)
Harald Mannl (as Fraenkl)
Friedrich Domin
Hans Fitze
Fritz Benscher
Otto Brüggemann
Peter Hansmann
Ferdinand Anton
Walter Janssen
Rolf Kralovitz
Georg Lehn
Wolfried Lier
Kai S. Seefeld

Long Is the Road (Lang ist der Weg)

Premiere: 1948
Also Known As: *Lang iz der Veg* (1948; USA: Yiddish title, YIVO translation)
Running Time: 77 minutes
Language: German/Yiddish
Director: Herbert B. Fredersdorf, Marek Goldstein

Production Company: International Film-Organisation
Writing Credits: Israel Becker, Karl Georg Külb
Producer: Abraham Weinstein
Original Music: Lothar Brühne
Cinematography: Jack Jonilowicz, Franz Koch

Art Direction: C. L. Krimse

Cast:
Israel Becker (as David Jelin)
Bettina Moissi (as Dora Berkowicz)
Berta Litwina (as Hanne Jelin)
Jakob Fischer (as Jakob Jelin)

Otto Wernicke (as senior doctor)
Paul Dahlke (as 2nd doctor)
Aleksander Bardin (as peasant)
David Hart (as Mr. Liebermann)
Misha Natan (as partisan)
H. L. Fischer (as Chodetzki)

Love '47 (Liebe '47)

Premiere: 1948
Running Time: 111 minutes
Director: Wolfgang Liebeneiner
Production Company: Filmaufbau,
    Göttingen
Writing Credits: Wolfgang Borchert
    (play), Wolfgang Liebeneiner
Cinematography: Franz Weihmayr

Cast:
Albert Florath (as Death)
Dieter Horn (as Jürgen)
Karl John (as Beckmann)
Hilde Krahl (as Anna Gehrke)
Inge Meysel (as Betty)
Erich Ponto (as God)
Grethe Weiser (as Frau Puhlmann)

Hubert von Meyerinck (as the Director)
Silvia Schwarz (as Monika)
Erika Müller (as Lisa)
Hedwig Wangel (as Mutter Beckmann)
Alice Verden (as Tante Eva)
Luise Franke (as Frau Kramer)
Paul Hoffmann (as Major)
Leonore Esdar (as his wife)
Gisela Burghardt (as his daughter)
Herbert Tiede (as his son-in-law)
Leopold von Ledebur (as the General)
Heinz Klevenow (as an infantryman)
Rudolf Kalvius (as von Wehrzahn)
Helmut Rudolph (as Alfred)
Kurt A. Jung (as Peter)
Erich Geschonneck (as a detective)

Marriage in the Shadows (Ehe im Schatten)

Premiere: 1947
Running Time: 105 minutes
Director: Kurt Maetzig
Studio: DEFA
Writing Credits: Kurt Maetzig, Hans
    Schweikart
Original Music: Wolfgang Zeller
Cinematography: Friedl Behn-Grund,
    Eugen Klagemann
Film Editing: Alice Ludwig

Production Design: Otto Erdmann,
    Franz F. Fürst, Kurt Herlth

Cast:
Paul Klinger (as Hans Wieland)
Ilse Steppat (as Elisabeth Maurer)
Alfred Balthoff (as Kurt Bernstein)
Claus Holm (as Dr. Herbert Blohm)
Lothar Firmans (as State Secretary)
Karl Hellmer (as Gallenkamp)
Hans Leibelt (as Fehrenbach)
Willy Prager (as Dr. Louis Silbermann)

Morituri

Premiere: 1948
Running Time: 88 minutes
Director: Eugen York

Writing Credits: Artur Brauner, Gus-
    tav Kampendonk
Producer: Artur Brauner

Studio: Central Cinema Company
(CCC), Berlin
Original Music: Wolfgang Zeller
Cinematography: Werner Krien
Film Editing: Walter Wischniewsky

Cast:
Josef Almas
Ursula Bergman
Alfred Cogho
Erich Dunskus
Catja Görna
Michael Günther
Annemarie Haase
Gabriel Hessman

Franja Kamienietzka
Klaus Kinski
Bob Kleinmann
Lotte Koch
Hilde Körber
David Minster
Winnie Markus
Peter Marx
Willy Prager
Walter Richter
Ellinor Saul
Sigmar Schneider
Carl-Heinz Schroth
Josef Sieber
Karl Viebach

The Murderers Are among Us (Die Mörder sind unter uns)

Premiere: 1946
Also Known As: *Murderers among Us*
(1948; USA)
Running Time: 85 minutes (91 min-
utes reissue)
Director: Wolfgang Staudte
Production Company: DEFA
Writing Credit: Wolfgang Staudte
Producer: Herbert Uhlich
Original Music: Ernst Roters
Cinematography: Friedl Behn-Grund,
Eugen Klagemann
Film Editing: Hans Heinrich Egger
Production Design: Otto Hunte,
Bruno Monden
Sound: Klaus Jungk

Cast:
Ernst Wilhelm Borchert (as Hans
Mertens)
Hildegard Knef (as Susanne Wallner)
Arno Paulsen (as Ferdinand Brueckner)
Robert Forsch (as Herr Mondschein)
Albert Johannes (as Bartolomaeus
Timm)
Hilde Adolphi (as Daisy)
Elly Burgmer
Wolfgang Dohnberg
Ursula Krieg (as Carola Schulz)
Marlise Ludwig (as Sonja)
Erna Sellmer (as Elise Brueckner)
Ernst Stahl-Nachbaur

Razzia

Premiere: 1947
Running Time: 90 minutes
Director: Werner Klingler
Production Company: DEFA
Writing Credit: Harald G. Petersson
Original Music: Werner Eisbrenner
Lyricist: Guenther Schwenn
Cinematography: Friedl Behn-Grund,
Eugen Klagemann

Film Editing: Günther Stapenhorst
Production Design: Otto Hunte,
Bruno Monden
Sound: A. Jansen

Cast:
Paul Bildt
Elly Burgmer
Agathe Poschmann

Friedhelm von Petersson
Nina Konsta
Claus Holm
Hans Leibelt
Heinz Welzel
Harry Frank

Arno Paulsen
Walter Gross
Undine von Medvey
Martha Hubner
Otto Matthies
Erwin Biegel

Somewhere in Berlin (Irgendwo in Berlin)

Premiere: 1946
Running Time: 80 minutes
Director: Gerhard Lamprecht
Production Company: DEFA
Writing Credit: Gerhard Lamprecht
Original Music: Erich Einegg
Cinematography: Werner Krien
Film Editing: Lena Neumann
Set Decoration: Otto Erdmann
Sound: Fritz Schwarz

Cast:
Charles Knetschke (as Gustav Iller)
Harry Hindemith (as Paul Iller)
Hedda Sarnow (as Grete Iller)
Hans Trinkaus (as Willi)

Magdalene von Nussbaum (as Frau
    Schelp, Willi's guardian)
Paul Bildt (as Mr. Birke)
Siegfried Utecht (as "Kapitan," leader
    of the boys)
Walter Bluhm (as Waldemar Hunke,
    thief)
Hans Leibelt (as Herr Eckmann, artist)
Fritz Rasp (as Uncle Kalle)
Gaston Briese
Karl Hannemann
Gerhard Haselbach
Lotte Loebinger
Lilli Schönborn

Street Acquaintance (Straßenbekanntschaft)

Premiere: 1948
Running Time: 90 minutes
Director: Peter Pewas
Production Company: DEFA
Writing Credit: Arthur Pohl
Original Music: Michael Jary
Cinematography: Georg Bruckbauer

Cast:
Arno Paulsen
Siegmar Schneider
Alice Treff
Gisela Trowe
Agnes Windeck

Index

Page numbers in italics refer to photographs.